JOCK
ITCH

The Misadventures of
a Retired Jersey Chaser

JOCK ITCH

Rosa Blasi

books

AN IMPRINT OF HARPERCOLLINS PUBLISHERS

itbooks

HarperCollins books may be purchased for educational, business, or sales promotional use. For information please write: Special Markets Department, HarperCollins Publishers, 10 East 53rd Street, New York, NY 10022.

FIRST EDITION

Designed by Cassandra J. Pappas

Library of Congress Cataloging-in-Publication Data is available upon request.

ISBN 978-0-06-199973-4

11 12 13 14 15 OV/RRD 10 9 8 7 6 5 4 3 2 1

Jock Itch is dedicated to the true loves of my life:
my Mom, Dad, and Kaia.

AUTHOR'S NOTE

Some of the names have been changed
to protect the guilty fucks.

Contents

JOCK ITCH

And so it begins . . .

ONE

Training Camp

Everyone has a type. Dudes tend to be either "boob guys" or "ass men." Some prefer blonds to brunettes. Few prefer redheads, mainly because their private parts resemble baloney and carrots. Intelligence-wise, some dig the hypersmart Tina Fey type, while others settle for those dumb bitches on *The Hills*—essentially blow-up dolls who rarely speak and seldom have opinions—to adorn their arms and blind them with cleavage. Types aren't just for the boys: Women have them too. Some like good guys, more like bad ones, and some just crave a big fat wallet—even if it comes with a guy who looks like George Costanza. You know what your type is. It's the one who gives you the uncontrollable urge that makes you go weak in the knees. It's the one who makes you a little bit dumber—and a whole lot giddier. Admittedly, we all have our celebrity crushes. And I'm no different. It's just that my itch is for athletes. I wish the cure were only as simple as buying a case of Lotrimin and being done with it. But it took a lot more than that to cure my jock itch.

There is a certain danger—a confidence and a swagger—that comes with professional athletes. It's what I call BDA—or Big Dick Attitude. I'm not insinuating that all athletes are hung. Believe me, height and stature have nothing to do with their . . . athletic equipment. What I do mean to say is that sometimes you meet a guy and he just has that certain *something*. Athletes are overly confident, and people are naturally drawn to them because of it. They're the fives who date tens. They have BDA. They carry themselves differently from the rest of us. And they know it. They simply have an air about them that you can't quite put your finger on—or around.

If you think about it, these guys have literally been worshipped since they were in junior high, when people discovered their talents. In fact it was probably even before that. How many unsuspecting, drooling infants have heard: "Oh, he's gonna grow up to be a linebacker! Look how *big* he is!" That worship continues through grade school until finally they become like pied pipers, whose adoring following only grows as they move from junior to varsity to college, and then on to the professional leagues.

If you're a guy, chances are you tune in to ESPN's *SportsCenter* at least three times a day, if not more. You worship a team, or several—maybe a player, maybe a city, maybe some dumbass mascot or school that you didn't attend. I'm pretty sure there isn't a guy out there who hasn't had the "I wonder what would it be like . . ." fantasy. Guys who don't fantasize about playing maybe just fantasize about looking around the players' locker rooms instead!

Some fans take it as far as obsessing about fantasy ball. Or as my friend Randall Slavin says, "Fantasy should strictly be used for storytelling and masturbation." In the same vein, imagine how you'd look at your girlfriend if she were sweating out and losing sleep over with whom she would potentially pair up in the latest Judd Apatow movie. Should the lineup be Cameron Diaz and Ben Affleck? Or should it be Ben and Jennifer Aniston? Or Kate Hudson? Or should we not go with Ben, because he once made a movie like *Gigli*, which was like watching a root canal in slow motion, with a windup drill. (You know I'll never get those two hours back.) Amplify this with the countless magazines dedicated to the fiction or fantasy of choice, along with websites, chat rooms, blogs, frantic phone calls, draft-pick parties, and even more frenzied sports-event watching. The behavior is really bizarre, I think.

If you've ever had a partner do this in front of you, it's almost like watching your once-adult mate travel backward in time, regressing and obsessing over this waste-of-time fantasy sport. But things could be worse. They could actually play the sport for a living. And you might even find yourself dating one of these "fantasies," or, in my case, one (maybe two) in every professional sport except soccer, tennis, and horse racing.

My infatuation with jocks all started with Ken Doll Donny Gothem. He was on the junior varsity football team. Donny was a public high school trifecta. He was hot, popular, and he wanted me because I had just thankfully grown out of my gawky junior high phase. (You know the look: when your teeth are too big for your mouth and go every which way but straight, your face hasn't caught up with your nose, and your monobrow is filing for a legal separation.) It was the late eighties, and I was sporting the big, teased, and highly flammable Aquanet hair that sprouted like cauliflower florets on top and curled under like a sausage down below. (My bangs could take gale-force winds without budging.) I completed the look with blue eyeliner—a color not found in nature—and neon fuchsia lip gloss. Who needed safety reflectors riding a bike with a makeup palette like that?

Donny was my "it guy," until I wouldn't put out, so he dumped me in favor of someone who would. You can only endure so much jeans-to-jeans dry humping before causing significant chafing and possible first-degree burns to the crotch. It was high school, so Donny just asked for his football jacket back and mumbled in that intelligible teenage angst garble: "This ain't working." Because it was high school, I acted like I didn't care, made sure I looked extra cute at school the next day (in case he changed his mind), and never bothered to ask him to expound on the reasons for our breakup even though I cried myself to sleep on my "Like a Virgin" pillowcases. (Ah, vintage Madonna, the first Lady Gaga.) After the whole brief Donny debacle, I realized I actually really enjoyed the attention of athletes. I felt cool—cooler than I did before. And isn't that the main objective of a high school education?

So I used my creativity to devise a scheme that would give me more access to them (as well as create a nice high school cash flow). Armed with a fake pregnancy bump and a shopping list "from my husband," I went to neighborhood grocery stores dressed like I was about to give birth any moment and bought alcohol for members of the football team. Due to my "delicate state," the clerks not only helped me gather the ingredients for "the barbecue we were having," they also carried the load out to my parents' woody station wagon. And when they asked "what I was having" and "when was my due date," I had to resist the urge to answer: "Bartles & Jaymes Black Cherry wine coolers, later tonight!"

They were innocent times. I came from Mount Prospect, Illinois, "Where Friendliness Is a Way of Life" our town's welcome sign boasted (unless that's been changed to "Home of 2010 *American Idol* Winner Lee DeWyze!!!"). A few years before meeting the Donny doll, I used to voraciously read anything by Danielle Steel. I would get lost in her world of romance and opulence. Since my childhood home was a modest, ranch-style house (similar to all the other houses on the block) I thought anyone who had white carpeting and an upstairs was "rich."

I also immersed my literary tastes in the grand dame of books—Judy Blume.

When I read what was considered the dirtiest book of all time, Judy's *Forever*, it felt very forbidden. The novel got its reputation because the two lead characters had sex in chapter 17, on lines 54 and 55, oh, and 56, and then in even more chapters. It was the summer before sixth grade. This was the time when I would have given my left leg to get my period and start developing breasts. My friend Tanya and I even went so far as to try to insert a tampon (with a mirror to guide us) in hopes that this might jump-start the real thing, because rumor had it that once you got your period your breasts could double in size! Sign me up.

Anyway, the guy in Judy's book actually named his penis Ralph. Judy wrote sentences like "Ralph was getting hard." This went totally over my head. Then when she wrote, "He came . . ." I thought, *Now why would that be a sentence? Where did he "come" from? Where did he go after he came?* And not only did he come, but then "she came too." Who were these visitors to Ralph's penis and where were they headed? She came. He came. It all puzzled me so much that I actually wrote a note to Judy's publisher: "Are you there, Judy? It's me, Rosa. I'm a little confused about people coming in your books."

While my serial jock dating started with Donny, my infatuation with athletes began when I was a midget-football cheerleader. Yes, back then it was actually called that, pre–political correctness. Today, it's Pop Warner. The Latin translation of Pop Warner is "little cocky egos-in-training program." As cheerleaders, we wore our ridiculously hyperthermal, nonbreathing polyester uniforms and pomponed our mighty men and their balls on to victory. We had no interaction with the football players. They were focusing on the game—while we were focusing on them. This would later become a recurring theme in my dating life. They never even extended a "thanks, bitches" to us, which would at least have been an acknowledgment. We just cheered our little junior asses off for them until we were so hoarse that our moms had to slather our throats with Vicks and warm hand towels at night, and also had to go without practicing: "We've got spirit! Yes, we do! We've got spirit! How 'bout *you*?"

The passion continued in college at the University of Kansas, where I was fortunate enough to be in a sorority with a girl that was dating one of the KU football players. They were like McDonalds supersized fraternity boys and as yummy as the inside of a chocolate ooze cake. But my sorority sister was the only one besides me who wanted to be in a relationship with these collegiate Neanderthals. My other girlfriends saw them as something to do on a Saturday night, while I (the serial serious girlfriend) saw them as my next goal. I think that everyone possesses a dark, masochistic side, some more than others. I craved the attention of these men: athletes who were infamous for being anything but monogamous.

I even padded my bra to make my waist seem smaller, but I don't think they saw past the freshman twenty, twenty-five, or thirty that I had packed on my short five-foot-two-inch frame. I was also considered *exotic* looking at the University of Kansas, like a love child of Frida Kahlo and Erik Estrada with just a dash of Charo. This was a time where it ruled to look like you were part of the Swedish Bikini Team and not the "now, exactly what nationality are you—Latin, Jewish, Guatemalan?" squad. It was a seriously challenging time, but I am convinced that J Lo changed the course of what typical Americans started considering beautiful when she played Selena.

After Kansas, I transferred to Columbia College. No, not the brainy Columbia University in New York City, but the one that even the Kardashian sisters and Bruce Jenner could get into in Chicago. Once there, I also got a job at a brand-new restaurant called Hooters. I had had a job since I started pumping hot, fake cheese onto nachos at the public-pool concession stand when I was fourteen, but the job opening at Hooters seemed potentially more lucrative (and posed less of a threat of coming home with jalapeños and melted soft serve on you). Despite the orange shorts and nylons, it seemed downright glamorous. It was an educational working environment, and at nineteen it gave me my first peek at professional basketball. I worked under my college fake ID of Molly O'Brien. Forget the fact that I looked nothing like a wee Irish woman. And forget that she had platinum-blond hair that I simply colored in with a brown eye pencil. Somehow the mixture of my saliva and the waxy eyeliner created a laminate effect. I was the Michelangelo of fake IDs.

Working at Hooters is not exactly on my résumé, but it was a big deal at the time. It even had fringe benefits. We received floor seats to the Chicago Bulls games, and all kinds of attention and swag. We were treated like celebrities and loved every busty minute of it.

This was before everyone and their mother had a boob job, although I was able to give myself what I called a "poor-man's boob job." I would twist a pea-sized amount of fabric and place it exactly where my nipple would be on my tank top. The end result was an indomitable Chicago-winter nipple hard-on look. That little trick made the Farrah Fawcett swimsuit poster look like her nipples were napping and increased my tips. My career at Hooters lasted exactly two weeks before I got fired for being a "sucky" waitress. Now, this is as insulting as a stripper being fired for having "no rhythm." But before I was canned, I met my first professional athlete. (It'd be really cool if I could somehow cue the *Jaws* theme music right now.)

I had never been to a football game. Nor had I ever watched one. There was a guy who used to come in all the time, with a group of football players, named Matthew Stonebricker. I knew they were football players because there was a definite shift in the energy of the place from the moment they came in, and they always traveled in a group of six. There was also a lot of Hooters managerial back-bending to accommodate them (with more than triple the normal wait-staff attention) and a general frenzy—as if they were *Zagat Guide* reviewers. The prettiest girl who worked there at the time was named Lisa. She had waist-length blond hair and a fifty-two-inch inseam of toned, tanned perfection that would have stood out anywhere, but especially in Chicago. She told me her boyfriend was a very famous (very married) out-of-state football player who lavished her with mink coats and spur-of-the-moment trips. I didn't know his name at the time, but many years later when I saw that in the press he was considered Mr. Family Role Model, I just thought, *Ewwwwww.*

Matthew had a slyness about him. He was a subtle flirt, like he wasn't that invested in whether I had feelings for him or not. He was also confident, and I immediately liked him because he was nothing like the frat boys or Chicago suburb boys I had met. He had a "rebel without a cause" attitude, complete with a motorcycle he liked to drive recklessly (which my parents "forbade" me to ride, so of course that was one of the first things I did). It was all very out of a movie—very *Grease 2*. I'd clutch the back of his motorcycle jacket, as excited as I was fearful. He seemed to live his life completely in the moment—as if he were permanently flipping the bird to all of society—and I found that intoxicating. He'd take me on the back of his bike and speed through the streets of the city, showing me all these Chicago haunts I never even knew existed. Those hip places and neighborhoods you had to be "in the know" to know about. We'd get stoned (while I nervously remembered the "pot is a gateway drug" movies I'd seen in Prospect High School health classes and prayed this wasn't the beginning of my demise). We'd gorge ourselves on crab legs at one of those bib-and-picnic-table places, making a giant mess and just laughing our asses off. Living at my parents' house in the suburbs, when I wasn't living on a college campus in DeKalb, Illinois, had kept me properly sheltered and I felt like this was my first taste of adult dating.

Career-wise, Matthew was a classic case of one of those guys who do tremendously well in college but "shit the bed" once they get to the pro game. Dating Stonebricker (born with such the quintessential badass football name) impressed the hell out of my guy friends, who all seemed to be champing at the bit and breathlessly waiting for any detail I could muster up about our dates. It almost seemed as if their heterosexuality could have been called into question. Athlete worship can do this to a guy. I've seen it firsthand. Dating Matthew was just an exciting diversion for me from sorority life, and as soon as he got traded to another team out of state, our romance (a generous description of the reality of it) ended. But like all things that are bad for you, I found myself craving more. It all felt dangerous and addictive and so much more exciting than the norm I was used to. I'd return to my college campus parties and crinkle my nose at the frat boy look-alikes (all standing about five foot nine with their braided leather J.Crew belts and pastel button-down shirts) trying to pass out trays of grain alcohol Jell-O shots—their only path to potential scoring—and find myself wanting more. Wanting another challenge. Much like the Lay's potato chips slogan, "Betcha can't eat just *one!*" And so I was hooked.

I MOVED FROM THE Midwest to Los Angeles at twenty-one, hoping not to become just another statistic with my attempt to break into the entertainment industry. I packed my bags and left Chicago with determination, a headshot, and my proclivity for athletes. The thrill of the chase only pole-vaulted my competitive spirit to find another guy as exciting as Matthew. But finding athletes while hating sports proved difficult. I lived in Los Angeles, where everyone and their dog was trying to be "an actor"—including all the men. Therefore they were all small, delicate, and prettier than me. The fact was, I was surrounded by guys who used fifty-dollar hair gel to try and look edgy, but only succeeded in looking *more* metrosexual (if that was possible). It was a massive turn-off. How hard could it be to find a date that didn't keep his headshot stapled to a résumé in the backseat of his car? Where were the manly men? Where were the guys who weren't getting facials while they were waiting to be discovered? Where were the dudes who ate meat and potatoes—or just ate for that matter? I knew where they were, and finding them became an addiction. They were playing at a field near you.

Like people do with all vices, I started rationalizing that dating athletes might actually be good for me—healthy, a distraction from all the stress of the business—if I could only figure out how to meet them.

Where there's smoke there's fire, and where there are Playmates there are athletes, so I had to devise a plan to get myself invited to the next *Playboy* party. I had a couple of friends (they worked on the television show *Baywatch* as Pam Anderson's double while Pam was getting her Tommy Lee groove on in her double-wide) who were actually invited to go. I asked them to describe to me exactly how the entrances to the parties were set up so I could Mac-Gyver my way in. Apparently, you drove up to the guard at the gates, they checked off your name, and you proceeded down a very long driveway to the mansion.

One of the friends, Cici (who would have been more aptly named "1,500 cc's of silicone"), had dated the famous director Michael Bay for a few years, and had bought him his beloved pet, a ginormous English mastiff. She often took care of both the dog and Mr. Bay's car, a huge black Chevy Tahoe SUV, while he was out making huge, successful blockbuster films such as *Armageddon* and *Pearl Harbor*, to name a few. The night of the big *Playboy* Halloween party, I crouched in the trunk of the huge SUV, every inch of me covered with a hairy old dog blanket we found back there. Big dogs smell, and this one weighed over two hundred pounds. So underneath the blanket it was unbearable. It smelled like it had been sprayed with Eau de Rancid Dog. But I successfully gained entrance to the party and hopped out of the trunk like an illegal alien on the U.S. side of the Mexican border. Sure, I smelled pungent, was covered in dog hair, and felt like I'd swallowed an angora sweater, but I was in.

The Playboy Mansion is surrounded by abundant, sprawling lawns. From the gates up to the mansion, it's literally a hike. Back then, you could drive up to the gate. Now, perhaps because self-smuggling missions like the one I just described were captured on security cameras, they have shuttle buses that take you from UCLA parking garages up to the entrance. This is after an elaborate check-in procedure that rivals international airport security and comes complete with a Polaroid photograph taken on the spot and a handstamp. On the grounds there's the zoo (with the monkey cages), the resortlike pool (with fake rocks and a moat), and of course the famous Grotto. I usually avoided the Grotto because it was very humid from the hot tub steam, and I didn't want to swap the effects of my carefully flatironed hair for an Ogilvie home-perm-looking mess. Plus, I didn't know how the extra fake hair I'd clipped in would react to the steam (unfortunately the package didn't come with directions from the previous owner). There was that, and then you could only spend so much time watching drunken public groping sessions. There was a rumor that Verne Troyer, a.k.a. Mini-Me, was once serviced by a Playmate in there. I can't back that up as factual. It just came from a really good source.

The grounds were mostly tented for the outdoor parties, with round tables set up everywhere, and catering that was as extensive and exquisite as you'd find on a cruise ship—ice sculptures included. The dance floor they had set up was always rocking, with the best DJ that Hef's money could buy. You can actually purchase DVDs similar to the *Girls Gone Wild* ones that feature this exact dance-floor scene and the people who frequented it. Thank God I had the sense to dodge the video cameras, because aside from a pic I have with Hef where I am wearing what could best be described as a tiny bikini made of fake leaves (it was a *Midsummer Night's Dream* party that night), there's no lingering evidence. Inside the party there were at least twenty hot girls to every guy. And by "hot" I mean if-you-polled-college-age-male-spring-breakers "hot." The parties were packed with girls who were barely out of their teens, hovered around a hundred pounds, were stuffed with implants (both in their chests and their lips), and dared to test their sense of balance by teetering on clear Lucite stripper heels. They had expensive, waist-length hair extensions, seductive false black eyelashes, and long shiny acrylic nails.

Sprinkled around the party were people ranging from A-list celebrities to oh-my-God-I-used-to-watch-his-show-when-I-was-little has-beens. There were half-naked and completely-naked girls frolicking everywhere. Nipple sightings were common. I remember once I was standing in line behind a naked girl to get a drink, and when she reached across the bar to grab a lime, she literally and unabashedly flashed me her vagina—in a manner usually reserved for gynecologists. This was back in a simpler time, before the trend of pantyless starlets exiting cars with their legs ajar—and being photographed doing it by the waiting paparazzi—so it was surprising to say the least.

There were also the girls hired for party ambiance who had endured hours of professionally applied body makeup. They had been *entirely* shaved to complete the effect, and an artist literally painted on an outfit. Not one of them had packed a warm sweater on this chilly fall night. Where were their mothers? As a side note, I believe this was how Kendra (formerly of *The Girls Next Door* and now of her own reality series complete with NFL husband Hank Basset) was discovered by Hef at one of his parties. He must have had artistic appreciation for her . . . canvas.

The athlete turnout was disappointing, not at all the tall muscle buffet I had anticipated. However there was no shortage of octogenarians, a.k.a. Hef's longtime friends. The cliché pickup line "So, what's your sign?" was replaced by "So, what month were you?" while the gentlemen gestured toward montages of past centerfolds flashing on giant movie screens and strategically placed throughout the party (as if to remind you where you were, in case you had been the recent recipient of a lobotomy). After a while, I just started making up months and excusing myself as politely as possible from the conversations. It was a little like being at a wedding with *only* horny fathers of the bride in attendance—or more accurately, great-grandfathers of the bride. I didn't want to be rude to these men (you never knew who you were talking to at these things), but I also didn't want to be engaged in any conversation that lasted longer than a commercial break. As exciting as it was to be at such a historical place, I never met one man I was remotely interested in dating. Not even close. If I was going to be successful at this athlete hunting, I was going to have to get a little more creative, and think outside of my box.

This is your sideline access to my dating experiences or, more accurately, my addiction to professional athletes. I wasn't a common whore: These were serious relationships, and I was just a young woman (like so many who came before me), with really bad judgment when it came to choosing men. People ask me all the time: "What was it about jocks that attracted you so much?"

I'm not gonna lie. It's as exciting as you think it is—a total rush—sitting in the stands and watching eighty thousand people go mental, screaming for your guy on the field. A guy on the field that only *you* are going home with later. The whole ride is a completely unique experience. But like most unique experiences, they come with unique ups and fuck you's. And being with a pro athlete has its share of the fuck you's. Trust me, having been a fly on that locker-room wall, and seeing the inside world of sports few have seen, *SportsCenter* doesn't cover the things I've been privy to. The difference is that unlike *SportsCenter*, I despise sports. Despise is a strong word. I really, really, really hate sports. I was bored to tears at the actual games and celebrated the end of each season like I had won the lottery. I was just insanely, irresistibly attracted to the players who played them.

For me it was the challenge. The sick challenge of knowing that professional athletes have their pick of the women who throw themselves at them, and the ultimate conquest for me was climbing Mount Monogamy. I always did aim high, and dating these guys was like participating in the dating Olympics. But are my "bad choices" different from any other woman's? We've all made them. It's almost a rite of passage. It starts after the first time we hear the words: "And they lived happily ever after. The end." Fairy tales read to us almost like an abusive how-to manual when we are little girls. The technical term I use for the sickness most women can't help but catch is "Cinderellafuckyou-itis." We wait for a prince. We believe he is out there looking for us. And all we have to do is grow up and find him. Then we grow up—and want to kill ourselves every time we walk out of a romantic comedy. Actually, that's not entirely true. We want to kill the person we are in a relationship with. The first half of the movie you may enjoy, engrossed in the plot. The other half you are thinking, *Would my partner do that for me?* I dreamt that my prince would come in the package of a monstrous, well-built guy, who would ride in on his white horse. Scratch that, his white G5 private plane. Towering over me, his enormous size would make me feel like a petite, delicate, more feminine little flower, and he would pick me up and carry me out like Richard Gere in the last scene of *An Officer and a Gentleman*. I just had a weakness for a different kind of uniform. The kind with numbers and last names embroidered on the backs.

It's not just me. I've met rock stars who turn all googly-eyed (specifically like the keyboardist from Bon Jovi), who I watched seem downright giddy to be hanging out with a group of NFL players one night. He actually said, "I'd give up my whole career just to get into uniform and play one down of professional football." Now maybe he was being polite to the present company (who had just played in a Sunday game a few hours before), or maybe it was his Jack-and-Cokes talking, but I believed him. You may have heard the expression "athletes want to be rock stars." Well, believe me, rock stars want to be athletes. Same goes for actors; don't kid yourself. They want to be athletes, too. How many baseball movies will Kevin Costner make before he officially exchanges his SAG card for a regulation jockstrap? I guess, in short, everyone wants to be an athlete. And the people who don't want to be them want to be near them. Unfortunately the athletes know this. Enter Narcissism (yes, with a capital N). They live their lives looking through, basically, entitlement goggles (which are far more reckless and dangerous than any beer goggles), and as a result there is something very alluring, and sexy, and dangerous about these guys. It takes "liking bad boys" to an entirely different level.

One of my best friends, Sarah, has a theory that I cling to in the hopes I seem less shallow than I look on paper. Once while meeting me for an emergency summit at a local bar after my last athlete breakup, she did her best to make me feel better about my constant craving for these guys. She said, as if she were stating a fact: "You are just *really* in touch with the basic human desire and instinct to procreate! It's survival of the fittest! Back in the caveman days, this would have totally made more sense, being attracted to . . . the biggest, strongest guys!" Sarah is a good friend. Who else but a good friend can put a publicist's spin on having bad taste in men? I love her for that. *That's* what friends are actually for. But, of course, I had to challenge her. "Yes, but let's be real," I said, awaiting her answer to the next question I didn't want to ask. "Do you think back in the caveman days I would have sought out the biggest asshole cavemen?"

"Probably, yes." she said a little too quickly for comfort. She could have at least paused.

"Sarah! I don't want to be this way! If there were a twelve-step program for this . . . for athlete sobriety? I would totally enter it! Where's *my* Betty Ford? I'd be all over it." I sighed. I looked around at all the guys standing in the bar area where we were talking, for reference.

"I just think all these guys look so frail." I winced as if I were surveying a collection of Fabergé eggs instead of people. "They're weirdly small and skinny and breakable. I feel like I could take them all down in an arm-wrestling tournament!"

Sarah knew the difference between being honest and sugarcoating, so she looked me right in the eye and left the sugar at home.

"Rosa, a lot of men's bodies are going to look like little prepubescent children to *you*, for a very long time! That is what *normal* guys look like."

Ugh! She was right. I was screwed up in the head. Every idea I had about what was "normal," what at least was *my* normal, had to be totally reconfigured. I had to detonate my erogenous zones and start from scratch.

I have always been financially independent. I have been fortunate enough to consistently work as an actress in television, and I bought my first house when I was just twenty-five. But for many women, the lure of these athletes is their financial status. They are trying to win the sperm lotto. I had one ex-boyfriend tell me that at an NHL players' association meeting for rookies, they had a speaker warning the guys about safe sex. The focus of the speech was the financial threat of getting trapped into paying child support for eighteen years. Now, you'd think that the terror of a sexually transmitted disease that could kill you would be enough of a threat, but these guys are athletes. Along with what should be illegal amounts of narcissism and entitlement is also a huge dose of invincibility—even in the sack. I consider myself a verbally persuasive woman who likes to toss out the term "deal breaker" when insisting that my partner wears prophylactics, but don't think for ten seconds it surprised me to hear all the Tiger Woods mistresses detailing their alleged condomless escapades. It's oddly and inexplicably the norm. In my experience, athletes seem to think the laws of nature (unwanted pregnancy and disease) do not apply to them. Those pesky little problems are for the common folk, the common penised.

I kind of understand where they get it—that invincibility—from. They are the closest things to superheroes we have to worship. Except superheroes generally do good in the world. That aside, the invincibility often gets in the way of the reality, especially when they are making decisions. In order to make these guys truly grasp the concept of say, condoms, the NHL players' association had to make the point where it counts—in their wallets.

They told the captive audience a true story about a woman who had sued a hockey player for rape. They had his DNA, and this guy was fucked. His reputation was on the line, there was a baby on the way, and this athlete was claiming he had never even *met* this woman. This guy was going down. It took a hard-core investigation—and a ruined reputation—before the hockey player could prove that the woman accusing him had in fact teamed up with a girl he *was* sleeping with. The woman the player was having a sexual relationship with would say she was "disposing of the condoms," when in actuality she was bringing them to the hotel room next door where her best friend (and accomplice) was waiting. Armed with some cruel creativity and a turkey baster, they would have had him trapped for eighteen years. The women planned to split the "proceeds" 50/50. The moral of this story is this: Boys, flush the condoms yourselves. I think the players' association should also have emphasized "Don't sleep with crazy bitches," but I wasn't running the meeting.

Jock Itch is a cautionary tale about my past, an exploration of the origins of my itch, and how I finally ended it—by marrying one! (A jock, not the itch.) It's also a story of redemption and my new itch, minus the jocks, that led me to finding salvation (and my self-esteem) with a five-foot-seven computer geek. I think it was Woody Allen who said, "Tragedy plus time equals comedy." This is my comedy.

Hello, my name is Rosa. And I'm a jockaholic.

SCORING

*I*f you do not heed any of my memoir warnings, and you still want to meet an athlete, here is your very own Where to Meet Athletes Guide.

1. At the Super Bowl (and the several days of events and parties leading up to it).

2. At their local postgame hangout, usually a fine restaurant because they are hungry and already in a suit. (Every team has one or two hangouts. You just have to befriend a trainer or someone who works closely with them or pay attention to your local paper about where players are spotted.)

3. Your local strip club. (I'm just saying.)

4. Individual player or team charity events.

5. Player parking lots (access is usually surprisingly sparsely or not at all guarded during the practice week).

6. Official team hotel (they check in around dinner time on Saturday night, in their "home cities" the night before the game).

7. NFL players usually have a "hot spot" nightclub on Sunday night. Monday night is their "weekend night" because Tuesday is their only day off during the week.

Sometimes, if the coach is in a good mood they will get off Monday after a Sunday win as well. Figuring out the hotspot is easier in say, Green Bay, Wisconsin, than it is in Manhattan.

8. *At the games (if you can get access to the VIP/family section via a "tip," even better). Also, athletes are generally fans of sports, so other sporting events with a several-day cushion of time from any scheduled big games usually have athletes in attendance.*

9. *Vegas on (NFL) biweeks—meaning the team does not have a game scheduled one weekend out of the NFL season.*

10. *Hanging out with me from 1998 to 2008.*

This one should have come with a warning label.

TWO

Pucked

It was 1998, and I was guest-starring as a lap dancer suffering from eczema on Ted Danson's *Becker*, when an old waitressing friend of mine named Amy came on the show to do a voice-over. She had a urinary tract infection, so I asked one of the production assistants to get her cranberry-juice pills. She had just returned from a Vegas trip and had all these pictures of her with her new boyfriend, who played for the Los Angeles Kings hockey team. I think she wanted a teammate, a wingman of her own, to go on double dates with. Perhaps it was my fast thinking that saved her from further bladder discomfort, but then and there she decided to set me up with a teammate of Sam O'Connell, her boyfriend.

I was concerned he wouldn't be cute. After all, it was a blind date, and she had unflattering photos of him drunk. I was also dating an übercute (albeit überboring to me) guy from the show *Baywatch*.

Despite *Baywatch*-boy's gallant Malibu-beach feathered hair and sun-kissed mahogany skin (as well as his slow-motion ability to run in red trunks while hoisting a buoy), I simply couldn't appreciate my time with him—unless I was stoned. I had started smoking pot when I moved to L.A., mainly out of boredom and loneliness. When I started waitressing it became a necessary evil to deal with the L.A. crowd. After 11:00 p.m., when the restaurant turned into a nightclub, I mostly served Persian guys trying to tip me in coke. Did they really think waiting on assholes was my hobby?

The not-so-blind date—is it really a blind date if you can Internet stalk, look up action shots, and figure out what sign they are, all before you've even had a chance to say "I'll be the one wearing the blue shirt at the bar?"—was named Mike. He was a baby! Only twenty-one (should it have bothered me that he couldn't legally rent a car in some states?), six foot five, and a Joseph Fiennes look-alike. Mike was beautifully built, adorable, very shy, sweet, and soft-spoken. This was so ironic, because he was an enforcer for the L.A. Kings, and his job was basically to intimidate and beat the living crap out of anyone threatening his teammates on the ice. And, yes, he had all of his teeth. (That's the first question everyone asks when they find out you're dating a hockey player.) I had never met more of a big teddy bear in my life. The four of us were not at dinner very long when his nickname came up. "Moose," I quickly learned, was rarely called by his real name.

"So, why do they call you Moose?" I asked naively. There was silence at the table—followed by a burst of laughter.

"Ummm. I dunno. Maybe 'cause I'm from Canada?" I noticed that Moose said this like he was about to tell a really funny joke. With a half smile, it was as if he were constantly waiting to deliver a punch line that never, well, materialized. Plus, it was hard to understand him. At first I thought he had just had oral surgery, but I soon realized he had an omnipresent tobacco-chewing habit. This explained the beer bottle he endlessly deposited saliva into. This was an act he had perfected. He did it so quickly you couldn't tell what he was doing—until you realized the "beer" in the bottle was dark brown, thick, and sludgy on top. And kissing him (with any sort of first-trimester protruding bulge going on in his lower lip) was just begging for a mouthful of tobacco surprise. That's the kind of teaching moment you really only need once.

The "I'm from Canada" thing seemed like a perfectly plausible explanation. But when I saw him naked, it all came together. The first time we were messing around it was dark. At first I felt what could best be described as a disturbingly large object pressing into my leg. *Did I really leave a rolling-pin in the bed?* I wondered. Then I decided maybe he was carrying one of those early-model cell phones, circa 1988. As it turned out, Moose had no such vintage device on him. I reached down and audibly gasped at what I unsuccessfully attempted to curl my hand around. *I must be drunk*, I thought. Then I gently lifted the thing up, so I could see the silhouette it made against the moonlight coming through the windows. My only thought was *Holy appendage, Batman!* If this hadn't been before *Punk'd*, I'd have expected Ashton Kutcher to jump out of my closet at any moment.

DATING MOOSE WAS a challenge of *Survivor*-like proportions. First, I had to understand what the hell he was saying. He mumbled like Rocky Balboa on Quaaludes. Our phone conversations required a combination of skill, concentration, and keen deciphering of something like Morse code. I felt like I was right there with Pat Sajak and Vanna on *Wheel of Fortune*, because I always had to fill in the blanks when it came to Moosespeak. As if the conversation navigation weren't challenging enough, Moose said to me one day, in our first month of dating, "I've never been faithful to a girl before."

What Moose was really saying was "You know I'm gonna cheat on you, right?"

Still, what I heard was, "I have never found a girl special enough to share all the comforts and sacredness that an adult monogamous relationship brings, until you, Rosa. Hence, the reason for my sharing."

I know what you're thinking. An enforcer in the NHL

with no high school degree would never use the word "hence." But in his defense, his favorite movie was *Braveheart*. "Hences" are plentiful in epic battle scenes, especially those containing the *pre*-racist commenting, angry voice mail leaving, rant master himself: Mel Gibson.

Instead of heeding his warning—which was a red flag as massive and unmistakable as the one in *Les Misérables*—I somehow took it as a compliment. Like all women in their twenties, I was in desperate need of a penile counselor, to guide me through this decade of my life, and to stand by my side until I reached my thirtieth birthday. The twenties are when most women make atrocious decisions regarding men time and time again. How different would the dating world be if having a twenties wrangler at your side was the rule of law?

"Why hasn't Moose said 'I love you' yet?" my girlfriends began challenging me after about six months, the female timeline for the window of opportunity in which you should have heard this already.

"He's shy. Not talkative. But I know I'm the first girl he's ever loved. We even waited to have sex!" I almost believed it.

"Hmm. Why haven't you been invited to a hockey game?" They heckled me like I was an unwelcome caller on a radio talk show. Clearly, they were not swayed by my latest defense of this "why didn't I see it?" prick.

"I think he wants me to like him for who he is. Our love is that deep. It isn't all about sex. He needs me to show him how to be loved," said the codependent dumbass inside me. I truly believed that because I had had this white-picket-fence upbringing, I could show Moose what love really was.

At fourteen, Moose had stopped going to school, moved in with a host family, and given up the comforts of home and friends in order to pursue his NHL dream. It was then that he discovered an awesome cure to the boredom of living with clueless faux parents: vodka. Miss Vodka became Moose's closest confidante, and she hid behind the dresser drawers in Moose's borrowed bedroom. It was just like being a child star in Hollywood, just as we see it detailed in the press: When the world around you is busy celebrating your talent and achievements, your potential problems take a backseat. Miss Vodka made the mornings come quicker and the long days fly by between hockey games.

I THOUGHT I COULD change him. I thought I could show him that he was more than just a stick, and there was a love stronger than Miss Vodka. Hockey or penile, he had more attributes and I saw them. He was an insomniac, and I thought it was sweet the way he would call me at all hours of the night. He needed me, and the comfort of me there, whenever and wherever he was.

I was filming the movie *Noriega* in the Philippines and missing Moose in the worst way. I also was paranoid about getting some crazy, explosive third-world diarrhea superbug. If you could get Montezuma's revenge going to Mexico—just a hop, skip, and jump away from California— then I didn't want to find out what could happen after a fourteen-hour flight to Manila. I didn't eat anything except papaya, even though I was staying at a five-star hotel. I worked out like it was my job and I was determined to come home and not only have Moose exclaim, "You look hot!" but also be so tempted by my re-formed body that he would throw in an "I love you" for the first time. I was running on a treadmill, which was new to me. I had always thought that doing any kind of exercise was the work of the antichrist, something for overachievers. Still, I was kicking ass! I couldn't believe how good I had gotten. Five miles a day? No problem! Anything for my Moose. Plus, with all the damn papaya and not much else, I was getting shredded. It wasn't until the week before I left the country, while I was bragging to my cast-mates about my recent cardio prowess, that I was informed the treadmills were marked in kilometers, not miles. Having a decent body, it's so annoying. There's always a catch.

Amy, who had introduced me to Moose, started seriously dating Sam, Moose's roommate, at the same time as my whatever-it-was with Moose continued on. Amy and I usually tried to make plans with the boys by being at their house when they returned from their most recent road trip. On this occasion, I had the cutest pink-with-red-cherries bra and panties all picked out from the famous store Trashy Lingerie. The pink said, "I'm nice." But the cherries warned, "I'm also kind of naughty, so don't trust me as far as you can throw my cartoon fruit." (Assuming your underwear could talk.) I was tanned and toned and couldn't wait to see him.

What I could have waited to see was the letter to Moose that had already been sent and opened. I didn't even have to snoop—well, at least not that hard. Inside the envelope was a photograph of some bimbo sitting on Moose's lap and a note recalling what a great time she'd had in whatever city it was a couple of weeks ago. Now, this was when I was in the freaking Philippines running kilometer after kilometer for Moose. I was so pissed and hurt, but after a few days, and many apologies later, I was also so forgiving. The good news was that it solidified that we were in an "exclusive relationship" and we were definitely boyfriend and girlfriend. The bad news was that if you were in a normal relationship, your boyfriend screwing someone shouldn't be the start of a commitment.

From that point on, the only smart thing I did was not trust him. I was always on the lookout for more clues. I became my very own Nancy Drew, and nothing got past me—except everything. I would be at his house waiting for him to come home from a game, secretly steaming his phone bill open while watching the game on TV. Maybe I remember this so clearly because—well, because it was a bit psycho—but also because it was Halloween, and the camera at the game cut to a live shot of a female fan. She was dressed as a bride and carrying a sign that said "Mrs. Johnstone"—Moose's last name. I'm watching, I'm steaming, both literally and figuratively, and I'm thinking, *Oh yeah, bitch? Not if I can help it!*

———

T HE NEXT TIME I caught Moose cheating I was following his car to his house, where we had plans. He usually talked to me on the phone during the half-hour car ride, because, well, we were both clearly codependent. It was strange this car ride, though. He was on the phone the whole time and, for some reason, I knew he was talking to a girl. We got to his house and when he went to take a shower I looked at the call log on his cell phone.

"Moose, who the fuck is Lori?"

"She's just this girl I was going to set my buddy Chris up with," he lied. "She reminds me of you!" he added lamely, as if that made it okay.

"Really? Because then you won't mind me calling her right now, right?" Moose looked extremely antsy—like Tourette's antsy. I called Lori by hitting redial, and in my non-confrontational way I told her, "You better stop calling my boyfriend."

Lori, without skipping a beat, said, "Um . . . boyfriend? Well, then I suggest you get a better handle on your Moose!"

Moose and I spent the rest of the night fighting. He had his ridiculous excuses, and I gave him all these idiotic justifications. I kept thinking, *I'm the first girl he's ever really loved. He doesn't know how to be in a relationship.* A seasoned serial monogamist, I had been in several. This was more about the girls throwing themselves at him. I would have justified anything at that point because I wasn't strong enough to leave the relationship. I loved him and I had delusions about us really working as a couple and ultimately I could just envision a beautiful engagement ring the size of an ice rink, followed by a wedding when Moose retired in a few years, the giant baby boy they would most likely have to remove by C-section, and finally the gentle yet effective tummy tuck for that special mom-orexic look.

This scenario left a nice stink, but we moved on. Moose got traded to Atlanta from Los Angeles, and we began a long-distance relationship. He clung to me more, because he didn't know anyone in Atlanta, and I was visiting twice a month. What better situation for someone you can't trust than to have him live thousands of miles away!

A couple of months down the road, I got a phone call at 3:00 a.m. from a guy who was a club promoter. I didn't actually check the message until the next morning, and when I realized this guy called me I freaked out. I knew him from my "going out" days. He was an acquaintance, and I couldn't believe he could get my number. I had never given it to him. To make things more alarming, his message said, "Rosa. It's Ronny. You have to give me a call when you get this. It's important."

Someone was dead? I thought. I scrambled to call him back, but, like most club promoters, he was not answering the phone at 9:00 a.m.

By that afternoon, still weirded out, I called him again. This time a girl answered the phone.

"Hi! Sorry to bother you, but this is Rosa, and I got a call from Ronny in the middle of the night, and I'm really worried. Can you please tell him to call me back? It's just really random that he called and his message sounded urgent."

"Sure. I'll give him the message. Rosa, you said?"

"Yeah."

"As in *Rosa Blasi?*"

"Yes. Who is this?"

"Lori."

Fucking Lori.

"As in *Lori* Lori?" I didn't know her last name. But at that moment I didn't need to.

"Yes," she said, like a surly teenager when their mom picks up the house line midconversation.

"Are you dating Moose?" I asked in full-on reporter mode. I was coming at her like Nancy Grace with bullets.

No answer.

"Listen, Lori, I want to meet up with you. I want to talk." I said this as sincerely as I could, considering the conversation.

"Um . . . I don't think that's a good idea." She sounded scared, which is funny because my biggest fear in life is getting into a fight, or having something hit my nose. I've seen *Extreme Makeover*. Unlike my upper eyelids, I still have my original nose.

"Lori, I love him," I continued. "If he's cheating on me, I'm going to break up with him. But I want to meet up with you and get the details. I'm not gonna beat you up or do anything weird. That's so not who I am. I just want to know details. I want to hear it from you."

I had a sick curiosity to see this Lori girl.

I finally coerced Lori into a meeting. It would take place at Ronny's house. She had been talking to Ronny about her boyfriend Moose. He knew I was dating him and decided to call and let me know that Lori and I were contestants in Moose's game of Musical Vaginas! Around and around and around he goes, where he stops . . . nobody knows!

When I got to Ronny's, Lori opened the door. I was strangely, extremely cordial, and just wanted to hear her side of things. I was visiting Moose every other weekend. She was there on the weekends I was not. Lori was infantile-young at twenty-two. She had a similar look to me, with the prerequisite nice Hollywood fake rack and petite body—or a "spinner," a.k.a., a petite girl you could almost "spin" around your penis, like a toy—as Moose often joked. She was a little meatier than I was, which surprised the hell out of me when I found out she'd had liposuction as well—and *that* body was the end result?

I could see why Moose would fuck her. She had just moved to L.A., and she was pretty in a low-rent Carmen Electra kind of way, despite the fact that she came from a really rich family. New money. Something to do with computer software or something. Her dad actually lived in the house where the television series *Miami Vice* with Don Johnson was filmed. But as everyone knows, you can't buy class. The house still had a very eighties vibe. There was actually a cheesy mirrored wall with an original Van Gogh hanging on it. I wonder if that's how the artist envisioned a piece from his sunflower series being displayed?

But back to Lori. I felt this need to tell her my side of things, and how Moose had deceived us both. Then I used my Second City improv skills to concoct an immediate rescue plan. I asked Ronny if he had a camera. He tossed me a Polaroid, and Lori and I took four staged photos. One was of Lori and me meeting in the doorway. One was of us faking deep conversation. One was of us fake-kissing. And finally both of us looked straight in the camera and flipped Moose off. We scrawled, "Fuck off!" to really drive the point home. Subtlety was never a fine point of mine.

Next up, we FedExed the photos to Moose. Then we recorded the following outgoing message on my answering machine:

"Hi! This is Rosa!"

"And this is Lori!"

"We can't come to the phone right now. We've both been busy fucking Moose," I stated excitedly.

"And we're tired!" Lori finished my sentence as if we were a couple.

"Leave a message!"

WAITING FOR HIM to get our FedEx and call was like being a kid before Christmas. It was awesome. He may have broken the record for stuttering and stammering, and when I finally took his calls I laid into him with the kind of vitriol you save up for an occasion like this one. For the next few days, he called, cried, begged, and called some more. I, of course, ignored his calls and played them for Lori. I told him I knew everything and that he'd better just fess up all his sins, because we were over, and it didn't matter anymore anyway.

I couldn't possibly have prepared myself for what came out of his mouth next. Perhaps it was all the hockey pucks, punches, and ice rinks to the head. He actually started rattling off all the women he had fucked around with. There was a creepy pattern, a familiarity to the list that I noticed immediately! All the women he named he had mentioned to me before. The sick part was that he had just conveniently left off the part about him fucking them. Like, if he had gotten a pair of jeans that day, he would tell me, "You know, the saleswoman was flirting with me."

"Really?" I egged him on—all the while silently praising him for being so truthful for telling me in the first place.

"What did you tell her?" I asked.

"That I had a girlfriend, dummy." He'd grin that killer smile, and I'd be oozing and dripping from the flatter sauce he'd just sautéed me in.

My mind raced. I started to envision every woman he had ever mentioned to me, at any time, for any reason. Meanwhile, he was breaking the record for the amount of times he could answer yes to each horrible inquiry.

"What about that teller at the bank that always says hi?"

"Yeah, her."

"What about your accountant you are always talking to?"

"Yep. Her too."

"What about your strictly platonic friend Angela?"

"Not so platonic," he replied.

"What about your masseuse who is here every week?"

"Of course. She's a rub-tug girl!"

"A *what*?" I screamed. The name pretty much said it all. It didn't take a thesaurus. But I wanted to hear him say it.

"Yeah. She gives massages. She's a real masseuse. But then after, there's a happy ending. But that's not really like cheating. All the guys get them!"

I knew he meant the guys on his stupid team, or all the guys he associated with. Surely, somewhere in the United States there had to be people getting legitimate massages! Or is *that* what was they mean by a "deep tissue" option?

"Um, Moose? A manual release is in fact considered cheating, for your future information." I'm still not quite sure why I felt the need to educate him at this particular juncture.

The list continued. It was longer than the one carried by Santa Claus. But on this list there were no good little girls, just bad ones.

I was so mad I did what any normal woman in crisis does. I went shopping! But I didn't buy the latest fashions or a killer bag. I bought something that would uncondi-tionally love me back and never cheat—an English mastiff that would grow to be two hundred pounds and I could use to assist me with illegal parking. I named him Jake Ryan, after every woman's fantasy guy from the movie *Sixteen Candles*. There's not an American woman over twenty-five who doesn't know that movie by heart. And anyone who didn't have a crush on Jake Ryan must have had one on Molly Ringwald, and may have emulated Jake Ryan's hair-cut while rocking in flannel at a Lilith Fair concert.

During the whole ugly process of talking to Moose about what had happened just frustrated me more. I asked him repeatedly, "*Why* did you cheat? *Why?*"

His response was always "I didn't have any balls."

IT WAS VALENTINE'S DAY, and he was still trying to get me to take him back and forgive him. He sent so many flowers it looked like Seabiscuit died. I wanted to send Moose a little something, too. Something he had expressed on so many occasions that he needed.

I wish I could have seen the expression on his face when he opened his UPS package. There was a card attached that simply read, "Heard you didn't have any. Thought you could use some of mine. Love, Jake Ryan."

In a mason jar, floating in vodka, were two small puppy testicles. Jake had been neutered the day before and, like a weirdo, I asked the vet if he could put them in a Ziploc for me.

The vet said, "You have no idea how often I get that request."

It was meant to be a joke, and Moose got my sarcasm and my sense of humor. He called me when he received it, laughing. "These are not what I think they are!" He giggled as much as an enormous man can.

"Well, they aren't gnocchi!" I snorted. They actually did look just like the gnocchi from your favorite Italian place, sans sauce. When I wasn't mailing organs, or missing Moose's, it became evident to me that I needed to get tested for every possible disease, including hoof-and-mouth.

Moose was a sex addict. He wasn't just a massive cheater but a sex addict, and he needed professional help. Let me rephrase that: He had had lots of professional help. He needed the kind where the pro didn't toss you a wet towel before she asked for a stack of money at the end! It was beyond my wildest nightmares. We had spent so much time together yet somehow he managed to screw all these other women. I was amazed his cock didn't fall off.

Most unbelievable of all was that in my sickness and dementia I befriended Lori. It was the least probable friendship, and she even ended up moving in with me in "Rosa's home for wayward women," as we jokingly referred to it. But it was weirdly healing, and I blamed Moose for what had happened and not her.

Then Moose dropped the T bomb.

He suggested we go to therapy together. Couples' therapy. I was shocked, flattered, and then hooked. I agreed to give him a chance with a therapist. I was so impressed that he wanted to heal and wanted to make us work as a couple that my armor began to break down. Everyone deserves a second chance, right? What guy begs to go to therapy? That's like a chick go-to line. I agreed to see him only in couples' therapy. We would go a few times a week and take baby steps from there.

Our therapist almost dropped his pen when I told him why we were there. I love therapy. I think everyone should go on their own and I think it should be the law that you have to check in at least once a month and take responsibility for your shit. But that therapist adventure with Moose was bullshit. If the doctor had any conscience he would have kicked us out after the first visit. At the very least, he should have refunded our money after Moose said softly and sincerely, "I love you, Rosa. I just don't know why you think blowjobs are cheating."

"It's the universal rule, Moose. It's not just a Rosa rule. Everyone on the planet thinks blowjobs are cheating."

I looked at the therapist as if to say, *Do you see what we're up against?*

The only real breakthrough came when the therapist said this sentence to Moose: "You are defined by a stick." He was talking about the one he uses on the ice to slap a puck with, and the one he uses between his legs at every opportunity that presents itself. He thought Moose might benefit from individual therapy and that he suffered from low self-image (of course, like all serial cheaters, he had not one shred of self-esteem). Moose finally broke down and admitted that he liked and craved the attention and "worship" of new girls.

While enduring couples' therapy, I started work on my first dramatic television series and my first starring role on the show *Strong Medicine*. I played tough, straight-from-the-inner-city, ob-gyn and single mom Dr. Lu Delgado for what would be the next 132 episodes (or six years) of my life. I had a grueling one-hour commute to and from the set and every morning had to pass Manhattan Beach, where Moose lived. He was always begging me to come over, and I was always trying to see him—but only in therapy.

One morning on my way to work, I decided to drive by Moose's home and leave a note on the windshield of his car. It would just be a little "I'm thinking of you" sweetness to start off his day with a smile. But when I pulled up to his house, I noticed that the front door was ajar. *That's odd*, I thought. I walked up to the door and noticed his friend from Canada, who had been visiting, crashed out on his couch, still in his clothes from the night before. I smiled to myself, thinking, *These guys must have gotten wrecked last night!* I decided to go in, climb in bed with Moose, tease him for a minute, and leave him wanting more. It was the least I could do. He had made such a great effort in our therapy sessions, and he was respecting the boundaries I was setting and the fact that I was basically in a permanent Heisman pose (one arm in a "stay away" position) with him. I wanted us to get back together the right way, with baby steps.

I opened the door to his room slowly, cursing the creakiness of the old wood, with the biggest smile on my face, anticipating his own big smile. He wearily raised his head and looked at me as if he were still asleep and not sure he was seeing what was actually right in front of him.

Much to my surprise, the brunette next to him did the same thing.

"Rosa?" Moose asked.

Oh joy! Oh rapture! He fucking remembered my name!

I blindly pirouetted out of the room and out the door.

Moose chased me to my car. I wish I could tell you what he said, but truly it all just sounded like the "wamp, wamp,

wamp, wamp" when Charlie Brown's teachers are talking in *Peanuts* cartoons. Moose and I were officially over.

A COUPLE OF MONTHS LATER, I had the pleasure of really "getting to know" Kara, the mystery brunette from that fateful morning. She was *Playboy*'s latest Miss December. (Rudely, that's my birthday month!) She was six foot two barefoot, *Playboy*'s tallest model to date. A beautiful, exotic-looking girl more suited to *Perfect 10* magazine than *Playboy*. I would like to tell you it's all airbrushing, but I'd be exaggerating to massage my own ego. She was a knockout and, I think, sporting real boobs. How dare she! In Los Angeles County, no less. Sure, she seemed dumber than rocks, but don't they all on that trifold centerfold? Plus, she was born in 1986, my freshman year in high school. It depressed me to know that she could have been my daughter had I been a big slut back then.

Shortly afterward, I heard that Moose ended up in rehab for drug and sex addiction. Now, this was before the press made "sex addiction" synonymous with "marital infidelity." It was back in the day, when normal people just called it cheating. I'm still not sure how that whole sex rehab thing works—especially with coed residents in sex rehab clinics. Wouldn't that sort of be comparable to leaving piles of drugs out on coffee tables at Hazelden? If you are confined to a place with other people who can't stop compulsively having sex, how does that work? And if you are a professional athlete it's particularly confusing, because isn't having frequent, anonymous sex part of the basic job description? It's practically written in the contract, and mentioned at the postdraft press conferences. I wouldn't be surprised if there were women servicing the new drafts under that podium as sort of a professional sports welcome-wagon perk. I wonder if that thing fans do at games known as "the wave" started when an announcer asked over the sound system: "Raise your hand if you have slept with someone down on that field?"

The problem that I have with it is why pretend to be monogamous in the first place? I don't want to hear that you're on a strict diet only to find you bobbing facedown in a three-tiered melted-chocolate fountain. Because then, really, won't we both just end up looking ridiculous?

Amy and Sam ended up getting married and divorced three years later. Moose and I stood up at their wedding, and it was the first time we had seen each other since the breakup. Never did a bridesmaid spend so much effort to look so hot in a mint-green-sherbet-colored bridesmaid dress. All that was missing was the matching Bo Peep hat and that sheep hook thing.

I FINALLY UNDERSTOOD THAT Moose was toxic to me, that he was my cancer, and I made sure he was permanently out of my life and deleted from my cell phone forever. I heard over the years from Amy that he was not over me, would describe me as the one who got away, and could he have my number? The answer was always "Um. No."

Finally, Amy caved. And armed with what she deemed to be a really good excuse she gave my number to Moose. He was on whatever step it is in Alcoholics Anonymous where you are supposed to go back in time, like the Ghost of Christmas Past, and ask forgiveness from people you have been a douche bag to. Apparently I was integral to his success in doing the twelve steps. I nervously accepted his phone call this time, hoping the sound of his voice wouldn't be like sexual kryptonite to me. I couldn't believe it when I listened to him rambling endlessly about "his sins" and "our Lord and Savior Jesus Christ." Was I saved? Moose wanted to know, eagerly awaiting my answer. I gritted my teeth and thought of Amy's genius idea giving out my phone number, and thought curtly, *Not from this phone call.* It was such a different Moose on the phone that day that I felt like I was having an out-of-body experience and an acid flashback. But I forgave Moose. He quit hockey and "found God."

Then I changed my number.

To this day, I have never seen anything like the man parts that levitated between Moose's navel and his knees. His cup truly ranneth over. Long after the relationship was over, I was in a sex shop with my friend Sheila. We had to buy joke gifts for a friend's bachelorette party. As we walked, intimidated, through a Hollywood sex shop we passed the fake vaginas, the funny and strangely clever porno-movie titles, the battery-operated artillery, and ended up at a section of the store that might be most people's worst nightmare—gag gifts, sex-shop style. As we approached what many, many before me have accurately described as a baby's arm holding an apple, Sheila simply squealed and said, "As if *anybody* is that big!"

Without hesitation and with the tiniest bit of wistfulness in my voice, I lamented,

"That was my Moose."

Seven ounces of self-worth and seven feet of regret.

THREE

Rebound

When you see a guy that is over seven feet tall, you would have to be Stevie Wonder not to assume he could be a basketball player. Lance was no exception. I was out at a bar in Hollywood with my new friend Lori when I saw a man whose head was only a few inches from the lighting fixtures, looming next to a casual acquaintance of Moose's. He was a friend I had probably met once, who was somehow connected to one of Moose's permanent hangers-on. All athletes have them. The friend that shadows them, hangs out with them at the athlete's beck and call, drops the athlete's name nonstop, and is always there like a personal assistant who gets paid not in cash but cache, unclaimed vagina, and game tickets. It's different from the entourage that accompanies music stars. The entourage screams, "Look how many people I roll with! Look at how important I am! Look how many people work for me!" In short, the recurring theme of "look." If you need ten other dudes on a payroll to make you feel important, you are either a rapper and in fear of getting shot, or you're just kind of a needy tool in my opinion. A hanger-on is different. It's more of a sycophantic one-man band. He is the guy who will approach the girl and get her number (for the athlete that is too cool to do it himself). He will set up the night's plans (specified by the athlete), secure the transportation (specified by the athlete—usually a big SUV for comfort and head room), notify the club of your arrival to reserve a VIP booth (it's not like the athlete's going to call himself), and generally kiss ass and spout off game stats to anyone in earshot—just in case you missed the part about being in the presence of greatness. He is "the friend of," which defines him more than his actual occupation, and not only makes him "cooler" than he would be on his own accord, but also gives him automatic proximity to hot girls he could never land by himself. If you could sell the benefits of being this "accessory" on eBay, there'd be record-breaking bidding wars.

This time, the hanger-on was seated next to the tallest blond man I had ever seen that close up. I was trying to blow off Moose's "friend," which made me the only girl in the bar that seemed disinterested in hanging around Lance, which in turn made Lance very interested in me.

Eventually, the hanger-on said something that made me almost want to reach out and hug him so hard that he risked a rib fracture. He looked at me seriously and sort of conspiratorially stated, "You know, you are better off without Moose. He's a great guy to be buddies with but not a guy you want to date. Kind of . . . a douche." I beamed. We were instant compadres; we had found common ground. I was ready to run out and buy those silly half-heart "best friend" necklaces. Maybe I was vulnerable and this was part of an elaborate hanger-on hoax ring, but something resonated with me at that moment, and it was exactly what I needed to hear. I sat down and took them up on their offer to buy us a drink. Lance and I had an effortless chemistry. His soft brown eyes were smiling like Santa Claus in the Coca-Cola commercials right before he winks. He was extremely conversational, and as we engaged in verbal intercourse I found myself listening not so much to what he was saying, but to *how* he was saying it. He had an accent from a foreign country, which made him hotter and a little more interesting than he was on paper. So did being over seven feet tall. I'm not gonna lie, and so did playing in the NBA. He was charming and had wisdom—a maturity and a Zen about him. He seemed very in control. I learned that night that he lived in Arizona (athlete capital of the world, second only to Florida), and that he used to play for the Chicago Bulls during the height of Jordan mania. It was only slightly embarrassing that I had never heard of him, as I had lived in the same city and been to some of the games while I was working at Hooters. If I hadn't been so busy people-watching in the stands around me, and adjusting my tank top with the Hooters owl on it, I may have been a little bit more informed.

He asked for my phone number and, intrigued, I gave it to him. This was fresh on the heels of the Moose breakup and I needed a distraction from mourning its end. Even breaking up with a serial cheater still hurts. I was in full-on postbreakup depression mode—the kind where you avoid watching romantic comedies and listening to the radio, because every lyric reminds you of what you had, or wished you had, and every word seems designed to stab you in the heart. At that point I was still celebrating the small stuff—you know, like not rocking back and forth in a corner, drooling, and moaning his name in a pool of tears.

Lance and the hanger-on followed us back to my house and we had a small party with the five of us (including my two roommates). Lance was drinking heavily and at one point rummaged through my underwear drawer trying to be funny and was trying on different lingerie (over his clothes) in front of everybody, looking ridiculous and making us all laugh. It was quite a sight. He looked like a tranny Big Bird after one too many Guinness beers. That night, after he left, I went to my information desk, a.k.a. my computer, and typed in his name. There was his picture and all of his basketball accolades, followed by one word I did not anticipate, and didn't even believe I was reading. But there it was: Married. My head spun. Okay, surely this information was outdated. I mean, there were at least a dozen websites where my age was off by a year. He certainly wasn't wearing a ring, he asked for my phone number, and he was not being subtle about the flirting in public. Plus the fact that he was seven foot two meant every pair of eyes in the bar was on him, whispering and watching his every move. If he really were married, wouldn't he have to be more covert, wear a baseball cap, or at least walk on his knees to blend into the crowd?

The next day Lance called, and I wasted no time. I think I interrupted him before he finished saying the last syllable in "Hello Rosa?"

"Yeah, hi Lance." I knew it was him. No one else called me with a foreign accent besides my father. "Are you married?"

There was a confirming pause.

"I am. Technically."

What does that mean—technically? He tried to explain as I pursed my lips, narrowed my eyes, and waited.

"I mean, not for long. It's at the end. It's a bit more complicated. But my marriage has been over for a long time."

"Does your wife know this?" I said as I channeled my inner Joy Behar from *The View*.

He sort of laughed and never answered the question. "I was wondering if we could meet . . . just for lunch."

"Just for lunch" is like when a celebrity says the person they are caught canoodling is "just a friend," an alcoholic has "just one drink," or a college guy says he wants to put in "just the tip." Justification for anything that has to be "justed" before doing it generally isn't a good plan. I had recently reached record lows of self-esteem on account of my Moose relationship and my taking it personally that he had cheated on me. So of course I agreed to meet him at the Ritz Carlton where he was staying. We had a great conversation. He was extremely nurturing, worldly, and complimentary. Plus, I was desperately in need of hearing the things he had to say at this particular juncture in my life. I explained the situation I had just gotten out of. He told me that "I deserved more." He explained that his wife did not have sex with him anymore, and I was so naïve I actually felt bad for him. I empathized. *How awful that must be.* I had never been married, of course, so at the time I didn't have full respect for the sanctity of marriage, which marriage deserves. Therefore, I didn't question the fact that this was just his one-sided version of the story—a story he was telling a girl he recently met in a bar, and telling her over "just lunch."

In my immaturity and naïveté I was able to hop aboard his justification bandwagon, right along with him. With that said, I too would like to bitch slap my younger self, but this kind of stellar thinking only affirms the need for a 24/7 midtwenties wrangler. They could be hired to assist the (not yet fully developed) brain of a young woman in decision making, particularly when it comes to relationships. There's a reason you can't rent a car in a lot of states until you're twenty-five. It takes life experience to undumbify and make healthy decisions. I was a novice and I had never dated a guy who had "marital problems" before (or since), so although I understand why I made the decisions I did at the time, it is the *only* thing to this day that I regret or am ashamed of. And I've done a lot of dumb shit! I am a strong believer in karma, in what comes around goes around, and even as recently as last year, I sat in my therapist's office and asked her, "Do you think all of these things happening are from my karmic backlash from the relationship with Lance?" I truly believe so, even if my therapist didn't have the heart to say, "Um . . . yeah, pretty much."

Lance treated me, well, like the mistress I came to be. Mistresses and cheaters are great for each other. They understand one another because although they don't address it (they are too busy being passionate and "really understanding" each other), if they are sneaking around then they have low self-esteem in common. Affairs are so unrealistic on so many levels, and generally puddle-deep. Although Lance was kind and passionate, he was still an athlete—a.k.a very self-absorbed. He'd ask me if I watched his game, yet never once watched my television show, so I felt like he really didn't support my career. He seemed to appreciate just my ass-ets.

"I can't find it on the television," he said when I questioned him.

"It's called cable," I answered. "It's not that hard."

I wasn't on Telemundo! He whined about "not playing," while getting paid millions of dollars a year to warm the bench. So, on a career level, I couldn't relate. I had been so broke I considered selling a kidney before, if only it wouldn't leave such a nasty scar. Lance and I would sneak off the beaten path to cozy restaurants and huddle in the corner booths talking for hours. He had been coached for many years under legend Phil Jackson, and Phil believed greatly in meditation, and making his players do yoga. This must have rubbed off on Lance because he became a regular Zen master, a stretched-out, skinny Buddha who gave me books with the word "Tao" in the title and spoke to me in such soothing, calming tones that I felt like I was at a spa during most of our conversations. Ironically, or maybe more conveniently, my new boyfriend (despite his impression of Gandhi in high-tops) and I didn't have any conversations about our own karma for engaging in this relationship. Lance said the things I needed to hear in order to heal from my Moosery. He was ecstatic with every touch, profusely grateful for every moment we spent together, and told me that he had never cheated on his wife before (whom he had been with for over ten years), although he'd had hundreds of opportunities to over his long and illustrious career as a professional basketball player, which made me feel as special as a dumb girl can. Strangely, I believed him. And stranger yet, he was treating me the way Moose should have been treating me all along, had Moose not been preoccupied trying to earn a gold medal in the fucking-strange-vagina competition. Lance was raising the bar for my dating expectations,.

I HAD LEGITIMATE CONCERNS getting intimate with a man who was seven foot two and wore a size 19 shoe. Size . . . matters. Especially to a five-foot-two girl who would someday need her uterus and didn't want to end up on a gurney. I had heard rumors of Shaquille O'Neal at

Louisiana State University accidentally injuring a girl with his basketball "equipment." I don't know if it's true, but it seemed logical and I also didn't want to have a suburban legend of my own. There was a two-foot difference in height between us and I looked like a kindergartner next to him. To have a serious conversation, I had to stand on the bed to see eye to (almost) eye. When the time came for nudity, and I stupidly justified that he was "near divorce" instead of "still married," I wasn't prepared for the unveiling. It was like a Salvador Dali painting, where things suddenly aren't what they seem, or what you'd expect—like your mind's playing tricks on you. Was I having an acid flashback from that one time in college?

Lance's penis was no different. There, at full attention, under what could be considered a slightly ginger-hued man-bush, was an incredibly wide but more incredibly short male sex organ that resembled a pale, half-eaten croissant. This was when I realized he probably wasn't lying when he said he had never cheated on his wife before, because he seemed proud of his half soda pop can. He was beaming at half (but full) mast! I learned that day that the myth about shoe size and dick size being correlated is just that—a myth. Thankfully, it worked nicely. And what he lacked in length, he certainly made up for in enthusiasm and effort.

O BVIOUSLY, WE DIDN'T see each other much. He was busy on the road (basketball has a brutal season of about eighty-two games a year, half of those on the road) in various cities, plus he was "trying to end his marriage." That's code for: having his cake and eating mine too!

Our "relationship" consisted mostly of late-night phone conversations and brief exciting rendezvous in random cities where he was playing. I could attend away games, but home games were off-limits. The risk would have been too high, and people would have asked too many questions about my presence at the games. A girl sitting by herself at a sporting event is anything but subtle. I would sit in the stands alone, in close proximity to the court, all decked out in my standard slutty-lite couture, as people around me tried to figure out who I was there for and since when were fuck-me pumps acceptable game-watching attire? Lance spotted me, smiled, and waved from the court at one game I attended. So many heads simultaneously snapped in my direction that it looked like a thousand fans were performing a sequence out of a Radio City Rockettes show. Once I flew to Rome, Italy, for just *twenty-seven hours*, for a date where Lance was playing for the Olympic team and the country he was originally from (not Italy—stop trying to guess). I was still filming *Strong Medicine*, so my time was limited and only allowed for that crazy brevity. Because I was young, I was able to pull off these mini jetting jaunts without a hideous travel hangover. The whole thing was such an odd affair, nothing like the ones you typically see in the movies. He never bought me any gifts (even on my birthday and Christmas) besides a couple of those Tao books, and I never asked him to leave his wife.

(I later learned from Oprah's show that only 5 percent of affairs end in successful marriages so it was a good thing I didn't.) It was also very lonely being a basketball widow. I had to occupy myself in these strange cities while he had practices or charity obligations. It was very isolating and lonely and I couldn't talk about him to my friends or co-workers because ultimately I was ashamed and craved a normal Blockbuster-movie-night boyfriend. I winced when he started with the "I love you's." The feelings were not mutually deep, but dating him was like a little boost for my starving self-esteem—or as much of a boost as a salacious and incredibly regretful affair can give you.

Our affair lasted a little over a year, and when the gnawing feeling in my gut (that had been there since the first night we met in a bar) said "end this, dummy," I finally listened. It seemed apropos to end our relationship over the phone, where the majority of it really took place. Lance was shocked, mostly I think because he had never been broken up with before. He scrambled to understand what was happening, and stammered that he would soon be divorced, and wanted to know what had gone wrong, and what else he could do. I tried explaining my "gut thing"—my reasoning—but I knew he didn't get it. My little speech was about as effective as him trying to teach me the physics necessary to sink a basket from half court—a waste of time because we'd both probably end up missing the points.

Shortly thereafter, Lance did eventually file for divorce. I hope his wife ended up with half of everything—because God knows, she was only getting half a dick all those years!

WARNING SIGNS YOUR MAN'S SPORTING A WEDDING RING (WHEN YOU AREN'T AROUND)

1. He answers the phone in hurried, hushed tones (as if he's at the movies) and he's not a librarian.

2. His phone always goes right to voicemail, he "never hears it," "forgets it in his car" a lot, or has chronic "problems with the ringer."

3. He knows the difference between the colors "white" and "ecru," plus he owns a fondue maker and a full set of china.

4. He can't believe you always want to have sex with him.

5. He can't believe you are willing to give him oral when it's not his birthday.

6. He knew what the topic was on Oprah that day.

7. He never sleeps over because he "has to get up so early for work."

8. He never suggests going out of town on weekend jaunts, or if he does, they're always work-related business trips in (nonromantic) cities like Des Moines and Toledo.

9. You never go together to large social gatherings, work parties, charity events, weddings, barbecues, or

anywhere really other than your bedroom and dark restaurants.

10. *When you Googled him, it said "married" next to his professional athlete bio.*

Pete and his curio cabinet.

FOUR

Out of Left Field

L ori, whom I revered as an athlete-bait savant at the time, had the genius idea that we should go to the Super Bowl in Tampa. It would be warm, festive, and crawling with men, specifically athletes. She couldn't have been more right if she were psychic. We did what any self-respecting duo of girls do before a vacation that mainly consists of looking hot and meeting people: We planned our outfits more carefully than an Oscar host. I called my publicist, Cheryl, and asked her to get us into all the best parties. Super Bowl week is all about the parties and has almost nothing to do with the actual three-hour game that culminates it all on Sunday night. The game is just an afterthought. We had no intention of going to it, nor could either of us care that it was being played or who was in it. The real lure was the hundred-guys-to-one-girl ratio—like a gay pride parade, but with men who enjoyed vagina. It was awesome.

Cheryl really came through and got us into the places to see and be seen. There were only two spots at the Super Bowl that counted in my opinion—the *Maxim* party and the *Playboy* party. Every other event just wants to be them when they grow up.

The *Maxim* party was off the hook. After a guest-list check-in table that practically included a cavity search and fingerprinting, there was a long, lighted red carpet to walk with eagerly awaiting paparazzi. I always have a love-hate relationship with these red-carpet experiences. On one hand it's incredibly exciting to have thirty people with flashing cameras screaming, "Rosa! Rosa, look over here! Rosa, to your left! Rosa, can we get one from over the shoulder? Rosa!" On the other hand, I have been on the red carpet when a bigger, better deal also arrives and it's equally humbling to watch those photographers rush in the opposite direction—leaving you standing (and smiling) alone. Inside, the party delivered. There was a sea of recognizable (mostly male) celebrities and so many athletes it was like my fairy godmother had waved her magic wand and put me in the middle of a literal ball. It was a blur of giant men lavishing attention all over us, and it gave an entirely new meaning to the phrase "sword fight." Meeting men there was easier than if I were a stewardess on a plane home from prison. We relished the attention, and I met guys all night that seemed superior by far to the little actor dudes with their hundred-dollar haircuts "trying to look like they aren't trying" and overpriced, faux vintage Kitson T-shirts. The men I met in Los Angeles did nothing but check their reflections in every remotely shiny surface and refuse to make eye contact—lest they lose their 360-degree panoramic view of everyone else in the room. These athletes, on the other hand, were fully focused on us.

The next morning we were invited to a boat party. It felt unusually early and I'm sure the name of who was throwing the matinee was mentioned to us, but it wasn't a name I had heard before. We met up with literally twenty girls, about four guys, and all of us boarded the boat. It was like a mini, floating Playboy mansion, but this time the senior citizens were not invited. I was surprised there weren't more men, but as an avid viewer of the TV show *The Bachelor*, I was used to "group dates."

Lori seemed to have an abundance of Playmate friends. I don't know if this is because she grew up in South Beach or because she's just attracted to dumb girls. In Florida it seems that aside from oranges, tit jobs and Playmates grow on trees as well. Regardless, one of the Playmates got us invited onto the boat. As it turns out, the captain that day was a charming, quiet, soft-spoken gentleman named Derek. As in Jeter. I knew people were throwing themselves at him, but I wasn't sure why at the time. I didn't have a laptop to Google his ass, so I was sort of lost.

Lori just said, "You're an idiot. We'll talk about it later. He's on the Yankees."

I couldn't name a single baseball player at the time, so while playing for the Yankees was impressive, I had no idea Derek Jeter was a legend of Wheaties-box, bobblehead proportion. I didn't see him hit on anyone all day; he was just the perfect gentlemen. If he went missing, I would describe him on a milk carton as being six foot three, brown-haired, with green eyes that were so stunning I could have sworn he borrowed them from the little girl from Afghanistan on that famous *National Geographic* cover.

It was a boat ride filled with dancing and music. Whenever we passed other boats and they caught a glimpse of Derek, it was as if Norm had walked into Cheers, where everybody knows your name. There was a "JEEEEETTT-TEERRR" drunken roar from passersby. The other men seemed particularly excited to see him and raised both arms up in a sort of male universal sign for "You rule!" It was like a caveman cheer, but instead of pompons they used beer cans.

As we were leaving, I felt the need to address the fact I knew he played baseball. I'm not sure why I felt this need, but I thought it was stupid to pretend that I didn't know since everyone else seemed to be fawning all over him. At the end of the all-day party, I hugged him good-bye, briefly imagined what our children would look like with those eyes, and said sincerely, "Well, good luck this year." I paused, for once at a loss for words. I suddenly remembered how frustrated Moose and Lance would get when they were just warming the bench for a game, so I knew just what to say: "I hope you get to play!"

Derek looked at me dead serious for a second.

Oh shit, is he retired? Had I hit a sore spot? I thought.

Then he burst out laughing so hard I thought I saw tears in his eyes. I sheepishly smiled back like I was in on the joke, gave him a feeble thumbs-up, and exited onto the dock.

Lori needed a lesson in giving me friggin' athlete Cliffs-Notes from now on. I wanted to kick her lipo-sculpted ass when we got off the boat.

That night at the *Playboy* party, we ran into him again. He caught my eye when I was walking past him at the bar. He was midsentence when he said to the guy he was with, "Hey! That's the girl I was talking about!" They both started laughing like I was Eddie Murphy circa 1980. Of course by this time I got the joke. Lori had already spent the better part of the rest of the afternoon mocking my lack of baseball knowledge. But baseball players simply weren't on my radar. The only baseball player I could name at the time was a dead one, Babe Ruth. And this was only because I enjoyed caramel with peanuts.

The night before, I hadn't slept more than a couple of hours following the *Maxim* party. And I had forgotten we were getting on a boat in the wee hours of the morning, a time usually reserved for morons who play golf. We basically left the boat party, fought through the infamous congestion that was Super Bowl–week traffic, and got ready for the *Playboy* party. I was beyond exhausted and jokingly asked the cocktail waitress if she would make me coffee. She mentioned to me that they carried this new energy drink called Red Bull.

"So what is this stuff?" I asked. "Is it like the Jolt cola?" I remembered Jolt, the overcaffeinated, crappy-tasting soda that got me through many a night writing last-minute papers in college.

"Kinda," replied the waitress, "but better tasting. People mix it with vodka."

"Well, that sounds like a plan," I said, unusually agreeable.

She should have asked me to sign a release form, or at least called the little devil by its real name: Really Bad Idea on the Rocks with a Lime. That night, I—the non-drinker—discovered Red Bull vodkas (plural, yes). Oh, and what blessings. I had energy! I had a previously undiscovered zeal for disco dancing! And I knew I'd better sit down, away from people, and preferably outside—before I vomited.

I scoped out some shrubbery in a quieter spot and wondered how to stop the *Playboy* party from spinning. A guy sat down next to me. The following conversation is what I imagine happened. I have no real recollection, just bits and pieces of the rest of the night that if painted would definitely be considered abstract.

"Are you okay?" he asked.

"Not so much. Will you watch my purse while I go to the bathroom?" This was a perfectly logical request to a stranger I'd just met. In fact, I should have just passed out copies of my Social Security card, my mother's maiden name, and signed blank checks for all the sense it made. Nevertheless, I had the wherewithal to grab a twenty and head to the rest room.

I broke a land-speed record for sprinting and thrust the twenty at the bathroom attendant.

"I need VIP access to the toilets! I need to cut to the front of the bathroom lines tonight! I think I might puke," I said.

As if I needed to punctuate that point, I went into a stall and threw up like a sorority bulimia champ. But afterward, I felt oddly better and clearer, albeit a bit like Linda Blair from *The Exorcist*.

Crap. Now I needed to find my purse and pretend I was not exiting the rest room postbarf. My twenty dollars entitled me to an array of perfumes, mouthwash, and leftover Halloween candy, even though it was January. Heading back outside, I wouldn't have recognized the guy, but I did recognize my Gucci purse. I thanked him profusely and wondered if he could smell the stench of puke as we spoke. Sexy.

Lori, my "good friend," was nowhere to be found, and I realized she hadn't so much as checked on me once during my absence. This guy was an angel, sort of my drunken stupor guardian angel. He waited with me until Lori surfaced hours later.

"Can I have your number? I want to make sure you are okay in the morning," he asked. I was so grateful to have been reunited with Lori at that point, I would have given him my car.

He called me early the next morning, while Lori and I were sleeping on the Anheuser-Busch yacht. (Don't ask. It was innocent. Lori meets random people and has a bloodhound's nose for men with money, like a hedge fund guy but with more hair and fewer morals.)

"Can I meet you for breakfast?" the guy, whose name I still didn't know, asked.

"Of course. But I only have an hour. We have a tight schedule, it being Super Bowl Sunday and all," I said, as if we had any plans to get anywhere near the actual game, aside from watching it to see the commercials.

"I'll meet you in your hotel lobby." I got off of the Busch boat and into the rental car with minimal effort on my appearance. He wasn't worth it, I reasoned. I couldn't even picture the guy's face to save my life.

It wasn't until I was actually in the hotel lobby that I remembered I didn't have a clue as to who I was looking for, or meeting for that matter. There was a guy staring intently at me. My heart sank. I visibly winced when I noticed a tattoo sleeve and what appeared to be the same horrid silhouette of a woman's body often seen on truck mud flaps. Then, like a scene from a movie, I heard the sweetest sound I have ever heard coming from behind me.

"Rosa?" I turned around. The voice was coming from a gorgeous man.

"Yes!" I said, a little more celebratory than I intended. Like I'd just won the Publishers Clearing House Sweepstakes.

"Hi. It's me, Pete. You look great all sobered-up."

I refrained from saying, *And you look lickable, gorgeous man!* I thought that might be coming on too strong, so I just thought it instead.

It made sense though now. Even though I was doing my best impression of an inebriated moron last night, I probably wouldn't have let some carnival-employee-looking dude hang out with me all night. And to babysit my Gucci? I was ecstatic about my good judgment even though I had been several Red Bull and vodkas deep.

We got into an SUV, and I saw that some other guy Pete's age (looking incredibly inconvenienced to be picking up a passenger) was our driver. I briefly panicked, thinking this was not an intelligent decision, but quickly decided that if this was in fact a gangbang, I could just focus on Pete.

Pete said, "Sorry, my car is in the shop." This I translated into "my car is in the store window of a shop, actually. Because I don't own one."

When I asked him, "So what do you do?" His loser friend held back a chuckle.

Pete answered, "Nothin' right now!"

I was right! He was a hot guy without a job or a car, and, oddly, I was okay with that. Damn, he was just so pretty.

It wasn't until the car ride progressed that they started talking baseball, and I noticed that they were referring to Pete as if he had a job in the industry.

"Are you in the field?" I asked. "I mean in the field of sports, not actually in a field like a baseball field or a field of . . ." I was thrown and starting to sound like I took the short bus to school. Finally I just asked, "Do you play baseball?"

"Yeah," he replied. Pete and his friend kept looking at each other.

"He plays for the Phillies," piped in the loser friend driving, who I now identified as an athlete hanger-on.

I had never heard of this team. The Phillies. It sounded downright equestrian.

"Is that professional? Or . . ."

"Yes. The Philadelphia Phillies. It's a baseball team in Philadelphia," his friend interrupted.

Okay, now he was just being a smartass. But I guess I deserved it. I had never met a baseball player, besides that Derek Jeter character the day before, so I didn't know about the baseball "type." Baseball wasn't an obvious look to me. Say, like the way you can spot a guy built like a brick shithouse (football) or a guy who keeps suddenly spastically ducking everywhere he walks (basketball).

We spent a brief morning with his friends. No gangbang took place, just the codependency of his friend, who was a confirmed hanger. We agreed to meet in L.A. in a week for our first date. We hadn't even kissed yet, but he was going to fly across the country for a date with me.

We talked on the phone endlessly every day and I was definitely smitten. Of course, I Google-stalked him and was shocked to find out he was the first-round draft pick his year. This was going to be his sophomore season. He was a newbie, but a newbie with a lot of talent, promise, and an ass like a gymnast.

The day before Pete was supposed to fly to L.A. something came up, some obligation, and he asked if I could please fly to see him if he sent me a first-class ticket.

"Um, okay," I said.

I flew out to see him, and the chemistry was palpable.

"I have been waiting to do this since the night I met you," he said breathlessly as he planted a kiss on me in the foyer of his condo. If it had been 1940, I would have lifted one calf during this particular kiss. It didn't stop there. We tumbled onto his ornate Oriental rug and almost crashed into the china display cabinet. I was too dumbfounded by the kiss to question why the hell he in fact owned a curio cabinet. Wasn't that for women in their fifties living in Michigan? Most typical young bachelors had just a couple of sad, black leather couches in front of the biggest television they could find (connected with rows and rows of electrical cords to multiple video game playing systems), and maybe, just maybe, a bag of chips and a stack of men's magazines hanging out on a ring-stained coffee table that accounted for all of their "decor."

When we both finally came up for air, Pete held my face in both his hands, looked into my eyes, and asked, "So . . . should we have a church wedding?"

I knew his question was only half serious, but the implications were 100 percent. And what guy says that after your first kiss? I was a goner. Officially smitten.

Don't take me out of this ballgame!

The weekend was fantastic. The chemistry, the conversation, the full-court press that this guy was laying on me were unbelievable. This was the best date I had ever been on, and he seemed to be a really good, sincere guy. Sure, he was tragically young, and I should have run in the other direction once I found out he was twenty-four, five years younger than me. But I got swept up in the romance of it all. He got my jokes, which was so refreshing after Moose, and the conversations seemed endless.

I've always been fascinated by the backstory, the story behind the story, that drove some guys into professional sports (aside from their freakish natural ability or growing into the Incredible Hulk). I've met guys who saw it as a way out of neighborhoods so rough they couldn't ride their bikes outside, ever, for fear of drive-by shootings. You'd be surprised how many of those guys end up back in the same gang-ridden neighborhoods because that's all they know, despite a marvelous financial detour in whatever sport they played. I mean I'd love to know, what were the odds that Dennis Rodman, a former airport janitor, didn't play basketball in high school but grew nine inches in height afterward? Then there are those athletes who are driven solely by their desire for attention and to appease their parents. I know another guy whose father pushed him into it so severely—he was practically a militant slave driver—that as a result his son (a well-known catcher) succeeded, but he absolutely loathed the sport that paid him millions. And another NFL player who used to go to games with his dad (when he was barely out of kindergarten, and one of the smallest kids in the class) stated to his father (an average-sized banker) while looking down on the field, "I'm going to do *that* when I grow up." Instead of telling his son there was zero probability, or that there were too many obstacles that said otherwise, the father simply said, "Yes you can."

Pete's backstory was that he had basically grown up on a farm and had no friends that lived close by. Because of this, he had to play with himself a lot. Not in the "Peewee Herman in a movie theater" way, but in the "imagine yourself in a field of dreams" way. He had drawn a target box on the side of an old barn and repeatedly threw and caught a baseball against it alone for hours and hours every day. He obviously got pretty good at it and attributed his success 50 percent to natural ability and 50 percent to those lonely days with just him, a baseball, and the side of a barn.

When things progressed in the bedroom and it was time to consummate our friendship, Pete paused as he was about to do his unveiling. *That's odd*, I thought. Usually guys are so spastically and eagerly wanting to show you their pride and joy. Even toddlers can't keep their hands out of their diapers. With his hands on the zipper of his jeans he sort of laughed and quietly said, "I'm, uh . . . well . . . I'm not that big."

He was doing his deadpan thing again. But I knew this time he had to be kidding.

I just laughed. I was in on the joke. His nickname was "the Bat." I had learned from Moose's nickname to take them seriously. All jokes are somewhat based in truth anyway, right?

Turns out I was a slow learner.

Pete had no "bat" to speak of. Where a penis would normally be located, there was a skinny, sad Popsicle stick. I was sure it could be bent and damaged upon touch. It was more beef jerky than hot dog (unless you left the hot dog in the Arizona desert for a week to shrivel and dry up) as it stared back at me, affixed between two completely shaven balls with traces of baby powder on them. To this day, I can't look at Dunkin' Donuts powdered munchkins without thinking about them.

I must have inhaled sharply and audibly, because it prompted a quiet "sorry."

So I did what any woman would have done in my position. I fibbed.

"You're fine!" I said, as if this were the third finger-sized dick I'd seen that day. We proceeded to have decent sex. I really just had to peer over his shoulder at his remarkable ass to appreciate him. I steered my thoughts away from his tragically underendowed appendage and considered publishing a twelve-month calendar of just his ass. It was like art.

And I was an ass-ficionado.

T HE BEST THING about Pete, other than the aforementioned pooper, was that he was very into "us." He was superattentive, he seemed very honest and communicative, and he was full speed ahead with our future plans and initiated the conversation almost immediately on the second date weekend. You know, *the* conversation. The one that people refer to when they are thinking about dabbling in someone else's privates and they justify it to their friends by exclaiming, "Well, we haven't had *the* conversation." It's a universal rule of thumb that you have to, in fact, have the conversation to officially make you a monogamous couple, which is the holy grail of coupledom. The beginning. Where the timeline really starts, because from there the pressures to "take our relationship to the next step" loom in the future: The first "I love you." The meeting of the parents. The moving in together. Then the shiny rock that better follow or you will hear about it from everyone on your speed dial. Pete initiated the conversation on his way to a company dinner—the company in this case being the Philadelphia Phillies.

I was in a nude-colored Herve Leger dress and looking fierce. Those dresses have the same effect as tightly bound duct tape. They suck you in at all the right Jessica Rabbit places but cost a crapload more than duct tape. When I was buying the dress, I must have been saying Herve Leger wrong, because the saleslady kept repeating it and emphasizing it, drastically differently, as if to correct me. I hate when you have to ask people the correct pronunciation of fancy shit. Herve Leger looks like it should be pronounced "Leg-ger" not "Leh-jay." Some high-luxury names are probably dreamed up solely for the amusement of the employees selling them. They get to make you feel dumber and a tad more classless than you might otherwise be. I had the same experience at Porsche. The Porsche people say "Porsche-ahhh." Most people pronounce it simply "Porsh," which ironically sounds more like douche, which is exactly how I would describe most of the people correcting you on pronunciations.

On our way home from Pete's company dinner, he

confessed to me that the general manager I had just met, an ancient-looking man who should be retired on Marco Island and not managing anything except his weak bladder and VCR recordings of *Gunsmoke* reruns, asked Pete outright if he was gay. We had a good laugh about that. I dismissed the thought that perhaps he had seen that curio cabinet in Pete's living room, and just thought that was a strange thing to ask a professional ballplayer. Perhaps that is why Pete was so gung-ho to introduce me publicly to everyone. Or perhaps, as per usual, I was reading too much into it and overusing the word "perhaps." It wasn't the most random of questions. With that said, I certainly don't think that Pete was gay. He had questionable taste in furnishings perhaps—but not gay. I have to say the more time I spent with athletes the more I noticed their . . . uniquely close relationships with one another. I'm sure that professional sports fans want to think that athletes' regular and frequent group nudity, communal showering, and the whole locker-room situation is just "customary." It's part of the job of playing sports, right? But the reality is that guys in most jobs (bankers, salesmen, lawyers, etc.) don't all hit the showers after a day at the office together. So at the end of the day I still think it's—well, peculiar. It's just *not standard* to shower with dozens of men every day. The last time I heard of group (same-sex) showering, it was going on in "bathhouses," a young Bette Midler was singing, a then-unknown Barry Manilow was accompanying her on the piano—and they were all surrounded by candlelight and lots and lots of gay sex! So excuse me if

I consider professional team sports as nothing short of homoerotic. I'm just saying you probably shouldn't know *for a fact* the details about your co-workers private parts—like whether they happened to be circumcised or not. You probably shouldn't be able to identify their junk in a police lineup. I can't imagine coming home from a day of filming on a television set and saying, "Honey I'm home! You'll never guess how [fill-in-the-blank famous actress] keeps her vajayjay manicured. . . ." Unless one was a porn star, and then I guess that would be typical as you reflect on your day at the "office."

I think if you find yourself in a group-shower situation, you can't help but notice the, uh . . . ambiance blatantly displayed around you. Professional athlete locker-room circumstances are no different. And they aren't as unaware as the typical hetero male fan would like you to believe. I have witnessed several conversations with "masculine" athletes who are proud to report which hulking player has a teeny weeny little thumb dick peeking out from his Budweiser gut, and which "brother on the team" puts Ron Jeremy to shame—and flaccid, no less! It's definitely ego checking for the, ahem, *inferior* white guys, to shower next to the superior black ones. And by "ones," yes, I mean dicks. The locker-room looking is not my only "hmmm, *that's* kinda gay" observation about sports. There are many to choose from. With that said, no one loves the gays more than me and Kathy Griffin, now that Judy Garland is dead. I have an impressive abundance of gay male friends. I have a stable of gays and at least two token lesbians, so I am coming into this study "in the know," or to use a more delicate term of endearment: I am a colossal fag hag. It was one of my gays who brought this whole male-team-sports-is-a-tad-homoerotic thing to my attention, actually, while he was styling my hair. Thank you, Shawn Finch.

First let's examine the names of the "positions." In, say, the sport of football. You have: tight ends (gay sounding), wide receivers (gayer), defensive ends (for rookie gays), and the O-linemen (sounds slightly orgasmic). They're all lining up in the backfield (hmmm . . .) waiting to pounce on the man that's ready to pounce on their man. Some are so excited to get at them they have a pre-ejaculatory "false start," and go what's called "off sides" (which also sounds like a gay synonym of sorts).

Then there are the names of teams: the Oilers, the Packers. Seriously? Were *all* the other non-homo-sounding names taken that day? Last I checked, Trojans are condoms and Astro starts the name of a famous brand of lubricant, not a team. At the root of every sport, there are either bats, sticks, or balls. Bats, sticks, and balls. That screams of more guy-on-guy action than the neighborhood porn store in West Hollywood.

Then there's the obvious scrutiny, the players ass-slapping each other, a.k.a. just your average obligatory congratulations for a job well done (which would result in an instant lawsuit in *any* other profession). The huggy huddles. The tight pants. The camps. Sharing hotel rooms with your chosen roommate. The on-field pileups that would be considered gang bangs anywhere outside a regulation playing field. There are football legends (with West Hollywood porno-star-sounding names) like Bob Griese (pronounced greasy) and Dick Butkus (yes, pronounced butt-kiss). There's even a pro football player whose jersey simply says "Gay." In his defense, it's his actual last name, and not, I assume, a reflection of his preferences. But probably the biggest acceptable homoerotic propensity is something I have never understood and I find myself frowning at as much as my Botox injections allow.

Why the constant touching, shifting, and juggling athletes do with their balls? What the hell is going on down there that needs so much attention? They seem nervous, as if they need to check and make sure the goods are still there! Is testicular burglary something I am unaware of? Fuck carbon monoxide poisoning, is nut-theft the *real* silent epidemic? It's like they are doing some sort of intricate crotch origami routine and it puzzles, fascinates, and confuses me. Why is this mild masturbatory movement the norm? More importantly, why is it always caught on camera? And what magnetic force is attracting their hands to their balls with such frenetic energy?

Just once I'd like to see a female ice skater in the Olympics adjust the crotch of her skate-a-tard (or whatever they are called) before completing her triple axel. Or a Best Actress winner nonchalantly remove a front wedgie from her designer gown live in front of millions of viewers before she accepts her Oscar at the podium. Would Hillary Clinton have fared any better on the 2008 presidential campaign trail if she just had adjusted her privates once or twice mid-debate with Obama? Perhaps more male voters would have related! I look forward to the day when the NFL caters to *all* kinds of men, and not just the ones who want to bang the cheerleaders.

Are you ready for some football?

A NYWAY, WHERE WAS I? Ah, Pete. His sophomore season started, and the press immediately got wind of our relationship: "The actress and the baseball player." There were even a few over-the-top references like "Where have you gone, Joe DiMaggio" newspaper articles. Now these Joe-and-Marilyn references I didn't mind of course!

I worked my ass off during the week and flew to be with Pete in whatever state he was playing on the weekends. Baseball players typically stay several nights in the same city, really giving the teammates time to have "girlfriends," and/or steadier sperm receptacles, in a multitude of places and not in just their home state.

Baseball players also seemed to have at least one stripper/ex-Hooters-waitress-turned-wife on each team. Hockey players tended to stay with the same woman since they first went into the juniors, an in-between league on their way to the pro circuit. These were homelier girls from Canada, who they kept like souvenirs of days gone by. The girls were a reminder of how far they'd made it—usually before they made it with some other American broad. I never really got to know the basketball wives, as I was kept hidden for most of the affair. From what I had seen, they were usually composed of either drop-dead-gorgeous women or more rotund "baby mamas." And on a typical basketball team it was not uncommon to have several baby mamas in the stands, preferably seated at a distance from one another, blinged out with so much conspicuous sparkly.

I T WAS DURING this time that Howard Stern's radio show asked me to do a "pre-interview." This is the interview that takes place before the actual live interview with Howard and his gang. As badly as I wanted to do this, and as huge a fan as I was of Howard's, I chickened out. I thought I could handle him and hold my own as a smart woman. But I also knew the dangers of the "So . . . do you like it in the butt?" conversations that Howard and company were so famous for. What if he skewered me for having been in a previous pro-athlete relationship? What if he called me an athlete whore on nationwide airwaves? What if he asked me how Pete was hung? I was a terrible liar, and I had a hard time not telling the 100 percent truth. It was his radio show, and Howard was in control. In the end, I didn't think it was the best career move to enter the gladiator arena with a hungry, horny lion like Howard Stern. I was sure to end up pulverized and, at the very least, embarrassing the hell out of Pete and Lifetime Television—the television for women . . . and gay men—that respectfully employed me.

It was also during this time that I was offered the chance to pose in *Playboy* magazine. The money was nice, and it was supertempting, but the thought of humiliating my dad raged in my head, as did concerns over Pete's family and the potential of hurting my career. Then, just as our relationship got more intense and we ventured into the meeting-of-the-parents-and-family stage, something else happened: Pete got into his first-ever Major League Baseball batting slump. He couldn't get a hit if his life depended on it.

It was often referred to as the "sophomore curse," and sportswriters were all over him like obsessive Trekkies at a sci-fi convention in line to meet Mr. Spock. I was glued to the television, or the radio, or, in most cases, in my dressing room and reading a play-by-play on the Phillies website in-between takes. There was a lot of hype around Pete, having been chosen in the first-round draft, well paid, and having come up from the minors so much quicker than most. The expectations (and the payday) were high, and he was not delivering. I tried my best to play the role of supportive girlfriend and give him what he needed on the other end of the phone, but at the end of the day the pressure was mounting.

I also tried to ignore the signs that Pete "enjoyed the beer." He seemed in control, but he definitely had an ongoing love affair with all things brewed with yeast and hops. I don't remember him ever slurring or acting drunk, but he could drink impressive quantities, And he seemed to enjoy those impressive quantities nightly and often alone and, in short, he would have made Ireland proud.

Pete was scheduled to play the Dodgers in Los Angeles,

and despite his less-than-stellar batting performances as of late, I couldn't miss the opportunity to invite most of my cast and crew to a local game. We joked around the set that we were all going on a class field trip. Knowing I could sing, Pete had often asked me why I never sang the national anthem at a baseball game. I had sung a cappella at a Lakers vs. Raptors game at the Staples Center. And I found out the hard way that when you're asked to sing and a Canadian team is playing as well, you have to sing their national anthem, too. As if the American national anthem isn't challenging enough, right? I was very nervous. I didn't want to be that girl who screwed up our anthem à la Roseanne, but somehow I zoned out Shaq and Kobe and got through it with a resounding ovation. Well, the ovation may have been because it was the national anthem and not necessarily because Rosa was singing it. But I did a bang-up job and the cheers were deafening, especially once I got to the "land of the free-ee."

I decided to surprise Pete by coming out and singing the national anthem at Dodger Stadium. I wore a Swarovski-crystal-beaded baby-doll T-shirt, along with shorts and tennis shoes with a heel. It was very "Sporty Spice meets Hooters waitress." At least forty people from the cast and crew showed up, and it was a nerve-racking and exciting day. I wanted Pete to be surprised, have fun, and forget about how much he was kind of sucking lately. I also wanted his teammates to be impressed. Few people knew I could sing, and I have a pretty belty voice for being a diminutive girl. I've been told I sound like an overweight black woman, which in the world of singing is the ultimate compliment. I sang it, nailed it, and I'm not going to lie: I was kind of proud. My stadium-performance buzz lasted all of an hour until it was Pete's turn at bat.

Pete was shitting the bed worse than ever! Three attempts at bat. Three strikeouts. I wondered if my focused wincing throughout the game would do any permanent damage to my impending crow's feet. After the slaughter, I headed down to the field as the crowd was leaving the ballpark. A few teammates gave me some high fives and props, and I knew I would only get to see Pete for a few minutes before he had to leave with the rest of his team. He was in a weird mood (no doubt embarrassed by his at-bats), so I didn't read too much into it. I had gotten used to his postgame depression and this was certainly not my first rodeo.

Pete's bad streak continued to get more attention, and the more attention it got, the more he was "in his own head" when he was up to bat. That might be the worst trait a baseball player can have. Pete was scheduled to have his own bobblehead-doll day (long before his batting slump). The beat writers rumored that the bobblehead day might be canceled, and the papers cruelly joked that "there wasn't much of a difference between a real bobblehead doll at bat and Pete in the flesh!"

They did end up unveiling his bobblehead doll that day. I wasn't there, but I know this because of the call I received. Pete sounded a little extra Bud-lit that night and began to ramble about how he didn't know how to focus on baseball anymore. I told him, "Look, I will be supportive and give you whatever you need." There was silence on the other end of the phone. I checked the bars to make sure we weren't disconnected and continued, "I will be there for you. You do what you've got to do."

"I know. That's my whole point. I don't know how to do both. I don't know how to do baseball and be a boyfriend."

Now it was my turn to be silent. Was he going to propose? Was he going to ask me to move in? I had no idea what was coming next.

"So I have to make a choice . . . and I choose baseball. I can't do baseball and be focused on us. I have to choose just one right now. Baseball."

Boy, I didn't see that curveball coming at all.

I was determined not to let him hear me cry and somehow got off the phone with my dignity intact. But before we hung up, he asked me one last question. "Do you want me to send you a bobblehead doll?"

No, he did not just ask me that.

No, he did not.

"Uh, no. I'm good, Pete. Thanks."

I went into my walk-in closet, an emporium of dirty-clothes piles I never seemed to get to, and closed the door so my roommates wouldn't hear me. Then I proceeded to cry my eyes out. I wailed so primitively and so painfully that I thought in that moment I might die, or at least lose weight from excessive-crying cardio.

A WEEK WENT BY, and in that week Pete had more hits at bat than he did the entire season up until our breakup. I couldn't help but feel worse, and knew that this validated his decision in his mind. You know what else really validates a breakup? Reading in the newspaper about Pete's new girlfriend, U.S. women's soccer team hottie Helen Motts. I remember his mentioning they were "friends," but I didn't know he meant friends in the way that Hollywood couples are always "just friends" when they are getting interviewed and then eventually married. Because "just friends" is such a better sound bite than "just sleeping together until one of us gets sick of it."

I wanted to throw up—mainly because it was impossible to find a bad photo of Helen Motts no matter how hard I searched on the Internet. It also completely disproved my theory that all female athletes are sort of mannish and dykey. This fictitious (and self-serving) theory helps me mentally come to grips with the fact that I myself have no athletic abilities whatsoever. I can't open a water bottle screw-cap without help, let alone envision myself spiking a ball, making a basket, or breathlessly crossing a finish line. So when I somewhat stalked Helen Motts on the Internet, with her feminine, toned body, classic girl-next-door looks, and all of her accolades, it truly made the breakup worse. Plus, she was younger than me. That's always a dagger.

Eventually the pain from being completely shit-canned by

Pete started to fade, as all shit-canning pain does. Maybe I should take this as a sign to stop dating athletes? Maybe I should try and date someone in my own industry who would really understand my life? Maybe . . . I should date a young bartender, from Chicago (by way of Iowa), who worships me? Now that's exactly what I did.

WHAT I'VE BEEN EXPOSED TO IN ATHLETE LAND . . . BESIDES ORAL HERPES

1. *A-Rod was kind of an a-hole. We briefly met while I was in the company of a half dozen New York Giants at Tao restaurant in Manhattan. Perhaps it's my imagination but he seemed to "fan" us (a.k.a. treat us all as if we should be excited to meet him, as if we were fans).*

2. *Michael Jordan does in fact glow in the dark. I waited on him when I used to waitress at Billboard Live restaurant in 1996. He wore an electric-blue suit, a smile as big as his wingspan, and his religious-figure-like glow. Seriously.*

3. *Marcus Allen is not a shut-in. He seems to have an active social life, as I have seen him out at several events and parties. So much, in fact, that I question if he was part of a twin set or cloned.*

4. *Mike Ditka is not against alcohol consumption. I have seen him appear to be sloshed at several parties.*

5. *Troy Aikman does not find me amusing. As evidenced by him either not getting my jokes at a dinner party, or purposely laughing on a ten-second delay at them as if English is not his first language.*

6. Tim Couch was not above hanging his own celebratory paraphernalia in his own living room . . . or drunk-dialing me.

7. I am just about as tall as both Barber twins. But not nearly as well dressed.

8. Tom Glavine is truly the quintessential "nice guy," and Greg Maddux has more accolades than just having a facial mole. (For a long time he was just "mole guy" to me, as I couldn't remember his name or long list of accomplishments. But not to his face. The one with the mole on it.)

9. Jeremy Shockey once asked me if I could set him up with actress Jessica Biel, but she was not interested. I think she might have Googled him and found old pictures of him hugging a smeary-eyelinered Tara Reid—not exactly confidence-building.

10. Athletes' accents can be broken down into three categories: foreign (including rednecks), mumblers, or both.

Matt and me on the not-so Love Boat.

FIVE

Reviewing the Play

During the brief long-distance relationship that I had with Todd the bartender, he flew back and forth from Chicago while I played "the man." I footed all the bills, made all of the decisions, and dressed him up like the little model doll that he was. One night we were in a restaurant when a woman approached our table and had this crazy story about how ironic it was that she was running into me.

"You're Rosa Blasi from that doctor show, right?"

"Yes . . ." I said. That was strange, I thought. Usually people don't know my name, especially in Los Angeles or anywhere outside of my hometown.

"I was at a benefit yesterday with Britney Spears, and some little girl was asking Brit if she could get Dr. Lu's autograph! Well, Britney didn't know who Dr. Lu was, so I filled her in on who the girl meant and from what show. Then she promised the little girl she would try and get her the autograph. We didn't know how to track you down, but here you are! Isn't it crazy?"

I didn't know what to think. It seemed like a plausible people-meeting-people story in Los Angeles; weirder stuff has happened. Plus, we were at the Mondrian Hotel's Sky Bar, so it seemed legitimate despite the random Britney Spears reference. This beautiful Indian woman, who introduced herself as Azaria, had large, unblinking eyes, and was decked out to the C's in Chanel. She gave me her phone number and wrote down the name of the children's charity she was referring to. Eventually, she asked if she could get an autograph for that little girl.

"Of course I'll do it!" I said to her, noticing that the address had Saint Rocco's written on it. My dad's name! I took it as a good omen that this meeting was meant to be. Azaria asked me to call her the next day to verify that that was the correct address.

When Todd the bartender got up to use the restroom, Azaria glided by and said as matter-of-factly as a doctor holding a hospital chart, "He won't last." But she didn't say it bitchy at all. "Call me tomorrow. We should talk."

I was intrigued. She was very confident and oddly mysterious. Sure, I had been schooled in "stranger danger," but I felt that rule somehow didn't apply to strangers with black

Amex cards. I phoned her the next day. She said she was a psychic but didn't do readings. She didn't take money, per se. She just "knew things" and gave advice. The psychic dropped more names than the late George Carlin dropped F bombs, and she invited me to a dinner at the Four Seasons in Beverly Hills she was having the next day. Fergie (of British royalty, not the Black Eyed Peas) would be there, along with some other heavy hitters, and maybe Prince William.

How could I not go?

I was seated at a long, impressive table with A-list Hollywood agents, prolific producers of hit television series, Fergie, and the random "what is she doing here?" chick like Mrs. Hasselhoff. I'm sure she had a first name, but all I knew was that she was David Hasselhoff's wife, she appeared to be getting tanked, and it cracked me up. Then I remembered that I too was a random chick at this odd dinner party amid some of the more recognizable names.

I had missed Prince William. He had "been there earlier." I also didn't know if that whole Prince William concoction was bullshit or not. Honestly, I didn't know what to believe at this point. It was like being on a hybrid episode of *Hollywood Squares* and *The Twilight Zone*.

AZARIA AND I continued to have a phone relationship. Her world was so interesting and she knew so many people from all walks of life. She lived in an affluent neighborhood in New Jersey and seemed to make a lot of money giving businesses, CEOs, and household-name people "career advice" based on her gut instincts, or psychic predictions. She had an impressive Rolodex, and if you Googled her, which of course is Rosa law, there was mention of her in several popular magazines. So when she called and begged me to go to Dallas with her for the weekend, I was tempted. She said she was dying to introduce me to a hockey player there who was "the nicest guy she had ever met."

"Az, you know I am allergic to hockey players," I said so seriously that I may as well have flashed her a medical ID bracelet as proof.

"Rosa, I'm telling you, this guy is different from Moose, and he is dying to meet you. He knows who you are and has vehemently requested this! Look, all we're gonna do is go to his game, do the spa thing during the day, and have a blast. You're going to have your own room at the best hotel in Dallas, we will always be in a group or together, and it's going to be fun!"

"Az, I have a boyfriend."

"He won't last, I told you. I know things."

How was I to argue that? I was intrigued that a guy, a pro athlete no less, was watching Lifetime. Either he was really in touch, evolved, and sensitive, or Azaria was Pinocchioing the whole story.

I FLEW TO DALLAS, checked into a gorgeous suite at the Rosewood, and went to the hotel lobby to meet up with Azaria, a few other of her friends, and meet this guy named Mark Modello. There was an instant spark and a "hellooooo!" look in Mark's eyes when we shook hands, and he naturally exuded class and charm. I was intrigued. The guy almost glided as he moved. He was like a Disney-movie prince galavanting at a ball, which shouldn't have surprised me: He was a finesse hockey player. He was the best of the best in NHL forwards and, appropriately, the star of the Dallas Stars. I had heard his name before and knew he was famous. I liked that his name was Italian and had a sexy sound that rolled off the tongue as you said it. I left our meeting looking forward to going to the game, but more so getting to know him at dinner afterward.

We sat in a luxury box and watched as Mark dazzled the crowd. He looked like Matthew McConaughey, but not quite as gorgeous and with just a teensy bit of an overbite. He definitely wasn't a replica, but he was close enough that if Mark's life was a Movie of the Week, for sure Mc-Conaughey would play him. Assuming of course McCo-naughey wasn't too busy exercising shirtless and being photographed somewhere.

After the game, we were finally able to talk and get to know each other, and I was impressed again by his class and warmth. He seemed like the ultimate gentle-man. He was articulate, confidant, and not a drunk. He walked me to my hotel-room door and asked if he could take me to lunch the next day before my flight left. He kissed me, but in a sweet "I really dig you" kind of way, and not at all in the prelude to getting inside that hotel-room door kind of a way. I said yes to lunch, and as I closed the door to my hotel suite behind me, I saw a giant arrangement of beautiful bright pink roses waiting there. This guy was on top of his game in every way.

The next day at lunch, one-on-one, he seemed nervous and eventually admitted as much. We had a great conversation, and I was flattered by his humble approach and vulnerability. At the end of lunch, he grew more serious. He talked about being successful but also being lonely. Somehow it was endearing and not at all cocky.

"I have a very full life," he admitted. "But there is definitely a piece missing. There is definitely someone I wish I had to share all of this with, and I so look forward to that." He looked deeply into my eyes as he said this.

I was surprised to hear him say this so soon, but there was also a "Well, what the hell do you have to lose?" attitude that came along with any potential long-distance-dating situation. You aren't going to waste your time if they aren't potentially serious and special people because, at the end of the day, you can get ass anywhere, so it better be worth it to take the time, money, and trouble to import it. The funny thing was we hadn't even really kissed yet.

Then, just as the bill was dropped on the table, Mark said, "So, I was asked to be in the NHL All-Star Game."

"Congratulations! That's great. You must be really proud," I told him sincerely. I hadn't been nominated for the Emmys, again. (Sometimes I felt like being on a basic-cable show was the same as doing a puppet show out of your garage. We were often overlooked when they were handing out respect cards.)

"Well, the thing is," he continued, "I have been in the

All-Stars a couple of times before. I wanted to skip it this year and take you on a trip instead. But I am only going to skip it if you say yes."

I waited for him to end with "just kidding." But it never happened. Instead he said, "We can take a private plane down to St. Thomas. My friend has a boat, a large yacht really, and we can cruise the islands of the Caribbean."

I made a mental note to self: I would definitely have to break up with the bartender.

"Are you sure you want to miss the All-Stars?" I said, knowing I would later Google more details about this event. Moose never mentioned them, most likely because he had a snowball's chance in hell of being invited.

"I'm sure."

Then he told me when we would be going: in two weeks. According to his time line, we would be returning during the same weekend as the Super Bowl. It was one of those moments when the record player screeches to a halt and the swelling soundtrack is abruptly replaced by stone-cold silence.

"Well, Mark, I would love to go with you, but only if I can come back a few days early. I have plans to go with my friends to the Super Bowl. We have already rented a house, and I'm supposed to shoot the cover of *Razor* magazine down there." (I left out the part about "Plus, it's my favorite holiday and my dating potential for the entire new year to come!")

Mark agreed and said he thought he could hitch me a ride on a private jet to the Super Bowl.

I felt like I'd been dropped into a romance novel. The only things missing were my ripped bodice, arched back, heaving bosom, and exposed clavicle—to Mark's gleaming, tanned chest and flowing Fabio locks.

I arrived in Dallas the night before we had to leave on the yacht because Mark had a game—that he kicked ass in that night—and we were scheduled to leave early the next morning. To celebrate the win that night, we went to dinner with most of the Dallas Stars and the wives that most of the players were actually cheating on. I was being introduced as Mark's girlfriend and getting interrogated and visually scrutinized by all of them. They all knew of our upcoming trip, and I just knew it was going to be heaven.

We were being joined on our trip by another couple, Kim and Brian, as well as a crew of six and a Cordon Bleu chef. Kim's dad owned the yacht, and it was sick! Gorgeous, stunning, and the kind of decadent you read about if you happen to get the *Robb Report*. The sheer mass of this private boat was incredible. Aptly named the *Fantasy*, it was occasionally rented out to other megarich families for two hundred thousand plus a week.

One of the first questions I asked Kim was "So, what does your father do?" This was the universally acceptable, more PC version of: "Okay, fess up. How the fuck does your dad have his own personal cruise liner?"

This wasn't the first time someone had asked Kim this. She smiled. "Well, you know what pavers are?" she sang in her heavy Texan accent, while fiddling with her conspicuous diamond tennis bracelet. The diamonds were so glaringly large—close to the size of tennis balls—that I thought, *What do you do at nineteen to warrant that kind of gift even if you come from a rich family? Pass your written driver's license exam?*

I turned my attention away from the chain of crazy diamonds encircling her wrists and forced myself to focus on the conversation we were having. I felt like a guy trying to talk to a woman with a huge rack. It was almost impossible to look Kim directly in the eyes—and not at her assets.

"Yeah, pavers . . . like on a driveway?" I guessed.

"Exactly! Daddy makes 'em!" I cocked my head, as this was not the answer I had anticipated. Maybe she meant he invented concrete. But I didn't feel like getting into a heated pavers debate. It didn't matter really. They were loaded in the vulgar way usually reserved for Aaron Spelling TV characters—the ones who lived in mansions with helicopter pads and had catfights in their Bob Mackie evening gowns beside their sexy, extravagant swimming pools.

Meanwhile, we never even saw the crew of six, except at mealtime, and we had several bedrooms on our floor to choose from. The one we chose even had a bidet. (God forbid you are out at sea with anything less than a fresh tush.) Before we had dinner our first night, Mark and I became officially romantic for the first time. In hindsight it was a little too soon, but I think I got swept up in the sheer Jackie Collins drama of it all out there on the high seas. However, it was just . . . okay. Average at best. Nothing to call your girlfriends on roaming charges at sea about.

Something happened the moment it ended. Something

not magical but jarring—that had never happened before or since. I only wish that a puff of smoke and a dramatic drumroll had followed, because I wasn't prepared to meet the new guy who emerged. I will call him Mark Deuce. Deuce, as in slang for "shit."

Mark's persona changed so fast it made me dizzy, and seeking Sybil's purple crayons. He became a completely different person before my eyes within seconds. The Mark I first met was a passionate, lay-it-on-thick, full-court-press perfectionist. Mark Deuce was a complete dickhead. The moment he got what he wanted he started treating me like a party crasher who'd jumped aboard uninvited from a blow-up raft in their wake. He wanted nothing to do with me. He was a competitor by nature, so all I could figure was that once he conquered he was done. I could have sworn I saw his eyes blink the words "game over." It was truly bizarre. I didn't want to dwell on it. I didn't bring it up, and I was hoping Mark Deuce would vanish as quickly as he reared his ugly head.

The next morning even the expensive, heavy brocade curtains couldn't keep out the blinding Caribbean sun, or the truth. Mark was one moody a-hole!

Actually he was a Gemini, which is the same thing as a moody a-hole. No, not all Gemini men are, but it completely made sense that he had this dual personality. Gemini is the sign of the twins. They are the guys who go "I love you, I love you, I love you. . . . Whoa, whoa, whoa! I need my space." It's like a theme park ride for your emotions.

I was bewildered and amazed that someone could have two distinct personalities. That may have been a bigger feat than anything he had done on the ice. Also, we were trapped on a luxury liner, so I was forced to observe him. When that grew tiresome, thank God there were plenty of cases of Cakebread chardonnay and Cristal champagne. I had also brought a slew of books ranging from self-helpers like *Codependent No More* to *When Your Lover Is a Liar* (I was still trying to get over the Moose situation) to *Linda Goodman's Star Signs*—my horoscope how-to guide for deciphering men.

When I wasn't engrossed in the escape that reading offered, I was racking up hideously expensive roaming charges and an almost four-digit cell phone bill. I was also dissecting how I had missed any clues to the two distinctly different Marks. The only theory that made sense was that this was a guy who had always gotten what he wanted. Yes, this is the case for most athletes, but it's ten times worse when you are in "the top ten" in your field.

So for Mark, the ultimate thrill was the chase. And because there were so few girls he actually had to chase, and pursue—as compared with the girls just lining up for a shot at being Mrs. Mark Modello—he was mentally engaged only for as long as the hunt was on. As soon as I was stuffed and mounted—so to speak—he was no longer interested in keeping the trophy. If anything, I was more annoyed at being stuck on this goddamned not-so *Love Boat.*

Once during the trip I could have sworn he magically morphed back into the first Mark: Mark Uno—the hot-on-my-trail Mark. Suddenly one afternoon he was supersweet, and superengaging for about an hour. My good-judgment button must have switched to OFF, because Mark convinced me to go downstairs to the bedroom for a "nap," and then just as swiftly turned back into a jerk as soon as the "nap" was over. Of course I blame myself for not seeing that one coming a mile up the 405 freeway, but when he turned it on he was Johnny Romance like you've only seen on the soaps. During this brief hiatus we were talking and I finally asked him, "What would your ex-girlfriends say about you if I asked them to describe you?"

He took only a moment to respond: "I am consistent at being inconsistent."

"That. Is. Genius," I cackled. He laughed too. He knew.

FINALLY THE DAY came when the boat was docked, and I couldn't get the hell out of there fast enough. Mark came through as promised and had arranged for me to fly on a private jet from Dallas to New Orleans. I had to "slum it" and share the G4 with Kim's dad (who owned the plane, fuckin' pavers) and a few of his friends on the short flight to the Big Easy. So it wasn't exactly a *private* private jet. Once there, I fled to my friends, who were already waiting for me, and we all began trying to figure out the mystery that was Mark.

We lost ourselves in the weekend parties and festivities when only a day later I got a call from him.

"Hey," he said, as if that meant anything.

"Um, hey Mark?" I said loudly so my girlfriends would know that the schizo had the audacity to call me.

"So, guess what? I flew to New Orleans to see you. Where are you?"

He *what*?

"I'm at some big sports agent's party. It's loud and hard to hear because Outkast is playing onstage. Later I'm going to a party at Anne Rice's mansion."

I definitely thought, *Hmmm, my life is weird*. But it wasn't as weird as what Mark Uno said next: "I'll meet you there!"

After a brief girlfriend summit, we unanimously decided that he was probably going to apologize for his hideous boat-ride behavior. Or he'd explain that he had a serious disorder and was not accountable for his actions. I couldn't believe he had stalked me all the way to the French Quarter. That was commitment.

Somehow he found me and got into Anne Rice's mansion party too. Her house was spookier than any book she could ever write. There were life-size religious statues everywhere that I was sure came alive when people weren't around. It was like a wax museum. Creepy eyes seemed to watch you everywhere you went. Some of the Jesus figures even had the thorny crown with so much blood on them they seemed more horror movie than religious artifact. And I'm a recovered Catholic! The whole place was like a sculpture-rescue facility. I wouldn't have been surprised to see a sign that read: ANNE'S HOME FOR WAYWARD STATUES— NO VACANCY.

As soon as Mark saw me, he was hugging me and introducing himself to my girlfriends. Did he think my friends would be impressed to meet such an accomplished jock? Maybe Mark had had some ice-rink blows to his head. Whatever the reason, his introductions were in vain. My girls already knew every detail I could manage to remember myself. Two out of three of them could probably have drawn a close likeness of his penis if they had to. (Women are more into descriptions and less into common male Neanderthal grunting.) He followed us around, unabashedly stalking, and started to lay on that famous full-court press again. He wanted to talk in private.

"Can we leave the party?" he asked. "I want to be alone with you."

Now, I know Dr. Phil would chortle, "The definition of insanity is doing the same thing, over and over, and expecting a different outcome!"

But neither Dr. Phil nor his 1970s cop/porn-star moustache were in Louisiana that day.

W E LEFT THE party, left my friends' confused looks, and took a cab the short distance to the house I had rented. As we walked into the bedroom, I thought I got a whiff of Mark Deuce lurking nearby, but dismissed that thought as pessimism. As I brushed my teeth, I thought of how truly surprised I was that he'd made the effort to fly here, alone, and find me at Anne's. With the long-distance stalking in place, I found myself feeling flattered all over again by his attention. By the time I was done brushing, an entire three minutes later, Mark was dead asleep, mouth agape, slightly snoring, fully clothed, on top of my bed. I was done. The night was still young. I decided to leave Rumpelstiltskin and find the girlfriends I had so foolishly, and prematurely, ditched. I called a cab and never called Mark Uno or Deuce ever again. He tried calling me a few times sporadically after that, especially when the Dallas Stars came to play the Los Angeles Kings. I just let the voicemail pick up and watched, amused at my own joke. I'd customized Mark's caller ID so whenever he rang, it flashed red on my phone: "Sybil calling!"

NOT THE RIGHT TACKLE . . . FOR ME

I was at one of the aforementioned Super Bowl parties that lead up to the actual game I have never been to, where I saw a muscular, six-foot-five mountain of a man, with a juxtaposition of delicate Botticelli curls and intricate tattoos peeking out of a properly filled-out shirt. He had a face so chiseled, with such high cheekbones that if he hadn't been so pink and Caucasian-looking, I'd have guessed he was an authentic Native American. More intriguing was that in an environment where women were in the minority (thus more attention on the women who were there), he was completely oblivious of me. Sniff . . . sniff . . . I smell a challenge! I patiently tried willing him to turn around and make eye contact. But he was talking animatedly to a man I did recognize. Being from Chicago, I had often driven past a restaurant and bar called Ditka's (after the longtime head coach of the Chicago Bears). And there in the flesh was Mike Ditka. Tonight I noticed that Mike's flesh was a lot . . . pinker than he usually looked on TV. Chances are he doesn't drink heavily when he's on television, and that seemed to be the culprit of his brighter hue this evening. That, or he was just really embarrassed to be wearing a mustache past 1976.

Finally the giant, cute blond man was sitting alone and looking very sullen. He made eye contact with me, and I noted that there was quite a bit of intensity bubbling

under the surface. Yet he didn't break his scowl, and
he didn't approach me. Ding! Challenge number two!
Game on. I decided to waltz by him and deadpanned,
"Gonna be alright there, big guy? You look angry. Or
are you gonna have a tantrum right here and now?" I
figured if he was worth my time, he had to have a sense
of humor. It worked. He cracked a crooked smile and
a few of his angel curls bobbed in delight as he joked
back at me, "Yeah, I'll try not to." We started talking; I
knew enough to know that he had to be a football player.
The only thing that would have made that more obvious
would have been if he had black smears of war paint
drawn under his baby-doll blue eyes. Hundreds of healed
scratches decorated his arms and competed with a half
dozen tattoos. He took pride in showing me the ones
that he designed and the stories behind them. He was an
athlete and an artist? This was epic.

Botticelli boy called me and we arranged for a first
date. By then, via our phone conversations, I had
discovered he was a first-round draft-pick offensive right
tackle, who lived within driving distance in the off-season
(which was when we became acquainted). He was very
open, articulate, and sweet. He had these great original
ideas for movie screenplays he wanted to write, he had
ideas for a clothing line he was designing, and he loved
his guitar almost as much as he loved his young daughter,
whose name was tattooed on his arm. Hmmm. That

would be a nice gesture, I thought. No one has ever tattooed my name or likeness on their body for me à la David Beckham. He was nothing like the scowling, yet intriguing man I approached while he was sitting idle at that Super Bowl party. He had just gotten divorced from a woman who was described to me as the second coming of Cruella de Vil. But instead of wanting to skin puppies, she was interested in skinning his bank account. He needed a female sounding board, and I was happy to oblige. I think one of the biggest things he was attracted to was the fact that I had a creative side like him, and the fact that I was financially self-sufficient. To him, postdivorce with the nightmare he was married to trying to take him to the cleaner's by way of the bank, that was sexier than if I were wearing see-through lingerie! I quickly learned that he was raised Mormon and he didn't drink or smoke. A Mormon with tattoos and longish hair who loved heavy metal? And I thought Mormons were just about plural marriages, sort of like Elizabeth Taylor, but simultaneously.

Because I worked nearly seventy hours a week, I naturally shared my life goings-on with my crew members, who were like family. Before our second date, the crew presented me with a Mormon blanket with holes cut out in case we had sex. The concept behind it was basically an ill-researched version of the common undergarments the Mormons wear to show religious adherence (nothing

to do with a blanket but equally as . . . interesting). We
never got to that point in our relationship. There was
something that just wasn't there—despite the fact that he
was my physical type, and despite the fact that he was
supersweet to me and had this creative, intense side.
Unfortunately we just didn't have the intense chemistry
side. It was more of a friendship than anything else, and
despite his tough-guy job description, he was even more of
a teddy bear than my ex–NHL enforcer. He fell under the
category of "too nice" during a time in my life when I was
more of a connoisseur of heart vandalization.

A couple of years after my short time with him, my
longtime agent John Kelly (who is also a huge sports
fan and my surrogate L.A. dad) sent me a videotape of
Botticelli boy having what appeared to be a nationally
televised helmet-throwing 'roid rage for everyone to
see. By no means was there any evidence of steroids,
but something with him seemed . . . not quite right as I
watched the tape. He was like a wild animal; even his
angelic curls whipping around were weaponlike! If you
have ever tried on a football helmet (as I did once) you
may have been shocked to find out how tight they are.
I don't know what I was expecting. It's not like helmets
could do their job if they weren't superfitted, but it was
alarming to me nonetheless. When I saw the footage
of the sweet man I once knew forcibly removing his
opponent's helmet and shot-putting it like an athlete from

113

ancient Greece, I couldn't believe what I was seeing. I reran the tape several times to make sure it was in fact Botticelli boy (despite his last name clearly spelled out on the back of his jersey). I was no less stunned no matter how many times I watched it. A few years later I heard Botticelli boy had also made a death threat against his coach, who in turn filed a report about it with NFL security. I'm no religious zealot but I'm pretty sure none of this behavior falls under the doctrine in the Church of Latter Day Saints Handbook, nor has Bill Paxton ever portrayed anything remotely similar on HBO's Big Love.

Lesson learned: By not having "big love," it seems I may have dodged a big bullet.

Hairspray: $7.00
Braces: $3,000.00
Not thinking you're a
hot mess . . . priceless!

Post Hooters Girl/pageant
survivor! (I heard fake
blue contacts, newscaster
haircuts, and crooked
crowns were making a
comeback.)

The Mannings and the Fishes.

Not George Foreman.

Ashley Manning and Tim
. . . wait a minute, *that's*
not the chicken dance!

A few good (football) men . . . and Tim. (Left to right) Tim, Amani Toomer, Tiki Barber, David Diehl, and Eli Manning at a party at Tiki's home . . .

. . . and the women who tolerate them.

All seven of Hef's girlfriends were there. Tim's were not.

The *real* me.

The smoke-and-mirrors me.

These are some outtakes from the cover shoot that just seemed
like a shame to waste. Enjoy!

HOW TO TAKE ON A HEAVYWEIGHT

*n*ot all of my adventures in athlete land ended up being hit-or-miss romances. Some were just little encounters that made for fun coffee talk. Several years ago, I was asked to pose for pictures and sign autographs at a cable convention, in order to promote my television series and appease advertisers. From across the room, I noticed someone staring at me who somehow managed to look childlike and sweet and menacing at once. It wasn't hard to figure out who he was, mainly because there was a giant billboard hanging above him that read: Evander Holyfield! Even though his name was familiar, I couldn't tell you if he was retired, still competing, or what he had accomplished. I knew it had something to do with boxing, only because people kept asking him to sign pairs of puffy gloves. I was asked to take a photograph with him, and his camp asked my camp about my contact information.

I received a phone call one day from Mr. Holyfield requesting that I visit him. Although I was amused, I knew right away that I was not interested in "visiting him," romantically or otherwise. I honestly didn't know the difference between him and George Foreman (who had a baker's dozen or so children named after him and probably a wife?), he wasn't going to win awards for being the most engaging guy I'd ever conversed with on the phone, and there were more sparks between me and the last guy working the drive-thru window at Taco

Bell. And that's just because I was hungry at the time. I declined his invitation as politely as I could without actually saying, "I am not interested, but I have to admit I am amused you are calling." But he didn't really take no for an answer and called me again the next day wanting to talk, and asking the same questions as if we hadn't just had that conversation. Hmmm, maybe boxing really is no bueno for the brain? How do I get out of this situation tactfully, I thought, and without using the word "ewwww"? The next night I was at a restaurant with a group of about eight friends, who I'd told about Evander Holyfield stalking me. Of course, he wasn't literally "stalking" me, but it made for a funny story.

Some of the details are fuzzy because we were enjoying margaritas at the time, but here's the gist of what went down: At that moment, my phone rang and I looked at the caller ID. "Oh my God! It's him! He's calling again!" My friend Kevin Connolly who was there (now best known for his starring role on the television show Entourage) grabbed the phone and said cockily, "Lemme answer!" Kevin is fucking hilarious and one of the most charismatic storytellers I have ever met. People are naturally drawn to him. He answered the phone with his classic gravel-voiced New York accent only to hear a somewhat puzzled Evander ask to speak with me. "Who is this?" Kevin demanded. He was basically yelling into the phone like a crazy man solely for our table's

entertainment. We were all trying to contain our hysterics
and not laugh the drinks out of our noses. He continued,
"Don't you ever, ever call here again! Do you hear me?
Or I will kick your ass!" He hung up dramatically and
we all literally almost pissed ourselves. Kevin probably
just wanted the opportunity to say he "once threatened
Evander Holyfield" and we just wanted the opportunity
to witness it, and have a great ten-minute laugh from the
safety of the corner booth in our Mexican restaurant.
Evander never called again so it was a win-win situation.
Unlike the last time I heard about Mr. Holyfield, who
shortly thereafter had part of his ear bitten off during a
temper tantrum from some guy named after a famous
frozen chicken franchise.

Marcus Allen, playmate NicHOLE, Tim, and me on
that fateful "Red Bull is the devil's spawn" night.

SIX

Mr. Not-So-Irrelevant

I was told two years after the fact that I first met Tim Fish that fateful drunken "Red Bull and vodka is Satan's cocktail" night, the same evening I'd also met Pete the "nonbat." It had been at the *Maxim* party, and as I walked by Tim said to his buddy, "Now *that's* the kind of girl I want to marry!" To make things more surreal, he actually kept a Polaroid that we took from that night. It's of me and some blond Playmate he ended up fucking. (Her name was Nicole, but unbelievably she spelled it Nichole. If you were a Playmate, wouldn't you do everything in your power to prevent the word "hole" from appearing in your name?) Also in that photo was Tim's childhood hero, Marcus Allen. I do not remember taking the picture, as evidenced by the fact that I had a drink in each hand, an ambitious party trick I hadn't dared since college. I also do not remember meeting Tim. A year later, at my annual Super-Bowl-minus-the-Super-Bowl trip, fate intervened and we met again.

When I was introduced to him at the famous *Maxim* party, frankly I was looking everywhere but into his eyes. He was just shy of six feet tall, which was short by my standards at the time. And with his brown eyes, brown hair, and olive skin, he looked like he could play my brother in an ABC Movie of the Week. I had yet to date a guy with this combo, so honestly he wasn't on my radar that night.

Since I was a little girl growing up in the Midwest, I had mostly Caucasian, blond, Aryan-looking friends, and then later, similar-looking boyfriends. I thought being beautiful meant looking like what I saw on TV, or inside my Barbie Dream House. Now that I think about it, Barbie can fuck a girl up! You know those seventies golden-tan California blonds? To me, that was definitively beautiful. I was absolutely furious when a brunette would win Miss America, and I actually felt sorry for *Three's Company's* Janet next to that Chrissy Snow character. How cruel to be the random brunette on a show with that sunny blond glistening beside her? But as a child I had warped ideas. Like Carol Anne Freeling, the little girl from *Poltergeist*, I was attracted to the light.

So I didn't notice nonblond Tim Fish right away. But the next night he was there again in the big group of us going out in downtown, pre-Katrina New Orleans. It was bedlam as we walked the streets of the French Quarter, and not just because of the "when in Rome" mentality of women flashing their breasts for Mardi Gras beads in every direction. It was like *Girls Gone Wild* but the girls were few and far between. At some point, I looked over and noticed that Tim had these beautiful Angelina Jolie–like lips. Something inexplicable drew me to him, despite the fact that he wasn't "my type" on paper. Maybe it was the fact that he had the biggest catcher's-mitt hands I had ever seen. I was curious to talk to him. There was definitely a lot of eye contact happening, and he kept jockeying positions to walk near me.

As the night wore on, I found myself doing research—you know, when a girl is basically interviewing a guy for the role of her vagina's next best friend. It sounds harsh, but I already had enough friends and a healthy stable of gays back home. The research was quick. I used painless, easy questions to either generate or diminish my interest.

"So, where you from?" I began, the way people always rattle off the top three: What's your name? Where are you from? Where'd you go to school? Except the conversation took an unexpected turn.

"Jersey."

"What do you do?"

"I play football." *Reeeeaaaaaalllly?* The antennas shot up. I couldn't help it; this was an involuntary reaction. If I were a dog and he were a bell, I'd have covered him in Pavlovian salivation.

"For what team?"

"The Colts."

"Where are the Colts based?" (Now, remember, I wasn't a sports fan. I was a fan of the athletes who played them, so this was a legitimate question.)

"Indianapolis," he chuckled.

So far, so good. Until . . . "How old are you?"

"Twenty-five."

Ugh. He was dead to me! I had just gone through that with Pete the nonbat, and that age just screamed, "Warning! Stop! Must abort mission!" So less than four seconds later, I quickly wrapped up the "interview" and forgot about Tim and his lips and turned my attention elsewhere.

About a month later, Tim asked the baseball player who introduced us for my phone number and called to see if "maybe you, me, and your friends could go to dinner while I'm in town for a golf charity?"

I knew he wanted to be set up with some of my hot friends (always a great accessory—women think it's shoes, but men would say hot friends over shoes any day of the week). I wasn't interested in him myself, so, being a good friend, I put feelers out to those in need as if I worked for the Red Cross.

The first girl I asked was Melissa. She was sweet, somewhat shy, and a naturally pretty girl, with no boobs to speak of and an ass you might see in a juicy magazine. Most people are cursed with one unfair body part—but blessed with another from the luck-out gene pool. Melissa had never done a lunge in her life, but her ass begged to differ. While normal people have buttocks that soften and flatten over time, Melissa's defied gravity—like two ripe cantaloupes—mocking inferior butts the world over. Despite this, we were able to be friends and I didn't hate her.

"Mel, come to dinner with us! You haven't had sex in three years."

This was not really much of an exaggeration.

"No. I have plans tonight with my grandma."

"Perhaps *that* is the reason you haven't been laid in three years," I pressed on, hoping for a different response. She wouldn't budge, though, and she didn't appreciate being reminded of her vaginal vacancies.

I moved on to recruit my sluttier roommate, Cici, who had lately taken to bedazzling anything she could get her hands on. Bras, bongs, and a set of balls were not off-limits. She was out of control with this new hobby, and I found sparkly beads all over the house and, once, on my dog's forehead.

"Come to dinner with us! It will be fun!"

"No way. He's a football player. I hate athletes. I like rockers. Not meatheads."

"He is not a meathead," I said defensively. We had had this conversation before. She didn't get my type, and I didn't get hers, which made us perfect copilots when we went out. Except that most men wouldn't even glance in my direction, mesmerized as they were by her circus-side-show-size tits. "He's just bigger than a normal human, who you can't share jeans with, nor bedazzle T-shirts for."

She wouldn't budge. My efforts were hopeless. It was like getting a stripper to go home with you for no money down.

So in the end it became Tim's and my very accidental

first date. Admittedly, during the sushi dinner our conversation flowed as easily as the sake and continued where we had left off that night in New Orleans. I learned he was close to his family, he went to an Ivy League school, and his parents, like mine, were still married. He seemed different—more articulate and less cliché—from the other athletes. It wasn't until they were putting the chairs on top of the tables around us that I thought to myself, *Forget the age discrimination, Rosa. He's a catch.*

We went back to my house, opened a bottle of wine, and did as much making out as two people can do when one of them has her period. Yes, remember this was *not* a date. My tampon remembered. We stayed up until the sun blinded us and seemed to mock me with its light, as if to say, "Aha, Rosa! You are all smoke and mirrors! So *this* is the real you, huh?"

Tim called American Airlines to extend his ticket. He charmed his way into bypassing the change fee, purred sweetly to the woman who answered the phone that he had just met someone very special, and even put me on the line all giddy to verify his information.

A WEEK LATER, PERIOD-FREE, I flew to Florida to meet him. On the plane I noticed that sitting became uncomfortable. *Ugh! Fabulous,* I thought. *He's gonna think I'm a freak show. I think there must be a bug bite forming on my ass.* I couldn't wait to land and do a full inspection. But the buildup of not seeing each other for a week was incredible! Except for my ass thing, which I tried hard to ignore, we were instantly making out like teenagers, until his hand swept across the bug bite.

I could have sworn I read his mind, which said, *What the hell is on your ass?*

His hand swept across it again, sort of a resweep. It was time to address the pink-elephant-sized bump-on-my-ass in the room.

"Oh! I think I got bit by something," I said lamely, embarrassed that I even needed a disclaimer for my ass.

The next morning the "bite" was pulsating. I'm pretty sure it had a steady heartbeat of its own. What if that urban legend about spiders laying eggs and them hatching in someone was true? My ass was now turning into *Charlotte's Web* the sequel! This was so ill-timed! I took matters into my own hands and called my dermatologist. I explained the situation in detail and asked him what I should do.

"Well, Rosa, it's probably an infected hair follicle."

"Um . . ." I tried lowering my voice, because Tim was there and the condo was small.

"I don't have any hair . . . um . . . on my butt." I had to let Dr. Rosenbach know this. He had only seen my face, and my face had only seen his needles.

"Everyone does, even if you can't see them," he continued, as if this was a logical explanation. "You have to go to an emergency room if it gets more painful or bigger. You don't want it to get abscessed."

Okay, you are a joke, I thought. What a dramatic explanation for what was clearly just a bug bite.

I looked in the Yellow Pages for a local dermatologist who would give me a diagnosis I liked better than my Beverly Hills doctor's. There was at least a two-week wait for every one! It seemed what the city was lacking in dermatologists, it made up for in golf courses and snowbirds. Sarasota, Florida, was literally becoming a pain in my ass.

The next morning, while Tim was out of the house, I bent over the mirror and attempted to squeeze the now-ping-pong-ball-size bite. The next thing I saw was green slime, like on Nickelodeon, but less kid-friendly. Then everything started to go black, and I almost fainted. As I stared up at the ceiling, trying to stabilize my vision, I thought, *Crap! Not the way I wanted to be staring up at a ceiling on this trip!*

When Tim got home, I asked to be driven to the emergency room.

He was almost giggling. "Okaaaaaaay . . ."

"I called my dermatologist. He said I should. It's probably just in need of a little cortisone injection." I left out the part about nearly blacking out midextraction and underestimating the complexities of reaching your unreachables. Fewer things were as difficult. It was the Cirque du Soleil of pimple-picking.

We went to the ER, which was weird for me only because I worked in a faux ER, playing a doctor for seventy hours a week. Now, living in Los Angeles, people seldom recognized me. I don't know if it was because I was on basic cable or because it's L.A., where people are too cool to acknowledge they know who you are. But that day in the real ER there were a lot of nurses and doctors visiting my room for what seemed like no reason, and a few who slipped and called me Lu—my television character's name. There, while laying facedown, I was fortunate enough to have a medical-grade lamp aimed at my menacing, mystery butt blemish.

To further my humiliation, the words "infected," "puss," and "hair follicle" kept getting thrown my way, in front of my new man! It was mortifying. When I thought it couldn't get any worse, they announced they would have to lance it, drain it, and stuff it with cotton. It looked like a Hershey's Kiss with a paper tail on top. Every girl's dream in front of a new paramour!

The next day, when Tim volunteered to change my lanced zit—which was oozing pads of green joy—I knew. We were falling in love. He was a keeper. I put a lot of stock in gut feelings and meant-to-be's, and all signs pointed to Tim Fish.

THE RELATIONSHIP WITH Tim was the easiest I'd ever had. There were no games. We couldn't get enough of each other. It was easy to fantasize about what our children would look like because we looked like sister and brother (if I were six foot, 255 pounds, and had ever gotten my lips injected with collagen). We both had that "we just know" feeling. We were from similar middle-class backgrounds. We had similar lofty goals and aspirations at an early age. When most kids just want to learn to ride a bike, or get the latest doll, Tim and I were dreaming about our careers, which we were eventually lucky enough to live out. Plus, as I did my "So what do you think?" meetings (you know, where you basically parade your new boyfriend around to the people you care about, so when he goes to the bathroom you can immediately get either the thumbs-down or the bridesmaids' gowns order together), Tim passed with flying colors. Each and every family member and close friend of mine said the same thing: "He seems like a good guy. He seems down to earth and warm." The icing on the cake was "You two seem really happy."

I loved that Tim was not a big "franchise" player. He wasn't a household name. He had to bust his ass to make it in his profession, and I could relate. It was obvious that we were the perfect couple to succeed at marriage.

Tim was actually about to drop the L bomb and tell me he loved me a week into our relationship.

"You know . . . I really . . . I . . ." He hesitated and I jumped in.

"You don't have to say it."

Tim waited two weeks before he couldn't stop himself. It was a classic, dizzying, whirlwind romance.

I met his parents, he met mine, and then we went to Cabo San Lucas to the amazing, over-the-top romantic luxury resort Las Ventanas—and actually met with a wedding planner to discuss the possibilities of getting married there. We had been dating less than a month. I just wanted to look into his eyes, photograph him, and inhale him like a fine French perfume. We even had the ever-important "time line" conversation. We would get married a year after the engagement, and have kids the year after that. I was ready and mama's clock was ticking louder than the opening credits on *60 Minutes*.

T HAT FIRST YEAR I enjoyed a very easy, very smooth relationship with Tim. I would work a long, crazy week on *Strong Medicine*, with its accompanying fourteen-hour days. Then Friday night I would take the red-eye and fly to Indianapolis, and then eventually to New Jersey, to see him for basically one day. It sounds brutal, but we had new-love adrenaline pumping through our veins. Tim would be sequestered in a hotel room from around dinner-time Saturday until I saw him on the field the next day in his uniform. Ah, talk about the ultimate foreplay. I'll take looking at a sweaty, dirty guy in an athletic uniform over poetry, massages, and long-distance dedications from easy-listening radio stations *any* day. Plus, it was nice to finally see an actual live football game after being at so many Super Bowl parties. Being inside the stadium with the deafening, thunderous cheers, I got it. I understood. And I was starting to drink the Kool-Aid just like everybody else.

Long-distance relationships never bothered me, but in order to make the flight home and on time for my day of filming (which started before even Starbucks opened), I had to leave before the game was over. I'd listen in the car to the end of the game, or stand in an airport T.G.I. Friday's with the other fans. Needless to say, we never snuck to see each other the night before at his hotel, or even attempted to break the rules. Their rules were crazy strict and the NFL are fine-happy. They made the FCC (even post–Janet Jackson nipple-gate) seem like slackers.

Tim once got fined for having one sock fall down. He wasn't trying to be all gangster or cool, it just fell, and he and his agent had to prove that it was in fact an accident. The fine was a few thousand dollars! My favorite fining threats came every Friday, when the guys got their weigh-ins just like the goddamned Ice Capades! If they weighed even one pound over their training-camp set weight, or preseason weight, it was two hundred dollars per pound. They are essentially treated like slabs of meat—albeit overpaid, childish, aggressive slabs of meat that will eventually need therapy.

I FEEL LIKE THIS is as good a place as any to apologize to God. I spent a lot of time praying while watching sporting events. It was selfish. I regret it. I know God has a pretty full plate, even fuller than Oprah's. I probably should not have wasted God's time by praying for another field goal, or for Tim to have a great game and "complete all his assignments." I remember that one mantra clearly.

There was also the looming threat, the virtual grim reaper waiting to knock on the doors of the athletes unlucky enough to answer, in the form of injuries. If the four-letter C word is the meanest, most vile thing you can say to a woman, then "injury" is the worst thing you can utter to an athlete, especially during the season. I've seen superfamous, superconfident football studs, guys known for knocking the crap out of their opponents, visibly cringe when some random person—who clearly hasn't been taught that it's sacrilegious—asks, "So, how you feeling? Any injuries?"

The reason for my sudden increased interest in religion was, of course, due to my sudden increased interest in the outcome of the games. You do not want to go home with a moody fuck after a bad game. It's the worst. It ruins the night, and sometimes even the week, until they can redeem themselves at the next game. It's actually an added stress on you: the girlfriend or wife. You know it's coming. As the game unfolds, first there's the uncomfortable shifting in your seat. Then the "oh crap" eye contact among the wives and girlfriends. As the scoreboard play clock ticks down, postgame dinner reservations are canceled and the mental preparation begins for what you are going to say after the loss, because you can't just say, "Sucks to be you." You have to get creative and think like a publicist after one of their famous client's really public screw-ups.

Postgame, go to any player-family area or waiting lounge, in any sport, and if the score was a tragedy, you'll see people looking like they are waiting to pay their last respects. Granted, most funerals don't showcase the latest wait-listed Louis Vuitton bags, blinding diamonds, or a fresh tit-job for almost every player-wife ticket stub. You don't have to have a neon VIP wristband or be in the player-family area to tell who's a girlfriend or a wife at a professional sporting event. Ray Charles could spot them. They are overly coifed with long, highlighted hair. They're also skinny and dressed in designer jeans and expensive stiletto heels, no matter how cold or gross or spilt-beer sticky a stadium might be. They (and I) want to look hot, not sensible. There are few benefits to being a football wife, or fiancée. Very few. But one of them is the "keeping up with the Joneses" tendency of most athletes to buy big, clear, sparkling diamonds the size of footballs. My diamond engagement ring was no exception. It was a flawless emerald cut (like mini football fields) just over three carats, in between two single-carat "bodyguards." It was hard not to notice, and while I didn't know it at the time, I would eventually "earn" every goddamned carat. One of my best gays, after seeing my ring, squealed, "Nice ice, girl! You musta sucked a lot of cocks for those rocks!" It would have been funny too, if Tim hadn't heard it. . . .

HANGIN' TOUGH

I never thought I would personally be "running interference" for Peyton Manning, but you never know where life is going to take you or who is going to step up to bat. This was sometime in 2002, or so I think, when the Colts completely shit the bed to the Jets. They lost something like 40-ish to 0, or something embarrassing like that. Maybe they had one field goal? No one remembers. No one cares at this point.

What I remember most about that game was sitting in the stands at Jets Stadium with Peyton Manning's wife, Ashley. She was a college sweetheart of his with a fondness for Burberry, alcohol, and my husband (or so I always suspected). The crowd around us did not know who she was. This is not surprising. The public only finds out who the wife is if she's:

a. excessively hot like Gisele Bündchen,

b. hounded by the press after her husband cheats on her (like Tiger's wife, and Kobe Bryant's "smart" wife for staying), or

c. some famous chick (like a Kardashian, Kate Hudson, or Carrie Underwood).

The crowd was going rabid in the throws of an epic Peyton Manning bashfest. He was the quarterback of the losing team (the Colts) for you women out there who may think he's just a really talented commercial actor and sometime host of Saturday Night Live. *The Colts used to kind of suck before they got really good and won Super Bowls and stuff.*

Ashley and I were forced to listen to the lunatics surrounding us screaming obscenities about how much the "Colts fucking suuuuuuck!" It was as if we had the power to read the minds of people around us, that we shouldn't be reading. Except we didn't have to read their minds because they were yelling deafeningly loud hate messages into our ears. In this case they were screaming the worst, most offensive crap you have ever heard, specifically about Peyton. I looked over at Ashley. She had that classic, glazed, Stepford-wife-meets-a-politician's-wife smile they must have to teach you in a school somewhere to perfect. Even I was humiliated to know the guy at that point. I decided to take matters into my own hands! She was catatonically smiling and I couldn't just sit by and watch her face crack. I needed to help in my own special way.

Just as another round of ear-shattering mud slinging started, and it seemed as if we were at the world's longest football game, I resurrected my cheerleader voice, the one I had long since buried. Using all thirteen years of my private voice lessons and the ability to connect with my diaphragm (not the ones that go in your vagina to prevent babies, but the muscle near your abdomen), I screamed just as loud as the biggest culprit trash-talker guy I could identify. He was a typical overweight cliché of a balding man, who seemed to be doing his best Artie Lange impression from the Howard Stern show. This douche bag had clearly been drinking and tailgating since 9:00 that morning (as evidenced by the stench of sour beer wafting over at me from a few rows away). Classy guy. If he is here . . . then who is working the tilt-a-whirl at the carnival? I thought.

I stood up and with my loud-ass annoying voice I screamed at him:

"Dude! Peyton Manning is hung like a horse! Unless you are too, sir? I suggest you shut your piehole!"

The crowd around us, including the faux Artie, fell silent.

I half expected people to start that awesome, dramatic slow-clapping thing from the movies, where a single guy starts from complete silence and then the crowd, looking from one person to the next, slowly joins in till the applause is thunderous! But that didn't happen, because this was not the movie Rudy *or* Lucas, *but real life instead.*

It did work though. The Artie guy (clearly hung like a raisin himself) said nothing for the rest of the game. I think he must have thought I was banging Peyton or "in the know," and in return had some sort of respect for me—even if Peyton was throwing more interceptions than passes that day, and getting sacked more times than

Lindsay Lohan after a week of clubbing. When Peyton got wind of this incident, I think he developed a whole new admiration for me. I know this because I was there when his brother Eli repeated the story years later and thought it was funny. Peyton and Eli's mother, Olivia, once told me that Peyton was a thirteen-pound baby (breaking records even at birth in his Louisiana hospital) and Eli was over ten pounds. I don't doubt it.

I had heard this little tidbit about Peyton's privates (which would be a great name for a garage band if you ask me) from the locker-room grapevine, and later heard the same thing about Eli, Peyton's younger brother.

Lesson learned: Who knew the Manning brothers were so gifted?

If only I had paid more attention to the signs.

SEVEN

Our Rookie Year

Things were smooth sailing the first year for Tim and me. Yes, we both were a bit opinionated and leaned more toward the argumentative than the lovey-dovey, but I thought what we lacked in fairy-tale romance, we made up for in passion. There was just that knowing feeling that this was forever. This was the father of my children. I knew with every fiber of my being that Tim would never cheat. From what I saw, the cheaters were generally the big franchise players (the players that were the pillars who held up the team, and thus, treated like gods.) Their god complex was worse than any politician's or surgeon's, so in turn these powerful men, like most really powerful men, tended to stray. I knew one NFL franchise player who took "playing the field," to a whole new level of creativity. It was "too easy" to find women to sleep with for this household name. I mean you can only bed so many Playmates before it becomes a case of same blond, different month bor-ing familiarity. So this NFL guy, who happened to be a huge NASCAR fan, decided that his next "goal" would be to bed the *wife* of one the biggest NASCAR stars. Game on! That at least kept him interested (for about as long as a commercial break) before getting bored with that too. Who says athletes lack creativity?

Tim was a scrub player. He was considered "fringe" and always in fear of being replaced and getting cut, particularly during training camp and preseason. He was the last pick in the year he was drafted, and they even had a name for it: Mr. Irrelevant. It seems kind of rude, but they throw you a big parade and give you a nice Rolex if you're Mr. Irrelevant. Personally, I'd be more irritated if I were the second-to-last pick of the draft, because you miss out on all of the fanfare.

T HE ONLY REAL, hard-core fight I remember having with Tim that first year happened on Christmas Eve. We were having a dinner with four guys from his team whom I didn't know well, plus Peyton Manning and Brad Scioli (who I'd spent time with before) as well as all of their significant others, which is like having dinner with six guys from the team and me. The wives don't contribute much to conversations, and the conversations are mind-numbingly dull, and about football for the most part. I became an expert at dumbing down references and small talk.

The fight started innocently enough, as most do. Some of the guys were asking me about Hollywood and working on a set. Who had I worked with? These were the usual questions because they weren't from L.A., where people act too cool to ask them. These are the questions you get when you go back home to the Midwest. They are the same questions I asked, before I moved out to La La Land.

Tim chimed in proudly, "She just worked with Apollo Creed!"

Tim's favorite movie of all time was *Rocky*. He worshipped the movie and this was a big deal to the movie's fans, I guess. Never mind that I had worked with Whoopi Goldberg and she was the executive producer of my television series. Apparently, Apollo Creed, whose real name is Carl Weathers, was a hot commodity with this particular group.

"So what was he like?" asked one of the guys, as if he were questioning me about a legend.

"Ummmm. Well, he directed an episode, and I wasn't really a big fan of him as a director," I said, slightly baffled by how much they were suddenly so attentive about a subject that did not include a ball.

"Why not?" chimed in another guy just as eagerly awaiting my answers.

"Well, he barked at me a lot, like we were on a field. It was as if he were coaching and yelling a lot, and that's just not the way you direct actors!"

I knew they appreciated me relating things back to their sport, and since many had had head injuries, this was also a thoughtful and somewhat necessary thing for me to do. That and repetition.

Now I knew I had their attention, which I figured pleased Tim. "Plus, he wore these ridiculous acid-washed jeans so tight you could tell he was circumcised!" The table laughed and while I thought I felt a kick to my shin (the universal sign for a verbal faux pas) I supposed it could have been an accident. We moved on, and had a great dinner.

The second the valet came up with our car, and the doors shut out the sounds of our voices, Tim laid into me.

"What the *hell* were you thinking? Do you really find it necessary to talk about Apollo Creed's circumcision?"

"His name is Carl Weathers," I muttered under my breath, confused about where Tim was going with this, but not so confused that I could leave out my go-to sarcastic nature.

"Whatever!" Tim was now officially raising his voice. "What is wrong with you? Who says that at a Christmas Eve dinner!"

"It matters that it's Christmas Eve? And since when is circumcision a bad word?" This conversation was so out there and so random that I couldn't have predicted it with Dionne Warwick and the Psychic Friends Network.

The shin kick was not imagined. And in the course of our relationship, investing in shin guards would have behooved me because there'd be many more to come. I had embarrassed him. I knew from that moment on that Tim might be reconsidering whom he had married. I threw in a couple of "perhaps your next wife can be a mail-ordered, less opinionated, fourteen-year-old Vietnamese mute! Because I have some fucking opinions and not a vacuous space between my diamond solitaire earrings like the rest of their dates!" I was livid. He basically wanted me to pretend to be someone else. Tim wanted Donna Reed. But I knew that wasn't possible. These guys were way too young to know who Donna Reed was. That night—that fight—should have been a red flag. He cared too much about what people thought, or how they would perceive him.

What seemed to bother Tim the most was that "some of those guys were the really Christian guys from my team!"

"So Christians don't have circumcisions? Now I'm really confused—because there were only three Jewish kids at my school and I've only seen circumcisions. I still don't get *how* this was offensive?" I was trying in vain to wrap my head around the whole stupid fight. What I understood after he calmed the fuck down was that aside from a few of his close friends on the team who were present, like Peyton Manning and Brad Scioli, there were also guys there from the team's Bible-beaters tight circle, who Tim must have felt judged him.

O N EVERY TEAM there is always a group of guys who are super into religion. If you are a football fan, you will notice that the guys who gather in the center of the field after a game and kneel down are praying. Some just join in, but most of those guys go to Bible study meetings hosted at one of the player's homes during the week. It's its own clique-within-a-clique on the team. In some cases, these guys are really judgmental about the guys on the team who aren't into religion like they are. Tim once called out a guy who was giving him a hard time for not attending Bible study. "But aren't you the same guy who was in a hot tub with a bunch of strippers before you found your wife and God . . . not too long ago?" Tim deadpanned. The guy Tim called out had nothing left to say. I loved that about Tim. Until that night, I thought he didn't give a crap about what people thought of him, and that he was honest to a fault.

Honestly, it wasn't the first time I had had a small run-in where I might have offended some "Christians." I once got into a similar argument with the late Rev. Jerry Falwell when we were both guests on Bill Maher's *Politically Incorrect*. Jerry Falwell had famously publicly chastised the children's television show *Teletubbies*. Yes, the Teletubbies (squeaky Muppetlike creatures on the UK-based television show for toddlers), because one of them carried a purse and was clearly "gay." I told Jerry Falwell on the air that day that "some of the most religious people seem to be hypocrites" and "regardless of what you believe in, the message of Jesus was about love—not judgment!" To really drive the point home I said, "Jesus hung out with whores and lepers, and there was feet-washing too. It was like a night at the Playboy Mansion!" I finished with, "to be honest, I have a problem sitting next to someone who has a problem with Tinky Winky!" But I digress, the moral of this story is, of course, that it's not ladylike for women to talk about circumcision. Especially on Christmas Eve. Particularly at dinner with Christians. What-ever!

My favorite shin-dangerment came when I was at another large football-player dinner. Tim's agent at the time had a yearly gathering in Florida at a resort for all the players (and their wives/girlfriends) that the agent represented. We were all in Palm Beach (home of the gaudiest jewelry and more kept women per capita than anywhere else in the United States). I thought the accents, the bright splashy flamingo-pink clothing, and leather-bag face tans were outstanding.

While in Palm Beach we met up with this backup quarterback and first-string ladies' man, Mickey Mahoon. Mickey was very good-looking, as an abnormally high number of quarterbacks seem to be. He also had the kind of classic stud/soap-star good looks. Mickey was not going to win any Mensa awards, but he was tall, with dark slicked hair and piercing Eskimo-dog blue eyes. I've often pondered what chiseled good looks have to do with your ability to throw a ball, but I've never formally done a conclusive study. Mickey also seemed allergic to any monogamous relationship that lasted longer than a week . . . end. This guy pulled more tail than a Beatle. He was also ahead of his time, explaining how easy it was to meet girls online at Myspace (this was the first I'd heard of it). I had to ask for clarification it all seemed so unbelievable. "So you just go to Myspace? To service . . . your space?" as I gestured to the space in his southern regions. Tim and I sat there, his attentive audience, as he explained that he met these girls online, and they just showed up for sex! This was another moment when I silently thanked God that I would never have to do this Internet dating thing, and was grateful to be engaged and have found my soulmate. I was shocked that women would just show up for sex like a cheese pizza from Dominos. We were warned that that night Mickey would have a different girl with him than the one we met briefly the previous night, before they holed up (literally and figuratively) in his hotel room.

"So, what does this girl do, Mickey?" I asked. I know that question was slightly loaded, as I didn't expect any answer other than student, nothing, or ass-bait for the Prince of Brunei.

"She is in real estate. She's an appraiser," he answered without skipping a beat.

I tried hiding my surprise. "Good for you! That's great! I can't wait to meet her!" I exclaimed earnestly. Finally, I could possibly carry on a conversation with someone who may also be literate. That was such a bonus round in these circles. The girl showed up, and she seemed normal and nice enough, although I did notice she could have cut back on the makeup a bit. She looked like one of those cosmetic-counter reps at the mall.

We were all a few drinks in, and laughing as Tim

shared a story about when he was single, how he believed so fervently in safe sex that he once used a shower cap in a hotel bathroom with a girl as a MacGyver-like, last-minute condom. (I tried to see the condom half full and thought, *What a good, responsible young man!* And then I tried not to picture some gross one-night-stand underneath my man, with excess plastic shower cap making a flower outside her vagina.) As much as a part of me hated how much "experience" Tim had had with women, I also appreciated it, knowing he would never have to wonder what it was like to be with a Playmate or what it was like to have a threesome, or. . . . We once attended a funeral near his hometown in New Jersey, and there were four girls there he confessed he had slept with. This confession took place in the car where he knew I was a safe distance from glaring and analyzing them to death. At least Tim wasn't going to be the guy having the midlife crisis, or cheating because he wondered what it was like to . . . because he had been there, and literally done that. Or them. Many of them.

We were all laughing and carrying on the conversation about girls, etc., when the subject of comedians, and particularly Chris Rock, had come up somehow. His latest stand-up special had been airing all month on HBO, and was piss-yourself-laughing funny. Genius even.

"The best line ever from that show was when Chris Rock was talking about strippers! He said something to the effect that if you have a daughter, your *only* job in life was to keep yo' daughta off the pole! Just keep yo' daughta off the pole!" I am a terrible impersonator, but I did my best Chris Rock impression on the last two lines of the sentence, and quietly praised myself for sounding just like him, especially the way I said "daughta."

Everyone was laughing when I felt it—the swift, subtle shin kick. I looked at Tim. He did not look back at me. Maybe it was an accident. *Oh hell no, he just did it again*, this time more determined. I was puzzled. The black guys at the table knew I was not even remotely prejudiced. *Could they have been offended by my Chris Rock impression? Should I not have tried to emulate his urban voice?* I shrugged it off, determined that what I'd said was not offensive, or inappropriate. Until Mickey's girl-du-jour excused herself to go to the bathroom. The second she was out of earshot Mickey put his head down on the table in an overly dramatic fashion.

A couple of the guys started laughing hysterically, and Tim just said, "Jesus Christ, Rosa! Did you have to tell *that* story?"

Everyone seemed to be in on the joke but me. "What story?" I was trying to remember what we had talked about that would warrant this kind of response.

"The Chris Rock story! She's a stripper, Rosa. That girl's a stripper!"

"Then why the fuck did you tell me she's an appraiser! What exactly is she appraising?" Now I was pissed at Mickey. "It's not like I'm Amish. Why wouldn't you have just told me?"

"She's wants to go to school to be an appraiser. But right now she's a dancer." Mickey said it as if that were the same as actually *being* an appraiser.

THIS SITUATION WAS another classic foot-in-mouth moment, like having accidentally offensive ESP where somehow the universe steers me into saying the most perfectly wrong thing out loud. This has happened many times, but it seemed to happen the most with Tim around, and with Tim's friends.

It wasn't the first time I'd put my foot in my mouth. It struck again when I met one of Tim's best friends, Marco DeRossi, a baseball player with the Atlanta Braves at the time. I was told that Hailey, Marco's wife, was a model. As soon as I met her, I could see why. She was stunningly beautiful, exotic-looking, and tall. I tried to compliment her (always a good way to put someone at ease when you meet them, particularly when it's sincere).

"You are beautiful, Hailey. It's so nice to meet you!" I said, feeling more than usually stumpy and stocky next to her towering physique and coltish legs. I had the same exact feeling as the time I was introduced to *Sports Illustrated* swimsuit model and actress Molly Sims. I did a body and facial scan for imperfections (strictly for self-soothing purposes) and came up with nothing to fixate on. Hailey, like Molly Sims, was freakishly, unfairly beautiful.

"Nice to meet you too, Rosa," she said as I was trying to

figure out if those were her pillow lips or if she had had the help of Rejuvederm. They looked (and were) real, it turns out, unlike her rack, which was compliments of a surgeon in her home state of Texas.

"So Hailey, Tim tells me you're a model. I can't tell you how refreshing it is to meet a real model, and not a Hawaiian Tropic girl that *calls* herself a model!" Hailey had sort of a delayed fake laugh. But I just figured that girls that stunning were maybe not blessed with a sense of humor as well. You can't have it all I suppose.

Cut to the next day when Marco called Tim.

"Nice job. Your girl Rosa throwin' Hailey under the bus like that!" Marco said to Tim in that ball-busting way that men talk to each other constantly.

Yep, you guessed it. I had hit the acrylic nail on the head. Hailey was in fact a former Hawaiian Tropic girl. She had done legitimate modeling locally as well, so I only looked like a semi-a-hole and not a full-blown one. Thank heavens for small miracles.

Our engagement continued, and Tim got traded from the Indianapolis Colts to the New York Giants. This was incredible for him because he was literally from a town that had Giants Stadium in its backyard. For whatever reason—alright, for real estate value reasons—the New York Giants were located in New Jersey. So our "glamorous" life relocated from Indiana to New Jersey, with the off-seasons in Los Angeles. Yes, it was close to New York, but nobody lived there except two guys on the team. I was turning into a Jersey girl whether I liked it or not. Even my diction got more annoying.

We were now around all of the family and the friends Tim grew up with all of the time. Tim was living a dream. His self-esteem was healthy to begin with, but the attention that his hometown and the media lavished on him boosted his self-image even more. He was loving it. We even got free use of a brand-new, loaded Ford Expedition in exchange for a couple hours of Tim's time signing at a car dealership. Everyone knew who Tim Fish was. Soon, I was known as the future Mrs. Fish, and, ironically, I was just a future trophy wife when I was on the East Coast. Regardless of the fact that I was making twice as much as Tim and that I had a very legitimate career, on New Jersey soil . . . I was Tim's girl. It was an afterthought when people asked me, "So, do you work?" But being in love and in that early blissful state, I was more amused than chagrined. Especially when I used it to my advantage to get out of speeding tickets.

I T WAS WHILE we were apartment hunting that it first really registered to me that Tim could rage, sort of out of the blue—like have these spastic little rage attacks. Almost like a burp: *bam*! There it is. Loud. It happened and then it was over. It was rage Tourette's, if you will. It was like a momentary angry verbal outburst (maybe about directions, me eating in his car, or just a regular couple's disagreement) but louder, and then it passed. It's like when you are trying to find a good radio station in a rental car, and it blasts offensive music stations as you frantically try to change it, but you're not familiar with how this radio works. "Ah! Make it go away! Not that one!" Then you change it and it's over. Everyone's relieved. I quietly concluded that Tim was under a lot of pressure and always nervous about getting cut from the team and looking bad in front of his hometown. Hence the tiny spasms.

I also chose to downplay the fact that he really liked going out "with his boys" while I was waiting at home catching up with the TiVo. That part of my brain, which was apparently lobotomized, quieted any concerns I had. *He's just excited to be back with his friends he hasn't seen in a long time*, I thought, hoping if I thought this enough— much like praying for your breasts to grow in junior high—it might actually be true. *Plus, he is enjoying being big man on campus! It's a once-in-a-lifetime situation. It will pass. It's a phase.*

The real Rosa (the louder, more vocal one) who couldn't stop herself from speaking if her life depended on it asked, "So how come you never went out like this in Indy?"

" 'Cause it was fucking Indy. This is New York!" Tim replied, like he'd been watching one too many *Sopranos* episodes.

"Actually, it's New Jersey. It's just called the New York Giants so that people will think you are cooler than you are and buy tickets."

Tim's deadpan look told me he didn't think I was funny.

But I wasn't deterred. That's why I had my gays. They thought I was funny. Plus I never had to explain my jokes to them.

I was the one who first told Tim, and his dumber side-kick—meathead, *Jersey Shore*–looking best friend Johnny—that they were considered "bridge and tunnel." Amazingly, they had never heard the expression before.

"There's no such thing. What does that even mean?" Tim challenged me as if I had just made it up on the spot.

"That's what they call the people from New Jersey that have to take a bridge or tunnel to get to their destination . . . New York. And as a means to keep out the undesirable, they charge them a hefty toll. It's a pretty common expression, and well, you guys are it. You're bridge and tunnel, dude." I knew I was milking it with the "undesirable" part, but it amused me and I was on a roll.

Tim's best friend Johnny just neighed. Or maybe it was a laugh, but with all the horse steroids careening through his body, it was in the neigh ballpark. Johnny was one of those guys who actually walked funny, due to bicep-itis. The symptoms of bicep-itis are when you intentionally overdevelop your traps and biceps in the gym so much so that you look like it would pain you to walk with your arms actually down at your sides, like regular humans. As if a constant airing out of each armpit were necessary throughout the day. They mustn't touch down under any circumstances!

That, combined with the carefully tailored shirts he bought at babyGap, made Johnny the perfect *Of Mice and*

Men sidekick to Tim. He nodded and smiled at most everything Tim said, seldom made a point, and even more rarely disagreed. He was there to be verbally abused by Tim when necessary, high-five him during many a threesome gone by, and love him like a brother, all the while maintaining an artificial tan that could rival Hulk Hogan's. They'd been best friends since they were eight. For me, having Johnny around was genius, because I was able to take advantage of his inferior brain, pump him for information, and later trap him into telling me things (by pretending I already knew). A classic Girl 101 trick.

If you have any acting ability at all and you word it just right (read: nonthreatening), it has an over 90 percent success rate. I endorse, recommend, and stand by this tried-and-true technique whenever you're fishing for information your partner would otherwise be unwilling to fess up to.

Aside from these boy outings and angry episodes, things seemed as calm as two people with occupations in the public eye, living three thousand miles apart, could be. We were planning our wedding and we wanted it to be a fun party of spring break–like proportions, minus the wet T-shirt contests and beer bongs. I've been to so many weddings where the brides have clearly pored over magazines and agonized about decor and flowers and chicken kiev. There are cake tastings (does anyone not know what cake tastes like besides Madonna, who hasn't had a carbohydrate since the nineties?). There are stupid hair run-throughs (if you want prom hair, then have some obliging hairdresser do your updo with curly tendrils plastered in hairspray down each side of your face). Finally, there are the live wedding-band auditions, or worse, wedding-band demo tapes people are forced to listen to. It's like getting a mixed tape from hell, because wedding bands are the antichrist unless you can afford Aerosmith.

Let me tell you what never happens . . .

No one leaves a wedding going, "Oh! That chicken kiev was to die for! I could look at those orchids all night long! Because of that—what a great time had by all!" You either love the music played, like the people invited, get a little shit-faced, dance, and enjoy yourself, or you want to sue the couple getting married because (much like epic films) most weddings last too damn long.

I've been to more weddings that feel like three-act play productions. You recognize the "actors" playing the bride and groom, but you question the "costume choice" (read: why the whore in the white dress is suddenly so desperate to channel the virginity she lost long before this guy). The bride and groom lose themselves in their "performance," but it costs way more than the average American income, and no one has fun but the florist, who gets to bill the newlyweds for all their overpriced flowers. Funny, at my local Ralph's grocery store, the roses cost $12.99 a dozen. My nine roses in each centerpiece cost $200. T-w-o h-u-n-d-r-e-d. That's floral rape.

I was committed to planning the antiwedding—and

having the ultimate party experience instead. For our wedding, 120 people flew to Maui to enjoy themselves and each other during that week. The rehearsal dinner was to take place on Friday the thirteenth (kind of a creepy date, but overlooked) because the wedding itself fell on the following day—February fourteenth, Valentine's Day—which just added to the romantic feel of it all, got all the male guests out of the pressure of having to come up with special Valentine's plans, and assured me that my future husband would never be one of those anniversary-forgetting guys. By the time the wedding happened, people weren't awkwardly meeting at a round table with number assignments. They were bonded from the weeklong vacation experience. Our wedding list was composed half of my show business friends (varying from struggling actors to hit television and soap stars) plus my fabulous stable of gays, and the other half of Tim's professional athlete friends (including Peyton Manning and Andruw Jones). We wrote our own vows, sharing with our guests specifically "what we loved about one another." The best part was that we didn't show them to each other until we were actually saying them, so they were a true surprise. The vows were both funny and touching, which included me telling Tim through happy tears that "I love that you are so anal and OCD that you label your socks with markers, so that they get washed the same amount of times." (Teammates of Tim's who were in the know about this laughed the hardest.) And

"Tim, I love that you are honest 97 percent of the time . . . even when I don't want to hear what you have to say."

Tim sweetly vowed to me that "I love you because I remember what my life was missing before I met you" and "I love that you think you are a real doctor." (The guests from *Strong Medicine* laughed the loudest on that one.) There was no priest officiating the wedding, but instead my acting coach and great friend Leigh Kilton-Smith, who got ordained on the Internet (like Joey from *Friends* did), and married us. The weather was perfect. The ocean was crashing behind us. And the sun was setting in a blaze of colors as we said our vows. People actually asked me if I was late to the wedding to wait for optimal lighting, which is something I would have done had I thought of it. But the truth was I was just late because I'm that girl.

DJ Kevy Kev was flown in from L.A. and everyone was dancing. Even Tim's mom was jamming down on the dance floor to the Prince song "Pussy Control." I don't think she quite heard the actual lyrics, which made it priceless. The wedding, many guests said, was "the most fun they had ever been to." Biased of course, I couldn't help but agree. We were in *People* magazine (they misspelled Tim's last name, which was amusing), our episode of *Pyramid*—that we got paid generously for, and then used that money for our liquor bill—was ironically being shown on the poolside bar television (it was Valentine's Day after all), and some of our wedding pictures were featured in *InStyle* magazine.

Just not the ones of Peyton's wife dirty dancing with my wasted groom.

My beautiful little sister, Tasha, who looks like a young Natalie Wood, ended up hooking up with one of Tim's friends from high school. Brian was from the same town Tim was from, and had come to the wedding with a girlfriend he'd dated off and on for almost a decade. Two weeks after the wedding, Brian moved out of the apartment he shared with his girlfriend. My sister and Brian started dating long distance (Brian was in New York and Tasha was in L.A.), and eventually they got married and had a baby boy five years later. But that wasn't the only hooking-up surprise to come from that week in Maui. Turns out I didn't even begin to have a cup of clue.

When Tim and I came back to our suite after "the best wedding by far—ever!" as we both excitedly exclaimed, we were greeted by a room completely decked out (compliments of the hotel) in lit candles, chilled champagne, and rose petals sprinkled everywhere—a path on the floor leading to the bed, on the bed, and even in the filled bathtub. Tim, true to form, complained that the rose petals were smashing into the carpet underfoot and were "making a mess." I started laughing so hard I literally felt abdominal muscles forming for the first time. If it was possible, I loved him even more in that moment—because only Tim could take the visual of the world's most romantic room, decked out like it was the final episode of *The Bachelor*, and see the potential mess that was there to clean up.

We officially consummated the marriage, and I was officially exhausted at 3:00 a.m. when I closed my eyes and went to sleep "a Mrs." that night. I couldn't wait to wake up the next morning and start the adventures of my life married to my professional athlete . . . *husband.*

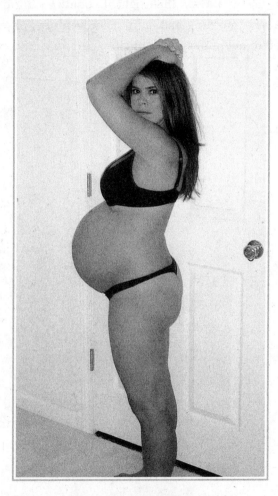

Days before giving birth.
I know what you're thinking . . .
that's one pliable thong!

Taking One for the Team

Direct from Hawaii, three days after our wedding, I flew to Japan with my hunky new husband. Without auditioning, I was offered my first major motion picture. It was a little horror film starring Sarah Michelle Gellar that was being made for just six million dollars. It was actually a horror film remake of a popular Japanese film called *Ju-on*. I was just psyched to be doing something that didn't involve Dr. Lu or a white lab coat, and finally a big movie! It was ironically called *The Grudge*. Ironic, because only days before the premiere, after I had told everybody and their brother about this film I had done, most of my scenes ended up on the cutting-room floor. It was the ultimate Hollywood cliché! I felt humiliated and, well, grudging, until the movie made $55 million and was number one at the box office just in the opening weekend. The movie continued to make a ton of money, and in turn I made a ton of residuals. (Thank you Sarah, megaproducer Sam Raimi, Sony, and all those people who like scary films!) It was our honeymoon I guess, of sorts. Tim stayed with me for a week, and then flew back to Los Angeles while I continued to film in Tokyo for a few more weeks.

I continued back on my television show after that, and Tim continued on with the Giants. It was always a vociferous, passionate, and argumentative marriage. I could have nicknamed him Old Yeller, and he probably would have given me the nickname of, well, Old Bitch.

I asked him early on in our relationship, playfully, "Babe? Am I a bitch?"

Without missing a beat, he said, "Well . . . you just like to point things out . . . and make *alot* of comments." I burst out laughing. He was honest. I'd give him that!

I wished our sex life was a little more impressive, but I knew you couldn't create the perfect person in your basement like the movie *Weird Science*. Otherwise, I would have married a cross between Tom Brady and Ferris Bueller.

At the very least I could trust Tim, unlike so many other athletes. Tim would never cheat on me. Why my confidence? Simply because he had the lowest sex drive of any guy past puberty I had dated. There's a statistic you hear about how men think of sex a bazillion times an hour. Well, I happen to have married the one guy to whom that didn't apply. On a positive note, I reasoned that if Tim barely even thought about it, chances are he wouldn't be specifically seeking it out from other people. For example, laundry is not something I am particularly into. I don't think about doing laundry until I want to wear something that's in the clothes hamper. So it's not like I'm going to go to my friend's house and offer to do a load of her whites just for fun.

Tim was going to be a great father and a trustworthy partner, and we both came from great foundations: our "normal" families. Sure, I wished he were funny, like my gays, or a planner, like my girlfriends, but you can't have it all. Our cyclical arguments would go something like this:

"Babe, I just don't get it. What guy doesn't want to have sex all the time?" I said, truly baffled. This was a first for me. This "not in the moodness." My experience with men was that they were closer to constantly starving animals. Just searching for a hole and a heartbeat.

"A guy who's never been in a monogamous relationship. This is all new to me, and I don't want the sex to get old." Tim replied as if everyone knew *that*.

"But that's weird. You get that, right? It's superweird. Even the fact that you aren't interested in receiving oral is weird. Did you know that some guys get oral as their entire birthday or anniversary present? Did you know that some women refuse to do that?"

"Did you know you talk too much and that life is not a John Cusack movie?" He snorted, all the while not removing his gaze from the *SportsCenter* crawl at the bottom of his beloved plasma TV. I knew better than to talk to him when he was doing his reading.

"What the fuck does that mean?" Now I was starting to talk just like him, Mr. Romance. It was catchy.

"It means life isn't a movie. There is no guy standing outside a window and holding a boom box with a love song on it. Do you want me to start talking like a pussy and writing poetry too? 'Cause I'm not that guy. *This* is real life, Rosa. Not a movie."

I didn't know whether to be depressed by what he had just said, or grateful that my wordsmith husband had doled out more than one sentence at a time. Maybe he was just more physically tired than most men because he had such a physical job. Maybe I could never begin to understand the kind of pressure he was under. Maybe he hadn't Googled: "What is the average number of times per week couples have intercourse?" the way I had. The answer was 2.5 by the way. I was confused by what constitutes a .5, and shocked by how far short we fell.

I was lucky to have sex three times in a month, initiated solely by me. And wasn't it supposed to get worse after you got older and had children? Then what? I tried not to think too much about it. The more emphasis I put on it, the worse I knew it would get. I didn't want to care so much, but I did. And I was right; it was weird.

I secretly and immaturely hoped to get a part in a film with a love scene, just so I could experience "real" kissing again and maybe ignite some sort of jealousy-induced passion in Tim. Why, after any significant amount of time, in any monogamous relationship, did making out go virtually extinct? And I'm sorry, but quick "love-you-bye" kisses as you exit a door don't really count as kisses. That's more of an obligatory exit salutation. I felt intimately burglarized! But at least I had the reassurance that with his low sex drive also came the high probability that he would never cheat on me. You have to at least want sex to seek it outside of a marriage, right? No one was perfect. I'm sure he wished I could misplace my vocal chords permanently. In short, we both just had to make do with what we had.

W HEN *MAXIM* MAGAZINE called and asked me to pose for them in a several-page spread and interview, on one hand I was superexcited for the chance to be the "hot girl." It was as shallow as goals come, but a goal nonetheless. I was also thirty-one. I was decrepit compared to the glowy, practically late-teen girls they usually featured. I was determined not to be the oldest, most airbrushed bitch in the magazine. I had to do something, and fast, once I got that fateful call. I decided to do cardio, specifically running, for the first time since my few-week stint while filming *Noriega*. I had never run before (unless you count running from the cops in high school when a party I was at got raided).

Perhaps more drastic than reintroducing my body to the concept of exercise was knowing I would need to cut carbs until the photo shoot, which was taking place in two weeks.

Now, two weeks is an eternity when you're eating nothing but boiled chicken and veggies. Sugar, my best friend,
would have to go bye-bye for a bit. I wondered how long
the withdrawals would last. Would I actually shake without my diet of Cocoa Puffs soaked in a pool of milk? Are
Lean Pockets considered a carb? My head was dizzy with
the prospect of the voyage that lay ahead in the coming
weeks. I had rested on my genetic laurels as well as my
belief that a few extra pounds were a "good influence" for
my female fans. I was sick of all the lollipop-head-looking
stick figures adorning red carpets, and tired of reading the
"tips" on how they stayed that way. Plus I was just lazy.

I knew the importance of this sexy pictorial. Hollywood
is predominantly run by men, and men subscribe to men's
magazines. This "spread" (as it's called—their words, not
mine) could catapult my career and put me on the fore-
front of an entirely different fan base. Not that I didn't love
and appreciate my female fans, but there was definitely an
allure to gaining fans with penises. This opportunity was
a penis gateway.

Back in the day, young men could only masturbate to the
sexy covers of *Cosmopolitan* magazine, or the underwear section of a Sears Christmas catalog. Where else, besides *Playboy*
or porn, could you see scantily clad women just sitting there
(in pictures), defenseless, for the (fantasy) taking? Thanks
to the makers of *Maxim* and its sister magazine, *Stuff*, the
roadmap of the masturbatory world had changed. Now each
month one could see an impeccably lit, well-oiled, tanned,
taut, scantily clad girl looking straight into the camera with

really only a few expressions. There's the famous, surprised "I had no idea there was a camera right here!", the deviant "I'm toying with the strings on my bikini bottoms and these could come right off!", and the mid- to postcoital "Mmm, you were incredible." These carefully manufactured expressions take all day (usually eight hours) and thousands of pictures to get the four or five they end up airbrushing anyway. You have to arch your ass like a stripper, suck in your stomach, jut out your tits, make your eyes scream "You want me?" or the aforementioned go-to expressions, all while trying your darndest to look natural and relaxed. It's almost as hard as the cardio it took to get there. And at the end of the eight-hour-plus day (with three of those hours in a hair-and-makeup chair), you definitely suffer from "stripper back." It's the acute cramping from the unnatural curve in your spine you have spent all day creating to make your ass look less flat. Plus, if you're like me and you have to give up eating for a few weeks, you are one cranky, tired, and hungry bitch.

I had a mini revelation during my brief carb-free stint. That look on a model—the look of extreme boredom mixed with angst that you see in magazines—is neither boredom nor angst. They aren't trying to be cool. They're trying to tough it out until they can eat again like regular people. That look just says, "Throw me a piece of goddamned bread! I'm not moody and aloof. I'm hungry and mad!" The vacant stare may not be drugs, as we all assume, but rather a longing look in the direction of the craft services table, tauntingly out of reach, like the distant mirage of an abundant oasis.

So it was up to me to suck it up, suck it in, and diet like a normal Hollywood actress, and not one who convinced herself that she's a better "role model" if she's ten pounds heavier. Here's a little something they don't advertise about the carb-free diet: The side effect is horrible, debilitating constipation. "No carbs" is synonymous with "no exit." I had become debilitatingly, hideously bowelly challenged. This was accompanied by hard-core cramping, a belly as distended as a starving child from one of Sally Struthers's third-world infomercials, and tantrums that put me in touch with my inner toddler, years before I ever had one. The magazine shoot was only a couple of days away, so I decided to take matters into my own hands, proactively. I went to the store and purchased some chocolate laxatives.

As I chewed and held the box of ex-lax in my hand, I thought, *They really took liberties using the word "choco-late" on the box of chocolate laxatives.* One is a tiny piece of heaven in your mouth, while the other tastes like what might come out of cardboard, if cardboard could expel waste products. But I chewed diligently, envisioning this as the icing on the carb-free cake. When food—carbs spe-cifically—become the enemy, it's impossible not to become obsessed with it. I couldn't wait for the next morsel I could put in my mouth. I convinced myself that I liked the taste of water, and I dreamt of my postphoto meal. I changed it time and time again, putting as much significance on that meal as an inmate on death row. Day after long day, I con-sumed sushi (no rice, no soy!), bland chicken breast (which tastes like gamey dead bird, minus the yummy sauces), and ground turkey with a reward dollop of ketchup so small it was as if the ketchup police might come and arrest me for dunk diving. A big dessert treat was coffee with fake sugar substitute, also known as crystalized carcinogens. If they can put a pig heart inside a human, why can't they figure out a way to make fake sugar taste real?

As I chewed the laxative, imagining it, willing it to be or taste like chocolate (as well as discovering I was not a method actor), I was sure I would be cured of my aliments in no time—in the "gentle and natural way" they advertised on the packaging. Unfortunately for my bowels, time had stood still. I panicked the next morning with the photo shoot only a day away. And I did what any self-respecting model-to-be would do, I pinched my nose and chewed another "chalk-olate" laxative. All day I waited for some sign of life from my outer space. Nothing happened. Pardon the obvious pun, but this was bullshit! I could barely believe it when on the morning of the shoot, I was two laxatives deep and still no sign of life. I said "fuck it" and bit into my third piece.

Somewhere between them rubbing bronzer on my ass, almost killing myself slipping on the baby oil they applied, and trying on every tiny piece of lingerie in the tri-state area with the promise that "if we see nipple, it will be Photoshopped out, no worries!" I felt a lower belly rumble. This was it! And in perfect time for the photos! I knew my hard work would pay off. I went to the restroom for one last stop before we would spend the day taking pics of me in various states of undress. I must have taken longer in there than I thought, because the photographer banged on the door and said, "We are ready to shoot!" somewhat annoyed.

I thought, *And so am I.* Definitely annoyed.

I had barely sat down before a rocket carrying bright, mustard-yellow baby poop took flight from my freshly bronzed and spray-tanned ass. I say baby poop because if you've ever changed a baby's diaper and cocked your head to the side like a confused canine, you know exactly what I saw. It doesn't resemble anything that should appear outside of an acrylic paint tube. I laughed at the irony of the situation, and wondered how many men, magazine in hand, were picturing what was really happening only moments before I gave them grade-A jerk-off material. Throughout the rest of the shoot I made more trips to the bathroom than Charlie Sheen in the eighties. I knew they thought, *She's doing drugs!* But I am also guessing they weren't thinking the little "mock-olate" chocolate kind, instead of the kind you find backstage at a rock concert. "We are almost done," the photographer tried reasoning with me as I went for trip seventeen. "The bathroom will be there when we finish!" I didn't have the balls to say, "But I need to finish before I finish." I had to come to terms with the fact that I was technically a crappy model.

I wished there were a loud white-noise bathroom fan, or something, as I reached for the sound of running water from the sink to drown out the more potentially embar-

rassing sounds. White-noise fans should be a legal requirement on all bathroom light fixtures. Particularly with
those powder rooms situated closely to living rooms, and
particularly when you are still in that first-date stage. If
the sound of pee humiliates girls, imagine how they would
feel with what was happening to me, echoing and in stereo
effect! I wanted to die.

In the end, the photos actually turned out great. Tim
said he was proud of me, and had always fantasized about
being with a girl from the magazines. He had conveniently
forgotten about Miss April and I had conveniently forgotten to remind him. I was sure this sexy photo layout, and
frequent locker-room high-fives once the magazine hit the
stands, would help us in the bedroom. Once again I was
mistaken.

A SIDE FROM OUR less-than-perfect love life, Tim had
a touch of OCD—obsessive compulsive disorder—
whereas I had a touch of "like-a-tornado-hit" messiness
(as my parents used to say) wherever I went. When Tim
added "Sharpie magic marker" to our grocery list, I knew
it must be "numbering-socks day." As I joked in our wedding vows, Tim had the genius idea to number his socks,
so they would get washed the exact same amount of times.
While this was amusing at first, it became less funny once
we shared a washer and dryer. God forbid one sock looked
more soft, worn, or faded than the other. That could ruin
a day. Once I borrowed his socks, just grabbed whatever

was closest, and had the audacity to match a number two with a number-eight sock, and then, just to screw with him and mostly to amuse myself, I took one of his markers and added fractions to his beloved numbered-sock collection. Like instead of "4" I would make it "4 ½." I could barely write straight I was shaking so hard from laughter as I did it. I couldn't wait for Tim to notice.

He did.

"You're not funny," he said dryly.

The folded clothing in his closet looked like a department store display, and he air-dried everything as if it were made of rare silk. He treated his T-shirts with the same respect you'd give your wedding dress the day of the ceremony. I was sure if Banana Republic ever found out, they would recruit him on the spot, and lure him into a life of folding, organizing, and monochromatic bliss an OCD person can only dream of.

Tim also kept that protective plastic sticker thing that comes on computers and various electronics. He never removed the film so it could "stay perfect." Just the way I'm sure Billy Joel is asked to play a little tune on the piano for friends, my friends would ask me to regale them with tales of Tim's latest *Rain Man* compulsions because they were so unintentionally hilarious. He was my go-to party trick.

One of my favorite memories was the story about his car. Tim's car was always a museum-quality picture-perfect shrine. Before training camp one year, he picked up a brand-new silver 750iL BMW. It was his dream car at the time. I think he felt somewhat pressured to make the purchase to "keep up with the Joneses" on the Giants. Guys on the team were giving him shit about his current 750 BMW, of the same color, because it was a few years old (the horror!). I guess it stood out in the VIP players' parking lot, which looked like a rapper's driveway from *MTV Cribs* or *Pimp My Ride*. There were all these crazy-colored, chromed-out cars—Bentleys, Ferraris, 911s—with rims so shiny they could beam signals into outer space on a clear night.

While sitting in the passenger seat of Tim's one-week-old car, I noticed a highlighted strand of my hair clinging to my black pants, and I casually flicked it to the floor.

It was literally one strand of my hair.

Although he was driving, Tim became totally distracted. He kept looking at me, then at the floor where the piece of hair landed. Back and forth: me, the hair, me, the hair, like watching a riveting tennis match by himself.

"You're kidding, right?" he asked spastically.

"What?" I had no idea what he was referring to. I knew I wasn't allowed to eat in his shrine-mobile, but I wasn't at the time, so what was his problem?

"You're gonna pick that up, right?"

"What?"

"That hair you just threw onto the floor."

I thought he was joking—a feeble attempt at humor—but I appreciated him at least trying. Too bad he wasn't. Half laughing, half wondering if I should be concerned about the number of head injuries he'd sustained, I started to look for the hair (singular) I'd laid to rest on the floor. Tim must have been so engrossed by my search that he wasn't paying attention to the road. He smashed his one-week-old car into another car. The entire front end crumpled up like an accordion, causing thousands of dollars' worth of damage. Worse, for the couple of weeks while it was being repaired, Tim had to explain why his brand-spanking-new car was in the shop, while I stifled a giggle. No one was hurt (except for the car and the lone piece of hair now missing and never to be seen again). I couldn't help but think that unlike Tim, those karma gods were blessed with a wicked sense of humor.

DESPITE THESE IDIOSYNCRASIES, I truly loved Tim and most of the time I tried to be amused by him, and less annoyed. We were both of the "once you get married, you stay married forever" school of people, an example set by both of our parents, who still were after thirty-plus years. At the end of the day I may not have always succeeded in staying "amused" (read: I bitched up a storm), but I tried, dammit.

We desperately wanted to have a baby, or maybe I did a lot more, but "we" sounded better on paper. Plus, my eggs were getting old, as in needing-walkers old, and the ticking clock was a deafening reminder. We agreed to start trying a year after we got married. And by start trying, I mean finally making deposits. I couldn't wait! I was ready. You know when you have something on your mind, you tend to see it everywhere? Like when I was pre-boob-job, I noticed more tits than a high school boy. There were constant evaluations, mental note-taking, and a lot of running internal dialogue. I was suddenly a breast-ologist overnight. Same went for wanting a baby. I noticed them everywhere and constantly puffed out my stomach and stood sideways in the mirror, imagining what my own bump would someday look like. I tried not to lunge and salivate at perfect strangers pushing itty-bitty babies in strollers. I tried not to reach for them when they were within touching distance in line at the grocery store. And I was only escorted from the Macy's infant clothing department once for crying uncontrollably and caressing a tiny layette display.

I asked my friends who were in the know if they had any helpful impregnation tips. The one that kept repeatedly surfacing was the "sit perfectly still and raise your hips at an incline, to help the sperm gravitate to your egg." And so I did. I took this tip immensely seriously. Postdeposit, I did not move a muscle and stayed stock-still for forty-five minutes. One time *American Idol* was about to start and I asked Tim to carry me upside-down, down a huge flight of stairs, and over our marble foyer to remain true to the advice I had been given. I even exclaimed, "If you drop me on my head resulting in my death—you better tell the baby I did it for him!" Which yes, made no sense, seeing as how it would be a challenge for a dead person to give birth. It got to the point that I was a slave to my ovulation sticks and early-pregnancy test kits. I almost didn't know how to pee without interrupting the urine stream with a testing device of some kind. You spend your whole life trying *not* to get pregnant, having panic attacks about it, and consuming yourself worrying "what if I am?" And when you finally want to have a baby—for people who aren't twenty—it's only that much worse. It's replaced by "what if I can't?"

Somehow, despite the frequency and bulk purchasing of my pregnancy-testing-related equipment, I still felt ashamed when I got rung up at the local Walgreens pharmacy. I know exactly where it stems from. It's residual anxiety from when I was seventeen and thinking for sure I was preggers. I'll never forget telling my boyfriend at the time, Kasey (shocking—a member of our high school football team), "My period is late. What do I do?" Kasey sort of shrugged his shoulders, only pausing a brief three seconds, before he continued to stock shelves at the Container Store where he worked that summer.

What a keeper. How did I let that gem slip away?

With a less-than-supportive partner at hand, I decided to ask my friend Erin to go with me to a place I found in the Yellow Pages that had a smiley face on the ad and an overtly friendly name, something like "Helpful Pregnancy Clinic." The ad said "free pregnancy tests!" and their warm nature jumped off the page at me. I'm sure it was designed for dumb-ass teens to gravitate toward, as I did. I was under the impression that when I got there I would get the test, and if it was positive I'd find out about the supersecret world of abortions. I was about to go off to college in a month, and although I knew it would probably devastate me for the rest of my life, I also knew I was not ready to have a baby at the time, or worse, have my parents kill me with their bare hands once they found out.

When we got there, I met a woman with one of those saccharine-sweet kindergarten voices. She asked me to urinate in the provided cup, and she said while we waited for the results we could go inside another "more comfortable" room. The more comfortable room just happened to be filled with medical models of things like the uterus and ovaries—with a few growing embryos thrown in for good measure. Strewn across the coffee table were books like *Diary of an Unborn Baby*. I cracked it open. Entries like "Today I grew my organs! It was a big day. Tomorrow I will have fingerprints!" It was unsettling at best. Particularly for someone who had to consider the possibility of making herself un-pregnant before the prom.

"Um, excuse me, Miss? How long until we get the results of the tests?" I asked timidly. I wanted to bark out a "What the crap, lady? It takes two minutes on a stick in my bathroom!" Erin, who had a wicked sense of humor, kept choking back the urge to laugh, which in turn gave me the inappropriately timed church giggles as well.

Finally we were called into the kindergarten teacher's office. "Before we get into this discussion, I wanted to give you some literature. There are several options for young people who find themselves with the challenges they may not be ready for." She took out a piece of paper with a bunch of statistics swimming around, and started giving us a dissertation about adoption options: how many people were on a waiting list, how long those people had to wait, and the high demand for a healthy baby.

I kept waiting for her to give us the results, and somewhere in the middle of her lecture I thought, *These are the results! This is the way she is delivering the news so I don't have a conniption and die on the spot.*

Then she really raised her kindergarten voice and started saying how a baby is a life even from the first moment of conception.

Erin couldn't contain herself or her church giggles any longer. "I'm sorry lady, but when it's not even the size of a lima bean, I have a real tough time thinking of it as a baby." The kindergarten teacher's eyes flashed before us. She did not expect an Erin on today's schedule.

"Well, then, what is it? Is it a *weed* or a *tulip*?" The lady spat, as if she'd been crowned Miss Vitriol 1990.

"Well, lady . . . know what I think?" Erin started, deadpan. "I think you been smoking a little too much weed."

The woman looked as if she were going to lunge across her prolife desk. I needed to interject because this woman held the answers to my pee.

"Erin! I'm sorry Miss . . . can you just tell me the results of the tests? Please?" I was now officially begging.

The kindergarten-teacher-turned-Satan-worshipper actually sat back in her chair, paused for what seemed like a three-day weekend, and said curtly, with a hint of disappointment, "No. You are not." I had never in my seventeen years been so elated, so I missed whatever she said next, and I didn't care.

Erin and I literally ran out of there, got in her car, and pissed ourselves laughing and repeating Erin's crack about smoking weed. I was beyond relieved and I had learned a valuable lesson about coming "this close" to an exit off of shit-highway. It was an exit that I needed to avoid for a good ten years.

N OW THAT I wanted to get pregnant, and was ready for it, those EPT tests I peed on were all I wanted to see. Two little pink lines. When you want something so bad, it's hard to wait those few minutes for the results and actually try to talk yourself into not caring either way or to believe that whatever is meant to be is meant to be during the wait. Then, at last, there they were. The stick revealed those beautiful (or horrifying if you aren't ready for it) pregnancy confirmation lines. They were more like ghost lines, so faint I swore my eyes were willing them to be there.

I was pregnant!

For about four to five weeks. And then I had a miscarriage.

And then a second.

And then a third.

I was getting really good at them. If people had the same gestation period as a gerbil, I would have several children by now.

To add insult to injury, I was asked to wear a huge fake

pregnancy pad, have faux ultrasounds on my television show, and act out the whole ordeal while my character discovered that she had become pregnant (without even trying of course). Crew members who clearly hadn't read the scripts asked me if I was pregnant almost daily. It was like rubbing salt on my wounds to have to answer no.

This was during the time when Britney Spears was pregnant nonstop for two years. Those babies were flying out of her with the ease of a T-shirt shooter at a concert or sporting event. I couldn't believe it the first time I received the call from my doctor and she explained that "Your numbers are low. We like to see them higher, and they are going down from the last blood test. So you are most likely going to have a miscarriage." I was waiting for her to give the statistic that aren't doctors supposed to give? Where was my "if you just think positive maybe you can turn this around" speech? But it never came. She continued, "You know Rosa, it's not uncommon, actually about thirty-three percent of first-time pregnancies result in miscarriage. It's completely normal to have a miscarriage the first or second time you become pregnant."

First *or* second? Who had two miscarriages? No one I knew. My mind went into a tailspin and I somehow hung up the phone without vomiting on our "dream home" Berber carpeting. So after the second one, I knew I had to see a specialist. I found out through an annoying fertility doctor's office receptionist that "they don't like to see you until you have had three miscarriages, but we'll see if the doctor will meet with you." It was like the worst consolation prize in the world. Yes, they like to see their patients completely shattered, not just semi-dismantled, but they may grant you permission to spend your life savings on overpriced fertility treatments.

It was so unfair. I was over thirty. I had the brains and the means to raise a baby and be a great mom. I was completely in the know about kids, having been a nanny my first year out here in Los Angeles. Everywhere I looked ,people, celebs, and friends seemed to get pregnant without trying. And living in a somewhat affluent beach community, it looked like the place was decorated in twin strollers and matching baby ensembles. My mom once marveled at the "phenomenon" of how many twins she saw down at the beach.

I informed her, "Ma. That's all IVF. It stands for It's Very Fair to assume you are having a set of twins if you gotta do that stuff!"

Of course, I wasn't opposed to it. At this point, I would have settled for adopting a small pet monkey if all else failed. I just wanted to be a mom, and I would have taken any route to get there. Tim was opposed to adoption, or donor eggs. I told him I was opposed to being married to him if I had to choose between being a mom or not. It wasn't a pleasant time, and it was the first time I thought to myself, *This could be the deal breaker for us as a married couple.*

All of Tim's friends from the team had young girls with fresh twenty-something eggs, taunting my starting-to-get-withered-and-fail-me ones. I did the fertility meditation tapes. I tried the Tao of Wellness fertility-expert acupuncture. I contacted psychics. I tried to "relax," which is the biggest bitch slap of advice you can give someone who is having difficulty getting pregnant.

"Just relax." The well-doers would say, almost in a soothing voice, as if *that* were a novel idea. I knew they meant well, but they weren't in the know. They weren't members of the exclusive "I'm having a really fucking hard time getting preggers club," of which I had so resentfully become a member. Therefore, I refrained from saying back to them, "Oh really? Will the baby fall out of me if I just relax? 'cause constantly hearing you're about to have a miscarriage from your ob-gyn isn't so fucking relaxing. You know what else isn't relaxing? Being told to relax all the time! It's the ultimate antirelaxant."

After almost a year of this rollercoaster, and many visits to a highly touted infertility doctor named Dr. Potter (not an alias, his real name, oddly, during the height of all the Harry Potter craze), I was pregnant again. But this time I was armed with needles and magical "pregnancy-sticking" drugs (not their real name).

My very own fertility wizard told me that "I would need daily intramuscular progesterone injections, and subcutaneous heparin injections." All I heard was the word "injections" among lots of syllables, and I briefly hyperventilated. Should I mention that I went to a pediatrician until I was twenty, at which point they politely told me it was time to find an adult doctor? I asked Dr. Potter to dumb it down for me, and "talk to me like I'm no smarter than a fifth grader." When Dr. Potter realized I wasn't making a joke, he explained that the progesterone was almost like a pregnancy steroid to help keep the pregnancy strong and stay put—or to "stick." The heparin was a blood thinner so I wouldn't clot, because maybe my body was "passing" the pregnancy thinking it was just some bad ol' blood clot. I had no choice but to get over the injections.

Having an athlete husband really comes in handy, I thought, as Tim iced my ass where the first injection would take place. He wasn't afraid of needles and had somewhat expert status after dabbling in human growth hormone (I didn't know where he was getting his human growth hormone, but I know it is often obtained illegally). The Botox needles in my face were nothing compared to watching the needle go into my belly fat for the second injection site, and eventually having to give them to myself while my husband was away at training camp (in the leg because I couldn't exactly reach behind me with ease). I wonder how long it hovered above my thigh and how many times I chickened out before plunging it into my muscle. Now that's fear factor!

Finally the moment had come, when the blood tests were all saying, "Welcome to the club!" Finally I got to say the words I longed to say to Tim. I took a deep breath . . .

"Babe . . . I'm pregnant." I beamed, and waited for him to pick me up and twirl me around like they do so effortlessly on *Dancing with the Stars*.

There was no twirling.

What he said next was not what I or any human could have anticipated. No one ever accused Tim of being romantic, but still, one hundred people surveyed on *Family Feud* would never have come up with what he actually said to me.

After I said, "Babe . . . I'm pregnant."

He said, and I quote, "Well . . . for *now*."

Exactly the three magical words that every woman who has had multiple miscarriages is yearning to hear: *Well. For. Now.*

He was an emotional godsend, that Tim.

THINGS I NOTICE *SPORTSCENTER* . . . *DOESN'T* COVER

1. *Most players are free-balling (a.k.a. they play without any athletic support cups cradling the family jewels because they are too uncomfortable). And the majority play without jockstraps, which are mostly considered "old school." Truly changing the notion of "contact sports."*

2. *Some players will pay cash for MRIs because they don't trust the team doctors, and/or they want to hide injuries from the team (and press). This is done with the intention of maintaining job security. Also a good tip for job security: not needing an MRI in the first place.*

3. *It is common for players to pay about twenty thousand dollars a year on a personal Lloyd's of London insurance policy so that when they get injured there's a potential payout. Yes, when.*

4. *Because surgeries are so common and so sophisticated, oftentimes insurance companies will deny players a payout, with the argument that "they could play with another surgery." (This, despite the fact that they may have already had a half dozen on the same ailing body part.) Insurance companies also deny calling this the "Joan Rivers clause" at office parties.*

5. Back in the day, steroids were (purportedly) openly kept in the MLB locker-room refrigerators, until the whole big bad BALCO scandal. Now, I'm assuming, they are kept in the players' (home) refrigerators, clearly marked STEROIDS for those players who thought they were something else. See Barry Bonds for details.

6. The NFL finally admitted in 2009 that recurring concussions are no bueno, and "urged players to get independent medical exams." This theory contrasts with the old method of acknowledging concussions . . . with a Vicodin or two, postgame.

7. "They" compare a typical NFL collision to the impact of a car wreck. I compare trying to convey simple messages to an NFL player as just as hard.

8. Doctors have recently discovered, through autopsies on deceased NFL players' brains, that some of the players have the same quality brain matter of a ninety-one-year-old Alzheimer's patient. Apparently, head collisions cause "much deeper brain damage than they once suspected." The dead players made no comment.

9. You can't detect human growth hormone on a standard, regulation, professional sports drug test, so some players buy it on the black market and use it knowing they will still get "a pass" when the old piss-test comes a calling.

10. Players do not get the day off even from missing practice, just because of a silly little thing like witnessing the birth of your child. However, if you are a franchise player, you get away with a lot more of these "frivolous" excuses and still get to keep your day job.

Fish family photo on the football field (say that five times fast!).

NINE

Our First Draft Pick

I loved every part of being pregnant, and almost every part of gaining those plump, precious fifty-plus pounds on my five-foot-two frame. My fetus developed on a strict diet of no soda, no caffeine, everything organic, prenatal yoga, and a Jack Lalanne juicer so I could actually ingest vegetables and not just intend to—like the New Year's resolution I forget by January fourth every year. Drink more water, exercise, and eat more vegetables. Sure. Aside from all that healthy living, I threw in nightly Lucky Charms (to bring me good vibes) and regularly stopped by L.A.'s famous hamburger joint, In-N-Out Burger, despite the fact that I rarely ate red meat prepregnancy. Now I was like a lion, albeit a lion that had an insatiable need for quiche and key lime pies as well. I would have eaten my Weimaraner dog if he came served on a buttery Pillsbury crust.

My senses were heightened to superhuman levels, particularly with regard to scents. I wanted to sue people who wore cologne in elevators. I was completely on edge from the minute I found out I was pregnant and worried about every aspect of what could go wrong. The Internet became my enemy. There really is such a thing as too much information. Every week I stayed pregnant I had a mini celebration in my head, because previously, of course, my gestation periods only lasted about a month. During this mood-swingin' time I didn't know how much to attribute to the hormones or how much to attribute to having a jackass for a partner who was more concerned about his upcoming season schedule than his upcoming offspring. I had heard from many friends that until the baby comes out of you, and they (the baby daddies) are holding it, the baby doesn't seem real to them. Plus, most men aren't really involved with the baby until it's able to communicate back and play with them.

I knew that if Tim was unable to imagine how a couch would look from a small swatch of fabric when we were redecorating, there was no way he was going to be able to picture a baby and how our lives would be tremendously impacted by it. Plus, I was pregnant during an "inconvenient time," according to Tim. The bulk of my pregnancy was during training camp. And during training camp everything else ceases to exist. My egg and his sperm must have missed that memo. So Tim went off to training camp and I, unable to work, watched so much Netflix it's a miracle that I didn't get bedsores. We weren't finding out the sex of the baby—we wanted it to be one of life's true surprises—but everyone—even strangers—told me I "was carrying like it was a boy." Whatever I was carrying stretched my belly out so far and so perfectly round that I looked like a cartoon character.

Two weeks before my due date, and conveniently on Tim's day off, we went to the hospital where I was given an epidural after a couple of hours of writhing in labor pains. Like any mother-to-be, I was scared of what actual childbirth would be like. I had seen enough of those TLC channel documentary-style episodes of *A Baby Story* to want to avoid delivery altogether, request a sedative that would render me unconscious for at least a couple of weeks, and *then* maybe become acquainted with the baby. The thing that worried me the most, however (besides having a healthy baby, of course), was the thought of Tim accidentally seeing the baby come out, and then losing what miniscule sex drive he had left. I had heard horror stories about this happening, where the mystery and wonderment of the great vagina becomes an awful sci-fi movie (the kind where you want to immediately change the channel) once the baby comes out.

I have no idea how women give birth without pain medication. I think if you are warrior enough to do that you shouldn't have to pay taxes, and you get to wear a special birthing badge, so people know you are a true badass!

After the initial shock that I had delivered a healthy little girl (not a boy like we had convinced ourselves I was carrying), and they were letting us actually leave the hospital with her, we knew we had to find a name for her first. I loved the name Kaia and had heard it from an actress friend of mine, Eva La Rue, who played Maria on *All My Children* for about a hundred years and now stars on *CSI: Miami*. She had a five-year-old daughter named Kaya at the time. But I didn't want to be one of those hideous name-stealers, so from my hospital room I wanted to ask Eva for her blessing to use the same name. I was ecstatic that Tim was agreeing with me on the unique name after many, many arguments about boys' names throughout my pregnancy, because we were 95 percent sure it was going to be a boy. Tim came from the school of boring name thought, and I thought it was very important to name the baby something original.

"Look. There's only one LeBron,"—it was the only sports name I could think of off the top of my head—"one Beyoncé, and one Oprah!" I argued.

Tim rebutted, "Yes, but I'm also pretty sure the baby wouldn't be born black."

"Okay, but that's not the point! There's only one Ringo!" My argument was hideously weak. But Ringo was the only original name I could think of in a pinch, and that must have worked because he agreed to the name Kaia. It wasn't until I was confronted by an employee at babyGap many months later, who asked me, "So what is your baby's name?"

I replied, "Kaia!" He smiled knowingly, sort of bobbed his long, superdreadlocks up and down (to the beat of music that was not playing), and said conspiratorially, "Ahhhh Kaya! A beautiful name." He said it strangely, like I was in on a secret. I wanted to be, so I mimicked his nodding. He leaned in, and in a hushed voice asked, "She's named after the Bob Marley song? Yes?"

Now I was really confused, but found myself saying yes as if that were obvious and nodding some more. Why was I mirroring this perfect stranger? I steered Kaia's little Bugaboo stroller out of the mall and Googled "Kaia Bob Marley" as soon as I got home. Sure enough, there was a song called "Kaya" all about Marley's marijuana needs.

"Got to have Kaya now . . ." he sang repeatedly. I had actually named my kid after a pot song without knowing it. Classic.

O N THE DAY we brought Kaia home from the hospital, Tim left to go to a teammate's house who lived in our same gated housing complex. I must have been engulfed in new baby love because it didn't strike me as strange that he was "going out" when we were coming home from the hospital for the first time. These days he was spending a lot of time with this guy Shaggy. Of course, like all guys in a locker room, Shaggy wasn't his real name but a nickname. He was called Shaggy because Tim said he reminded him of that dopey character from *Scooby Doo* with the long shaggy locks. He was a badass in the NFL, sort of a modern-day Brian Bosworth. Shaggy's jersey number seemed to be on the backs of most of the fans at Giants Stadium, even more than the quarterback's! He was also known for romancing as many women as possible, and because he had never had a girlfriend in his life, it was sort of accepted and okay. He wasn't considered a scumbag, just a normal pro athlete. I considered Shaggy a harmless friend, because although he liked the women, he liked the weed even more. Shaggy was stoned most of the time he was awake, ripping off bong hits as if he were at Woodstock—except you'd expect that at Woodstock. Shaggy was a highly paid star player for the Giants—when he wasn't injured (which was more often than not). He even bought an oxygen chamber that he slept in like the late Michael Jackson was rumored to have done. It was supposed to promote the healing of cells, and for the price tag of thirty thousand dollars plus, it better have. I'm no cell expert, but I'm guessing not smoking such an incredible amount of weed would also possibly aid in the healing of cells.

Shaggy once told me that he often pissed his pants on the sidelines when he had to go to the bathroom.

"What am I s'posed to do? Go have a potty break durin' the game?"

It made sense. The players had to constantly keep hydrated, so they wouldn't get severe cramping, and eventually even Superman's bladder would get full. I couldn't help thinking, though, that that was one of the many random facts not "out there" for public consumption. Once we were talking about this (as I was freakishly attracted to what could be categorized under bizarre random facts), one guy said he knew a lineman that hit a guy so hard he shit his pants right on the field. He literally crapped himself in his tight white football pants in front of a stadium's worth of people and television crews. Now you know people just thought it was field mud. That's not exactly something the announcers would stop and focus on making small talk about. It's just not something you think about when you think of these athletic superstars. After all, that's what my newborn did.

I loved and embraced being a mom from the minute I realized she was not going to die of jaundice when she was three days old. I thought she just looked "sorta tan" when we brought her home, golden even. I must not have noticed that the whites of her eyes were golden as well, because when I took her in for a checkup the doctor seemed startled. And it wasn't because she was so damn cute. Sure enough, when the doctors told me that she had to stay in the hospital for one night (days after we had left the hospital) I had a full-blown Shirley MacLaine *Terms of Endearment* moment. The nursing staff warned me that "you need to calm down immediately!" and "your baby can feel your anxiety!"

I literally couldn't stop crying. It was like being seven years old again and not being able to catch your breath, saying the same thing over and over in a broken-record stammer. "I . . . I . . . I . . . I . . . I . . . I . . . I . . . I . . . caaaaa-aaaaan't!" Of course "I can't" didn't matter, because I had no choice and I really just needed to calm the fuck down and admit my newborn back into the hospital. They put her in this little tanning bed and put goggles on over her eyes. All I could do to try and soothe her was put my arms through the holes in her little incubator, but my daughter would not stop screaming. Laced with new mommy hormones, breasts engorged with milk that wanted to make its stage debut, and lack of sleep, I was nothing short of a train wreck. And it was just newborn jaundice (which 60 percent of new infants get). Common as cradle cap.

Like a good NFL wife, I kept it to myself because Tim was out of town for a game that day and I didn't want him to be distracted. Jaundice scare aside, I was able to take home my little yellow-eyed baby and start motherhood officially.

My parents flew into town and lived with Tim and me in New Jersey for the first three months, so between that and the new baby, I didn't dwell on Tim's shortcomings as a father or his frequent trips to Shaggyville. I think Tim appreciated my parents being there because not only was their help invaluable, but it kept me nicely distracted from his frequent outings. Sure I had visions of leaving him and getting an apartment by myself back in California, but I chalked it up to all the new mommy hormones rampaging through my body. And football season. The damn football season that always seemed to come before anything else. I couldn't wait to do a happy dance when the season was over. Despite this, motherhood was everything I thought it would be. There isn't a description I could come up with that wouldn't sound cliché. I was prepared for the amount of love I would feel, just not for the amount of worry. After the difficulty of getting pregnant, I just kept feeling like the other shoe was going to drop. Like someone was going to take this little baby away from me. I also had to think of getting back into actress shape after gaining more weight than I could justify with a seven-pound infant. How much does water potentially weigh? I was never good at math, but I figured that the sur-plus of kids' crappy sugar cereal and all things piecrust were also not recommended by leading health professionals. I was determined to get one of those "Oh my God! You don't look like you even had a baby!" bodies.

I longed for mom-orexia. You know those moms you see on television who are photographed just weeks after giving birth and look so slim you could have sworn they adopted? That was my postbaby goal. Also, I had to find another tele-vision series now that *Strong Medicine* had ended its six-year, 132-episode run about two months before I got pregnant.

I had no choice but to lose weight. Hollywood doesn't take that "extra ten pounds" look so lightly.

On the recommendation of Tim, when the baby was six weeks old, I started kickboxing *and* personal training. I was pretty sure I was the only person lactating in the gym, which was sometimes evidenced by the dark round stains that showed up on my jog bra and caused my workout to end prematurely. But I knew that if I didn't have an ap-pointment to work out with someone, I would blow it off. I needed someone abusive and hardcore. I once had a trainer I could talk into skipping the workout and going next door to the diner for waffles. That wasn't going to cut it this time around. Enter kickboxing. I had tried it once before, but I thought, *No one needs this much physical activity on purpose.*

It was outrageous to lace up my Nike's and "just do it" unless you were trying to shed your body by high fructose corn syrup. From the day the baby came home from the hospital Tim asked me to sleep in a separate room from him because the baby waking him up all night wouldn't bode well for his ultraphysical job. Except straight guys don't say "ultra." He couldn't "be tired all the time." That was my job. I couldn't really argue, seeing as I wasn't working at the time. Although in hindsight I should have made him get up with the baby on his days off. I didn't mind sleeping right next to Kaia on a twin bed in her room. The paranoid overprotective side of me even preferred this. I lay her down in a Moses basket on the floor next to me, so I could make sure she was breathing all through the night. Kaia's strong-willed little personality showed its true colors right away. She would cry and I would have a mini panic attack trying to make her stop. I lovingly bounced that baby so much it's a miracle she didn't become a victim of shaken baby syndrome.

I asked my parents to watch Kaia while I attended all of the Giants' home games, and pumped breast milk in the disgusting stadium bathrooms (unheated and freezing in the dead of winter) at halftime. Thank God it was so noisy in there because the sounds that come from a breast pump are more humiliating than the actual act of pumping itself. It sounds like a sad, repetitive donkey noise, set to a mild drumbeat: eee-haw-eee-haw-eee-haw. That combined with stadium bathroom smells made for a very unpleasant home-game halftime ritual. Once, famed running-back-turned-*Today*-show-correspondent Tiki Barber was generous enough to let us sit in his luxury box on a freezing day at Giants Stadium, so that I could bring Kaia to a game and we could get a family photo on the field with Tim in uniform. We knew the time was ticking on Tim's athletic career (he had played eight years and the average football career was 2.5), and we wanted to take advantage of the once-in-a-lifetime opportunity.

On the car ride home, Kaia was hungry, miserable, and screaming her seven-week-old lungs out in the crawling stadium exit traffic. I climbed into the backseat, facing the cars behind us, and tried nursing her from the carseat she was buckled into. I swallowed my pride so Kaia could swallow her dinner. I didn't care who may have looked into the car windows, seeing this crazy woman hunched over a car seat with her boobs flailing out, I just wanted that baby to stop crying. Plus I knew that Tim was silently fuming over a missed block during the game that landed him on his ass, looking as bewildered and graceless as a blindfolded team mascot.

I felt like I was being held captive in New Jersey, with flyaway hair that needed Static Guard sprayed onto my brushes (so I wouldn't look like I had stuck my finger into an electrical socket), and nothing to do except wait for football season to end. I had no potential jobs on the horizon and no real clothes that fit, so all of my energy went into mother-hood, losing the baby fat, trips to Starbucks (which were counterproductive), and channeling my inner paparazzi through daily photo sessions with my very willing (read: she had no say in the matter) participant, infant Kaia. I did manage to set alarms when late afternoon rolled around, and I realized I should brush my teeth at least before Tim got home from practice and noticed—or rather smelled—

that I hadn't. I knew I would never be one of those bouncy, hair-blown-out, together-looking country club moms. But I also thought that plaque and visible "sweater pills" on my teeth from the night before kind of crossed the line into gross territory. As I squeezed into my old skinny-ish jeans, my moment of victory was instantly squashed by the muffin top that always greeted me when I tried buttoning up my pants. It was so annoying. No one ever, anywhere, in any book mentioned that I would have a hideous, fatty, extra skin roll hanging over my jeans that would completely throw off any otherwise desirable silhouette that might have once been. The worst part was that this new mommy fat was softer than anything else on my body! It was about as firm as a water bed filled one-eighth of the way. I tried tucking it, wearing girdles, pantyhose, anything that would suck it in. And that worked, if you didn't mind the overspill at the top of the "helpful" garment, which looked even worse and drew more attention. It had to go somewhere! I someday intend to invent the muffin top postnatal girdle specifically designed for this time. It was as if my midsection were under attack, and the only weaponry I had in my arsenal was black, loose, flowy clothing. Extra camouflage was a BabyBjörn carrier containing a baby. I recommend one even if you don't have a baby. They are very forgiving.

My friends back in L.A. hadn't even met Kaia yet, and my gays and I always planned a yearly trip to Big Bear Mountain in California. Most go there for the skiing. We went there to try and hang out with each other, play mindless board games, sing show tunes, and laugh our asses off.

I flew with three-month-old Kaia, and decided to drive up the mountain in the middle of the night because Kaia *hated* the car. On the drive up, at about 1:00 a.m., there were tons of construction detours and I ended up getting lost and having to pull off the freeway and get gas. It was like a ghost town and I didn't want to wake up Kaia, so I locked her in the car, and left it running. I had keyless entry, so it was no big deal. I walked a few feet away to the window of the gas station attendant so that I could ask for directions.

When I walked back to the car to get in, I noticed that one of the buttons on my keyless entry had fallen off! I couldn't get back in, and there was Kaia sleeping (and technically trapped) as I panicked from outside. I called the police, and two officers showed up and helped me jimmy the lock. They scolded me for what I had done, and told me I was lucky that here in Compton someone hadn't jacked my car with the baby inside it. I felt like an ass. I had no idea I was in the city of Compton, a place I had just heard about in rap songs. And I felt lucky because this could have gone the other way completely and ended up on headline news. The police asked me where I was headed, and I told them Big Bear.

"By yourself? Now?" They asked like I was most certainly not going to win mother of the year. It seemed like they were seconds away from a "tsk-tsk" arrest.

"Yeah. Why?" The police looked at each other, shook their heads disappointedly, and yelled, "You better watch out for the *black guys!*" I was utterly shocked and I couldn't believe they'd just said that to me. I started to open my mouth to say something about their outward racism, but instead I just buckled myself into my driver's seat, shook my head in disbelief, and drove away. I had heard and seen sometimes-racist police officers depicted on television, but this was the first time I had witnessed it firsthand. *Should I report them?* I wrestled with this question for the rest of the drive to Big Bear. What would Tyra do?

After the fun weekend with my friends, I decided to drive home really early in the morning, in hopes that Kaia would sleep on the two-hour ride back, too. When I got outside there was a fresh six-inch snowfall. I was not used to driving in the snow, and wanted to concentrate on the road, so I traveled slowly down the hill at a snail's pace. I felt the car slide a bit here and there, which is petrifying, and just wanted to get the hell off that damn mountain and back on a straight road. All of a sudden I tried to turn the car left toward the curve of the road, but the car refused to obey and I swerved into the side of a telephone pole in what seemed like slow motion—as all bad things do. The back passenger side window smashed to pieces all over Kaia (whose infant carseat was right next to the window), and I scrambled out of the car to rescue her. I was hysterical, as expected, but Kaia was oddly calm. I thought I had given her brain damage. Luckily, this accident happened outside a tiny dive café.

The owners and few customers came running out and called the police and the paramedics as I hyperventilated and tried to pick shattered glass off my newborn while stuttering, "My baby! My baby!" It was like a mantra I couldn't stop repeating. Kaia had only one scratch on her head. It was like she'd just gotten in a little scrap with a kitten. Nothing more. After they calmed me down and assured me that Kaia was fine, they asked me to replay for them exactly how it happened. After I got out my story, through sobs and a few "what if?" breakdown tears, the police said, "Yeah. You really gotta watch out for the black ice." But this officer had better diction and it actually came out black *ice*. Not black *guys*. I realized at that moment that I was officially the dumbest person on the mountain that day. Maybe ever.

Near-death experience and muffin top aside, football season was finally over. No one was happier to close in on Super Bowl time than me, because that signified the end of my football season prison sentence in New Jersey. I was just five pounds away from my "normal" weight, although the rule of thumb I had heard is that it takes ten months to gain the baby weight and ten months to get back to any semblance of normalcy. And by normal I mean not waging a full-on self-hatred war every time you get out of the shower and look in the mirror. Finally, we were able to return to California with our new four-month-old baby, where I could try and get a job, and Tim could finally take on some of the baby responsibility as well. Plus, it was just one month until we celebrated Tim's thirtieth birthday with a surprise group trip I had organized to Cabo San Lucas. Little did I know that I would end up being the most surprised when we got there.

The Cabo trip . . . right before "Hurricane Percocet" hit.

Time Out!

I t was going to be Tim's big thirtieth birthday! I wanted to do something really cool for this milestone (he was considered one of the oldest guys on the team, and his body definitely echoed the same sentiments). But I was also grateful he was finally out of his damn twenties! Thirty sounded much less infantile. I was convinced that at thirty he would finally start to grow up. Plus, we had a twelve-week-old baby, so if that doesn't give you a knee-to-the-groin maturity check, nothing will.

I decided to plan the surprise trip to Cabo for February 2007, after the season had ended but before Tim's annual shoulder surgery took place. I wanted just a handful of his closest friends to be a part of the special trip. I rented a private house on the beach with a pool and Jacuzzi and hired chefs and bartenders, chauffeured transportation for any outings, and an English-speaking concierge who could get us anything we wanted. I invited Johnny, Tim's best friend since he was eight, and Johnny's girlfriend of the moment, whose name escapes me because they all looked the same (really young, exotic, stacked brunettes), and Gary, a Wall Street Republican and functioning alcoholic who was one of Tim's roommates from Penn, and his soon-to-be fiancée, who was so poised and preppy it wouldn't have surprised me if she dotted the *i* in her name with a Polo insignia and kept her Hermès purse equipped with madras panty liners. It was plausible. I also invited Ted and Torie, an adorable, have-been-together-since-college couple, who represented the 1 percent of football *couples* I genuinely liked (who were also friends of Tim's). Torie was an even rarer breed because she was a football wife I truly enjoyed, which put her in a category populated by .0001 percent of the wives and set her firmly apart. Torie was cooler than cool, just like one of the guys. She was a calls-'em-as-she-sees-'em kind of girl. She had a nose-ring stud so subtle I mistook it for a piece of sand, and a giant smile plastered on her face as she gutted you with her searing sarcasm, all the while sporting a brand-new Floridian boob job. I loved her. Ted, like most NFL players, had played for various teams, and had even won a Super Bowl ring when he was with the Patriots. That ring weighed more than an Olsen twin and was nearly as big. The hardest part was planning the trip behind Tim's back, which was only second to my concern that one of his friends would accidentally tell him. Some had had more head injuries than others, so it was definitely a legitimate risk.

About a day into the blissful trip, I noticed that Tim had brought with him a bottle of prescription pain pills called Percocet. According to the label there were thirty pills in the bottle just a couple of days before. I didn't think it was too strange that there were only a few pills left. I had once stumbled upon a giant bottle of these Percocets in the walk-in closet in our New Jersey residence. And when I say stumble I mean literally. It was more like a mayonnaise jar than a bottle—about seven inches tall with a wide mouth—and I nearly tripped over it one afternoon. I didn't like it. I certainly felt like it was my wifely duty to bitch about it. But I also respected the fact that I couldn't possibly know what it was like to be in the kind of physical pain Tim was in from blocking for Tiki Barber for a living. It was basically Tim's job to be a human battering-ram, to absorb some of the displaced anger the opposing team's defense had for the yardage Tiki was gaining on their watch. In short, while Tiki was busy breaking records, Tim was busy breaking down (his own body) to protect him.

The secret to Tim's career longevity—and really just in order for him to function on the field and be able to get out of bed in the morning—was to have ART treatments twice a week. ART stands for active release technique. Thankfully, it has nothing to do with a hand job; it just sounds kinda dirty. It is basically the most hard-core, legitimate deep-tissue massage you can get and it left him with bruises the size of softballs. These sessions were so intense and so painful that I was told pain pills were a prerequisite to get through them. A man came to our living room to work on Tim, in addition to a woman who came twice weekly to give him acupuncture treatments. He looked like the cover of a *Hellraiser* DVD with the hundreds of pins all over his body when she was done with him.

The last night of the trip we were all set to go to a famous scenic restaurant in Cabo, overlooking the sickest view you'd ever care to toast your margarita next to. The restaurant was high on top of a cliff, with the "caves" of Cabo, the setting sun, and the ocean crashing loudly below. As we were exiting our chauffeured SUV to go in, though, I realized we were missing the birthday boy.

"You guys! Where's Tim? Did we leave him at the house?" I giggled at my own joke. Were we all that tequila-fied?

Luiz, the concierge who brought us there, laughed and said, "No señorita, Tim is getting más pills."

I stopped in my tracks, and turned to Johnny. "What does he mean? Tim is getting más pills?" Johnny didn't answer and did a half-assed shoulder shrug, like a teenage boy saying "mmm-nnnn" to the tune of "I dunno."

Johnny thought he could defer my questions by giving me a quick language lesson instead. "Más means more, in Spanish . . ."

I cut him off midsentence. "Thanks, Johnny. I know what más means!" I was directing my anger at the wrong person, and knew I had to pull it together before I frightened him. *Shake it off, Rosa,* I thought. *Use your Jedi mind-*

trick to make Johnny think you are already in the know. I tried a softer approach.

"Look, Johnny, I already know he brought a bottle of thirty Percocets here. What does he need *more* for?" The blinking, spastic shoulder shrugs and steady eye contact with the ground affirmed my suspicions.

"Rosa. Relax. Okay? He's quitting cold turkey on Monday," Johnny said, as if this was not news to me.

It was, in fact, just that. News.

And isn't "cold turkey" an expression they use when someone's an addict? Or when there's a problem? Although I was freaking out, I had to act cool. I had to act like this was a casual conversation and not a mind-blowing discovery.

"So Johnny . . . how many pills a day do you think Tim's taking? How many you think he's up to now? What's your guess, big guy?" I said, sort of lightly punching him in his humongous bicep, distracting him with the "big guy" compliment, and using the same tone of voice one would use to causally inquire about pizza-topping preferences. *Cheese or pepperoni? You a thin- or thick-crust guy?*

Johnny started his shoulder-shrug dance again. It was his go-to move. I wanted to place both of my palms on his shoulders and command him to stop. Then, I don't know whether to thank Don Julio Tequila or Johnny's momentary lapse in judgment, because next he said, "I dunno know . . . twenty?"

What I did following Johnny's guesstimate goes completely against the advice I just gave about acting cool to extract more info. In a loud, annoying wife shriek (complete with a Chicago accent I thought had long been laid to rest), I yelled, "A . . . day?" Stranger than the newly extracted info was the fact that nobody seemed shocked except for me. Which is code for everybody knew, and I was "that girl." The clueless spouse everybody surely whispered about, and shook their heads in solidarity. It seemed as though Tim was a full-blown, *ABC Afterschool Special* pill addict—and I had no idea.

If there were an award for fast-forward catastrophic thinking, I'd have won hands-down. Would Tim need rehab? Rehab is hideously expensive—like thirty thousand dollars a month at least. How many months would he need? And would he go? Or would it be like the television show *Intervention* (a show we both loved and watched so many times—*had he not learned anything*)? Would we all have to sit in a circle with his loved ones and talk about "how his addiction has negatively affected our lives"? And while he was at rehab I would practically be a single mom. How much of our baby's childhood would he miss? Would he get anally raped at rehab or did that just happen in prison?

I wanted to ask Tim a million questions. I wondered if our marriage was over. I wanted to kill him for ruining this trip I had been planning forever and a day. But at the same time, all these little things suddenly came into really clear, sharp focus. Oprah calls it an "aha! moment." And like all things Oprah, I related to it. I realized: *Duh! This is why he had no sex drive! That's why he was sweaty all the time like Whitney Houston in concert (he wasn't just a moody guy with a quirky metabolism). That's why he was lethargic and lazy, and why he couldn't give two shits about anything except the couch and the plasma TV mounted in front of it.* As if marriage wasn't challenging enough on its own, now I felt like Tim had really fucked me at the drive-thru.

Tim must have accomplished his pill mission, because he showed up to the restaurant as well lit as the Christmas tree at Rockefeller Center. I approached him and his two humongous pupils and sarcastically whisper-hissed, *"Good to know you're quitting cold turkey on Monday!"* Now he knew that I knew. And then he wanted to find out how I knew.

An addict spends most of his energy on obtaining his drug of choice, and then keeping it a secret (in that order). Now that his secret was blown, he needed to blame someone else. Like most guilty parties, Tim put 100 percent of his focus on *who* had told me, and less on the actual issue at hand—or, at digestive system in this case. Tim and I had the rest of our lives to fight about and deal with this discovery, not to mention you can't argue with a guy who is high from swallowing who knows how many *más* pills. There was no room for logic in any conversation that was going to take place that night. So instead, I smiled and seethed and put on the happiest press-conference face I could muster.

Next, Luiz took us to the beautiful One & Only Palmilla Restaurant. We were seated at the special "chefs' table," which was actually located inside the kitchen so you could watch the chefs create their masterpieces. This table was for honorary guests, and was considered a privilege. Long ago, I learned there was no shame in pretending to be a publicist over the phone to get what you want when making reservations at snobby establishments. So I'm sure they were excited to celebrate with some NFL players—until we showed up that evening. Tim, in an effort to escape the reality that I was now in the know about him, did exactly the opposite of what you'd expect from someone trying to convince you there was no problem: He proceeded to get completely obliterated—and it was worse than I have ever seen. It even trumped the awful night we celebrated New Year's Eve in a New Jersey nightclub with his old high school buddies, when he got so wasted that he urinated in a fake plastic plant in the corner of a bar. He thought no one had caught his stealth public urination in the jam-packed bar. And then we were politely asked to leave. There was an apology the next morning. To me. Not the plant.

In the once quiet and sophisticated restaurant, Tim dropped not one, but *two* glasses, which exploded against the Mexican tile floor (and punctuated the universal sound of an inebriated dumbass, just in case anybody missed the part where he also became an aficionado in slurring). He was so over-the-top he looked as if he were part marionette, part newborn colt when he tried to walk—and we were all horrified to be a part of this display. If slow, disdainful head shaking by a wait staff were a language, I became fluent that night in "get the fuck out of our restaurant."

It was at about this that point Tim excused himself to go to the bathroom. We (who remained at the table, grateful for the opportunity to discuss the train wreck we were all now a part of) had a little powwow while he was absent. But it seemed like Tim was gone a little too long, and we started to assume the worst. Had he thrown up? Passed out and hit his head? Died on the toilet like Elvis? We elected Ted to do a restroom check. Tim was not only alive, but apparently seated at the bar doing shots of espresso, and Red Bull and vodkas. I think this was his "fuck you" to his impending Monday cold-turkey sobriety, and to me for finding out. He staggered back to our table eventually.

At one point, he took off his shoes—and placed his bare feet on the pristine white linen tablecloth. Torie—never one to mince words, who speaks in a monotone like a bored, hot version of the late Bea Arthur—simply demanded, "Tim, get your gross, dirty, *pirate feet* off the table." All the while stabbing at her overpriced ahi sashimi.

We all started laughing so hard we couldn't breathe. Because really? What else could we do? We were stuck with Mr. Pirate Feet until he sobered up.

The next morning all the other guests had departed from Cabo, but our plane wasn't scheduled to leave until a few hours later. This gave Tim and me a chance to sit alone on the beach, where he admitted everything. He said he knew that he had "gotten in deep with the pills." He knew they got in the way of his being the father he could be, or the husband. Knowing I only had a slender window of opportunity and that it was only a matter of time before he would say, "Enough with the questions!" I asked him everything I could think of that day—like a speedy Barbara Walters on a handful of Ritalin.

"Where did you get them? How often did you take them? Why didn't you tell me? Were you selling them or was that giant bottle, not so hidden, in our walk-in closet all for your consumption? Are you going to go to meetings?" I fired the questions and he gave me the answers at a machine-gun pace. And he made me promise *not* to tell his family.

Then I did what I always did when a crisis struck. I called our couples' therapist (she was on speed dial) and made an emergency appointment with her—and then she made an emergency appointment for Tim to see a psychiatrist (sort of like a fairy god prescriber) who was asked to wave her magic wand (pen) and get him some Subutex. Subutex is like a "magical pill" that helps your opiate addiction dissolve. From what I understand, Tim took the Subutex for a week, and it worked! The spell was broken. It really was like magic—no withdrawals, no cravings, nothing. Also, no meetings. I wish Tim had gone to AA or Narcotics Anonymous, but he feared someone might recognize him. I, on the other hand, feared that his "no pills, no problem" attitude was a cliché Lifetime movie waiting to happen, but I couldn't control him. *And just look at what Brett Favre accomplished after his pill battles*, I reasoned. I tried not to overthink, but my mental hamster on the wheel was spinning so fast that (if that counts) I was burning some wicked calories! Luckily it seemed as though Tim's pill situation was just a snag in the pantyhose, and much like pantyhose, it was a just a passing phase.

DECEMBER 2007, ALMOST four years into our marriage, we downsized and moved after selling what we called our P. Diddy house. The P. Diddy house in this case was a monster *Cribs* home, complete with a movie theater, elevator, wine cellar, and a four-car garage. It was a dream home of sorts (aside from the nightmare mortgage payment). The P. Diddy house drained us financially (there was a two hundred thousand dollar roof-leak lawsuit) and emotionally, and we were looking for a fresh start. Plus, with Tim's pending football retirement, my television show now over, and my status as stay-at-home mom in search of a new series, it seemed the wiser financial thing to do. Or the "stop living like we are P. Diddy and start living like normal people" plan.

Almost as soon as we rang in the New Year in 2008 and unpacked the boxes in our new home, Tim started going out probably five nights a week "for the business." Everything was "for the business." He would come home sober and at a reasonable hour, so although I didn't love it, I understood he was making sacrifices and networking to make his new start-up company actually start up. Plus, this diversion did a great job of taking his mind off the fact that he had sat on the couch the entire previous football season and watched the New York Giants win the friggin' Super Bowl! He didn't even get a sidelines invite to the big game. Sure, being placed on the injured reserve meant he got paid for the entire season (including playoff-game bonuses and extra pay for winning the Super Bowl). But I had to imagine that watching it from our sofa, despite getting paid for it, was about as exciting as playing *Madden NFL* on an Xbox. He would have traded it all for the chance to actually play in the game and have that ultimate NFL experience. Plus, if we had a *dollar* for every time someone asked, "So, did you get a Super Bowl ring?" I could buy my very own Jonas Brother to perform in my living room twice a week just for shits and giggles. Assuming I could tolerate their music, which, unfortunately, I cannot.

I was excited for the Giants to win, especially for Eli Manning. I fondly recalled his permanent "aw shucks" hunched-forward posture, and his baby, baby, baby face. He barely looked old enough to drive, let alone drive a team to Super Bowl victory! Eli reminded me of my own little brother, but paler and much better compensated for his job. He seemed superhumble and just naturally possessed a certain sweetness. Tim, on the other hand, started to have a chip on his shoulder. He *allegedly* had the balls to bet his playoff game salary (about twelve thousand dollars) against the Giants during the playoffs—and lost. He seemed to think there was no way they were getting to the big game, but instead he got a whiff of some strong karma cologne. I mean what were the odds that over the last three years every team that had drafted Tim would make it into the Super Bowl—and win it? Bears. Colts. Now Giants. The curse of Tim Fish! If he had been a part of a fourth NFL team, I would have bet my life savings on the next Super Bowl prediction. What are *those* Vegas odds?

BESIDES TAKING CARE of Kaia, who was almost eighteen months old now, my life pretty much consisted of crashing out most nights in front of my beloved and faithful companion TiVo, going to bed, and starting all over again the next day like the movie *Groundhog Day.* One odd night Tim was actually beside me on the couch for a TiVo night. He had been so absent from our home after sunset that I was beginning to wonder if he had secret vampire tendencies I didn't know about.

"You know, it's weird. . . . It's like, we're roommates." I stated flatly, eyes still on the television as I fast-forwarded through a commercial. I was just stating a fact. I had said it a dozen times before, and he had scoffed at my implication every time. I wasn't trying to start an argument. I felt more defeated than anything else.

And then his next two words threw me entirely. Mirroring my calm, Tim stated, "I agree."

I was so surprised I might have even paused the television. I slowly turned to him, like a child not wanting to scare away a rabbit in her backyard, and we proceeded to have a completely calm, normal conversation—almost as if it were about two other people. It didn't get argumentative like all the others. We didn't yell. It was downright sane and composed. Then things got a little odd. He actually said at one point, "I will always love you," and "It's not you; it's me," along with "I think we can be best friends if this doesn't work out, like Bruce Willis and Demi Moore."

I couldn't believe he just Bruce and Demi-ed me!

Tim Fish was talking like we, the Fishes, were going to break up, and worse, like he was just breaking up with me for the prom—as opposed to the magazine-featured, life-long commitment with child we had both signed up for.

Despite the fact that I was shell-shocked, and in denial about what had just taken place, I was also hopeful. The conversation was depressing, but it was also a relief that we were finally able to talk about it. It was very adult, even with the hideous clichés and the A-list celebrity references. We agreed we needed to talk to Kristin, our marriage therapist, about it as soon as possible that week. Our session with her was like all the sessions with Kristin. You leave the office expecting that somehow fifty minutes of therapy have changed you and given you the "tools to better communicate," but the reality is that you're just $150 shorter in the pocket, and more focused on how fucked your decision was to marry.

That night, after seeing Kristin, like most nights, Tim went out. I, using my female intuition, stayed in—and went snooping. Something felt off. I started looking in his closet. What for? I had no idea, but I felt like I should be looking for something—perhaps some kind of insight into him, into why he was this impossible-to-live-with partner. Just as I was about to give up, I stood on top of a stepladder and placed one of my hands in Tim's enormous Air Jordan sneakers. I felt something hard and plastic, and when I pulled it out, I had a prescription pill bottle in my hand. It had just been filled that day. I read the bottle, wondered silently what the hell Norco was, noted the pill count, and quickly subtracted how many white, horse-sized pills were missing. As if on cue, the creak of our automatic garage door opening halted my snooping, and I almost broke my neck scrambling down from my perch. By the time Tim walked into our home moments later, I was pretending to be sound asleep. *Norco. Norco. Norco.*

What the hell was it? I might have been overreacting. Maybe it was just a muscle relaxer? But if it was just a muscle relaxer, why was it hidden in a Nike? I made a mental note to Google it. But I couldn't ignore the feeling that I didn't have to. *Shit. He's back on the pills*, I thought.

This discovery was thoroughly ill-timed, as we were leaving in a few hours to fly to the East Coast with Kaia, to play the perfect-marriage charade in front of an abundance of his family and friends. Tim was being honored by his old high school at a Hall of Fame dinner banquet, based on his being a phenomenal football player, alumnus, and role model.

On the second day we were in New Jersey I had an opportunity to snoop in Tim's travel bag while he was showering, and I found the same prescription bottle (from the Nike) that I had found before we left. Only now it housed *one* lonely pill. Perhaps inspired by the Nike I decided to "just do it" and confront Tim. By then, I'd had time to do some research and found out that Norco was basically Vicodin. I was trembling (which made the pill bottle sound like a really unpleasant baby rattle) as he toweled off, and I said to him in a hushed voice, "Can you tell me why the fuck you're taking six Norco a day?" As much as I wanted to wait until after the big celebratory "you're a good man Charlie Brown" dinner, I literally had no control over the words falling out of my mouth.

"Jesus! What—are you counting?" he hissed at me.

He didn't acknowledge my question. He was just irritated that I was monitoring him, which in effect perfectly answered my question. Some bullshit was exchanged about how "it isn't going to be a problem like last time. Norco was different. Plus, I'm only taking a few, three times a day."

"Oh . . ." I said, as deadpan yet sarcastically as possible. "My bad."

We had the world's most brief and hushed argument. First of all, there wasn't time. We were running late to this damn awards ceremony. Second, we were in his parents' small, old house that was built in the 1930s. You could hear everything echoing off the original hardwood floors, so the entire conversation was more like a heated stage whisper. Most memorable was one of the last things he said as we were leaving to go to the event.

"Well, it's not your problem anymore."

First the Bruce-and-Demi red flag and now the "it's not my problem anymore" sound bite? I was just an okay English student, but I was quite certain that Tim was no longer speaking about us in the present tense. What the crap?

We got out of the car at the banquet hall, and I proceeded to give the finest Oscar-worthy performance I've ever delivered. There were lots of bulbs flashing, lots of smiling and congratulations, a few journalists interviewing us, and more times than I could count that someone said to me, "Tim, he's such a great guy!"

"Yeah . . ." I smiled, a little too big.

"He . . . is . . . somethin'!" I guessed their version of "some-thin'" and mine differed slightly. Mine included an econ-omy-size pill bottle shoved up the "man of the hour's" ass.

The next morning we boarded the plane back to L.A. You could almost cut the tension between me and Tim with a plastic plane knife.

Like all women in crisis mode, I needed some serious phone time with my girlfriends. I couldn't wait to tell them about *all* the loveliness and adventure they'd missed out on since my weekend departure. My first call was to Kelly. She was like a sister—very honest, very blunt, and very di-vorced from a drug addict. I remember being at her home years before and her confiding to me that she suspected her husband at the time was smoking pot again. He was a former hard-core drug addict, so this was a no-no, as he was supposedly sober. I went straight to her ashtray. They were both cigarette smokers, so they had them ly-ing around and easily accessible. I started digging through them and inspecting the contents with my fingers.

"What are you doing?" Kelly didn't know whether to be concerned or amused as I fingered my way through the ashes in various trays.

"I'm looking for nuggs." I said, as if that was a perfectly logical explanation.

"Okay, Vanilla Ice . . . what's a nugg?"

"A nugg. A nugget. If you are smoking pot, then you dump out the little clump, like the resin, when you come to the end of the pipe. The nugg should be in there . . . and heeeeere's Johnny!" I held up a little black clump for her inspection.

We proceeded to place it in a Ziploc bag and scrawled across it with a marker: EXHIBIT A.

Not that there was an exhibit B or any exhibit whatsoever to follow. Sure enough, with our evidence glaring him in the face, her ex fessed up to nugg-gate, his drug use, and their divorce proceedings weren't far behind.

"You have to search his stuff. Remember nugg-gate?"

"Yeah, Kelly, I remember. But I have searched! That's how I found the pills in that shoe in the first place."

"An addict always has a few stashes. That was not his only stash, Rosa. Look in his car. Look in his closet. Look in every shoe. Use that female instinct and hunt for shit. Trust me."

She was right. How could I have been so mediocre in my pursuit of clues?

I hung up the phone and told Tim I would be right back, that I had forgotten my purse in my car. "Can you watch Kaia for a second?"

"Well . . . I'm kinda busy. Can you?" he said without looking up from the computer. I didn't have the patience to explain to him that ESPN.com wasn't going anywhere, so I picked up Kaia and put her on my hip.

I went outside to his car, which at the time was parked across the street and not in our driveway. I unlocked the doors and put Kaia down in the front seat. I knew I wasn't going to start the car, so it wasn't as vintage Britney Spears car seat–less and cavalier as it sounded. As soon as I shut the car doors, I saw a wild-eyed Tim looking at me in horror from across the street.

"Rosaaaaa!"

I didn't recall my name having quite so many vowels.

He looked like a rabid animal, but he waited for traffic to clear before he sprinted across the street like he was getting timed in the NFL combines.

I went into an immediate flash of armpit sweat and started spastically pressing every button within arm's length. *Why oh why was it so hard to locate the locks? Why did BMW feel the need to make their car more complicated than a rocket ship? Crap! What was wrong with old-school car locks?*

Just as Tim approached the car, I heard a beautiful *click*. The doors had locked. Tim was pounding his fists against the glass so hard I half expected it to shatter. I knew there was only one reason he was having such a strong reaction to my being in his car, and it wasn't because I was going to reprogram his preset radio stations. He had something to hide and I wasn't leaving the car until I found out what it was, or until he smashed a window. Whatever came first.

"You're a fucking psycho! You know that? Get the fuck out of my car you mother fucker!" He was screaming Ike Turner–style, in a way I had never seen, except in *What's Love Got to Do with It* and sometimes on the *Sopranos* right before some thug gets a bullet to the forehead. His eyes bugged like a crazed animal, with a fury I had only witnessed on a football field (and through binoculars).

In concert with his fist-pounding symphony, I located a

little button on the middle console rest, and watched as the two console doors simultaneously opened with the kind of quiet ease that only a ninety-thousand-dollar luxury car provides. There, looking back at me, was a Ziploc bag filled with at least a hundred Vicodin.

Wow.

I slowly nodded my head. I couldn't pretend I hadn't seen that. Now I knew definitively. *He's knee-deep in a pill habit*, I thought. I could hear Dr. Phil's imaginary voice chirping in my ear: "Well if it walks like a duck, and smells like a duck . . . it's probably a duck, by God!" *Shut up imaginary mocking Dr. Phil voice! What do you know?* But it was displaced inner anger at Dr. Phil.

I took a deep breath and picked up Kaia. As I got out of the car, gripping our baby in a protective mama bear hug, I avoided eye contact with Tim.

His screaming continued. "That's it! It's fucking over! I'm outta here! I should have never had a baby with you! You fucking bitch!"

I stopped walking, lowered my voice to almost a whisper, and in an exercise in futility I replied, "Tim?" I mean really, what do you say in a situation like this? "Please don't swear in front of the baby."

He stormed off, packed a duffle, and left the house for good, with one final requisite door slam just to prove he meant it. That was April 2, 2008, our official date of separation. That also meant that the last day of my marriage to Tim Fish was April Fools' Day.

That night I did that thing where you try to sleep because you are exhausted, but only end up thinking and thinking and thinking yourself more awake. I wondered how much Tim could potentially have spent on these pills, assuming of course that pills you keep in a Ziploc bag weren't covered by our health insurance. I couldn't wait for it to be the next morning so that I could call our accountant, ask some questions, and hopefully find some way to assess the financial damages. Was it possible I was just overreacting? Was he "Dr. Drew needs to help him on *Celebrity Rehab*" bad? Or just "functioning addict" bad? And was there even such a thing as a functioning addict?

Nine o'clock in the morning *finally* came, and I got hold of my accountant's assistant. I gave her the PG-rated Cliffs-Notes on what had happened the day before and asked, "Is there anything unusual about Tim's spending lately?"

"Well . . . not unusual." She faltered. "But you know he goes through a lot of cash."

No. I did not know.

He was never one of those guys to carry around a wad in his wallet, because he was so OCD that he got bent out of shape if I put a gift card in there for fear his wallet would get "stretched past ideal capacity."

"Well no . . . I wasn't aware he went through a lot of cash. What's a lot? Like what were the last few ATM withdrawals?"

Maybe it was "a lot" to her, but it's all relative.

"Okay . . . a thousand dollars yesterday. Eight hundred

dollars the day before that. Twelve hundred dollars the day before that . . ." She started ticking off numbers like an Olympic judge.

My heart did a perfect-ten swan dive into my abdomen.

"Give me the total for the last month in ATM withdrawals." I was almost whispering, grateful I could make sounds that were audible.

There was a lot of computer clicking, a long pause, and then finally, "Sixteen-thousand, four hundred and eighty dollars."

"What?"

I immediately went into another flop sweat.

"Tell me what the total was for the last six months."

This time I was grateful to hear all the clicking calculating sounds, because I needed a moment to catch my breath. "Rosa. Are you sure you want to hear this?"

Yes, bitch. That's my final answer . . . just get to the info! Instead, I composed myself and squeaked out a "Yeah! Go ahead!"

"Eighty-six thousand, nine hun- . . ." She may have continued talking but I just heard a ringing in my head. There was no way. No way. In my drug education (thanks in part to the television series *Intervention*), I had learned that black-market drugs cost about five to ten dollars a pill. And if he was up to so many a day he had to be damn near overdose levels if all that money was spent buying drugs. There was no way!

I remembered the threats Tim gave me. "If you ever tell anyone in my family . . ." This was regarding his "first" drug problem. And I didn't. I kept silent (except to my best friend Jennifer—but everyone has to tell one person their secret so she doesn't count). I felt that even though I hated it, I owed it to him as his wife and partner. He, in turn, promised me that he was so committed to sobriety that "*if* I ever did the pills again and it was a problem, *then* I could tell his family." It was his way of promising sobriety back in Cabo, because he liked keeping his family in the dark about who he was, what he was doing. I was pretty sure this all fell into the category of being a "problem."

I got his sister Carrie on the phone and asked her not to tell her parents yet so we could use that for ammo if we had to. Then, through her tears and mine, I surprised the hell out of her with the new information about her brother. Without missing a beat she said, "Go to the bank and put all the money in your name before he kills his stupid self." Carrie had a thick New Jersey accent so it came out more like "stupit self."

I went to the bank with the intention of putting all of our funds into a new account that couldn't be accessed by anyone (or extracted in bulk) until we could reassess and regroup during all this drama. I hadn't yet showered or brushed my teeth. My hair was wild from me running my hands through it screaming, "no . . . noooooo"—my latest morning mantra. And I was wearing the shirt I had slept in, complete with old traces of dried zit cream and pregnancy sweats. All in all, I looked homeless, crazy, and a little bank-scary. On top of that I couldn't stop shaking from nerves and raw adrenaline. Then I waited for the call that would inevitably come once Tim found out he had no access to cash.

Sure enough, about an hour later Tim called. He was so livid it was palpable, even over the phone. For the first time since I knew him, or at least since yesterday's car freak-out, I was a little afraid. I didn't know who this person with all these secrets was, or what he was capable of doing. His personality changed throughout the conversation from crazy to calm, while he admitted that "the money was *not* spent on drugs. I used to have sort of a sports gambling problem. . . . But it's over now!" He pleaded with me to give him access to some money and that he was "just catching up on some gambling debts and he had learned his lesson." He sounded eerily like he had in his parents' bedroom a few days before, trying to convince me he had no problem with the big white pills he took several times a day.

I explained to him during that phone call that he "still had access to his credit cards. Anything he needed could be bought on them, the way *normal* people did. I personally only needed cash money for Starbucks and valet parking. He should be no different." It was a miracle if I went through a hundred dollars a month using ATMs. I thought that with my mathematic deficiencies it was better to have a credit card trail for the accountants and taxes and all that crap so I didn't end up all Leona Helmsley-ing myself.

"How am I gonna eat, Rosa?" he screamed.

"You can put everything on a credit card!" I replied. "Ev-

erything except illegal things, asshole!" Now I was screaming too. Tim Fish did not like my game plan one bit.

The next week was a blur. I had no idea where he was
living, and I was waiting for him to acknowledge his mistakes, apologize, and commit to change. Just one week ago
we were in a therapist's office trying to work it all out!
Stranger than that, he didn't seem remorseful, just annoyed with my sudden financial control and discoveries.
Despite our problems, I let him see Kaia every day for a
couple of hours (which was more quality one-on-one time
than he had with her when he lived with us).

Next, I saw a divorce lawyer and had an out-of-body
experience walking into his office, like I was an actress
hired to play the part of a character getting divorced (and
not really doing it myself). I was sure this was all a brief
and traumatic hiccup in our lives that would somehow put
us on a better path. Ironically, during that first meeting the
lawyer asked me the same thing that the interventionist I
sought advice from did. "Do you think Tim was cheating?"
That just made me laugh. "No. No way."

ABOUT A WEEK after the separation, I called Tim
one night to update him about a lawsuit with an ex-
manager in which I had been forced to defend myself for
the past five years. There was finally the chance of a financial settlement with it (that would have to come from
our joint funds), so I needed to talk to him about it. He
sounded very weird on the phone, and "didn't want to talk

about it now" in sort of hushed tones. Tim was as obsessed with money as he was with superior clothes-folding. Since when did he not want to talk about our money?

I had an instant flashback to when you have a boyfriend in high school and you're on the phone with him, and he gets that completely different-sounding voice in front of his friends. He treats you like the plague when he is with his boys, but then reverts back to the mushy boyfriend you fell in love with when it's just the two of you. And that's how he pulls you back in!

I heard a tiny gut instinct whispering in my head, so I asked aloud, "Where are you anyway?"

"I'm at Jamie's house."

Jamie was his trainer, married with kids, and a superstable guy. He often gave great guidance to Tim and I hoped he was talking sense into him while he was there.

"Oh good! Well, ask Jamie if he thinks settling is a good idea."

"No! I have to go . . . I just . . ." He was stuttering. Something was off.

"Let me talk to Jamie," I said, as my intuition kicked into red alert.

"No . . . I'm . . . Jamie isn't here. He's in Vegas with his wife. I'm house-sitting for him." He couldn't stop stuttering and seemed inappropriately frustrated.

"Then let me call you on his house line," I challenged him. Now he knew that I knew something was up, and that he was lying.

"No! I gotta go . . . I'm not doing this now. I'm hangin' up," he managed to stammer before I heard the *click*.

My head blazed. I hit redial as fast as I could. I was past instinct now. It was clear, as if I truly believed the next lie that came out of my mouth.

"Tim. *I know for a fact* that you are not at Jamie's. I know for a fact that you are with a girl. I had you followed and I know exactly where you are located. So you can either tell me what the fuck is going on, or I am coming over there myself."

"We'll talk tomorrow." And again, he had the ball-sack to actually hang up on me!

Trembling, I texted the following message:

Tim. I am changing the locks within the hour. All of your shit will be on the front doorstep. But first, I am e-mailing every person in your address book and telling them the truth. That I THINK you're a degenerate drug addict and gambling addict. Enjoy.

I pondered whether "degenerate" was too big a word and that he may have to look it up before I pressed SEND. Guess not, because he called back within the minute.

"I'm coming home now." He sounded out of breath, like he was running. I knew I'd hit a nerve with the threat to blow the whistle on his secrets. I remembered that an addict's biggest fear is being discovered—and revealed. Plus, he was looking for investors in the new business, and the words "gambling addict" most likely would not instill fiscal confidence.

"Who is she, asshole?" I asked, white-knuckling my cell phone.

"Okay! Okay! Her name is Carlie. I met her at a bar a few weeks ago and went home with her and we slept together. I'm coming home now. Don't send any e-mails. Don't do anything, please!"

Now it was my turn to hang up.

He cheated.

Carlie. She had a name. An annoying name that ended in "ie" that she probably dotted with a big, circled smiley face, but a name nonetheless. Who is named Carly besides Simon? And rock stars don't count, or it would make perfect sense for me to go the store to buy diapers in a metal sphere à la Lady Gaga, if they were what was considered the norm.

He fucking cheated a few weeks ago *while we were still married!* Is that where he was living now? My thoughts went completely bipolar—from blind rage to a scary calm unlike any I had ever achieved through yoga. I went from mourning our failed marriage to planning the ultimate revenge, all within the speed of a thirty-second commercial break. And who was this mystery femme fatale who had lured him away from our marital bed? And how fucking dare he be the one who cheated? He didn't even want sex when it was readily available! Aren't cheaters usually people who actually want sex and aren't getting it? Mr. Two Pump had cheated. The sexless wonder that was my husband had cheated. Irreparable damage had been done and I knew it. There was zero chance of any reconciliation now that he had crossed into foreign vagina territory.

It dawned on me that if I were wearing a jersey, the name on the back would now read "divorcée," or "single mom." I was *not* the exception to the rule. I was the kind of clueless girl that I have made fun of on so many occasions: Dumb Girl Marries Professional Athlete.

Athlete cheats.

Girl is surprised.

"Cliché party of one . . . ?"

Your table is now ready.

They say a picture's worth a thousand words:
This one may be worth more. Tim and Amy on the night
of our wedding . . . yes, really.

ELEVEN

All-Out Blitz!

I was thirty-five and newly single, complete with a lovely side effect from having given birth: I still peed (just a tiny bit) every time I sneezed. Men dig that. Although I searched, I simply couldn't find a T-shirt that said, "I married a pro athlete and all I got were these big-ass diamonds, *and* oral herpes." Plus, I had made a terrible decision just a few months prior to our separation to chop off my once-gorgeous, long, midback brown hair. Apparently, I was itching to look very average-soccer-mom, and less recovered bimbo. Things always look different on Posh Spice than they do on a mere mortal.

But old habits die hard, and I soon wanted a part of my once-familiar bimbo look back. So, via a referral, I tracked down the hair-extensions-to-the-stars lady and got some very expensive hair remains that Eva Longoria must have "passed" on. They were fabulous, overpriced, and very Beyoncé.

The baby had sucked the life literally and figuratively out of my breasts, so I got those a tune-up too. So what's a girl to do that feels celebratory? I settled for some retail therapy. For the first time in six years, I was going to be single again. I knew I had to pony up about seven thousand dollars and redo my so-old-they-should-be-in-the-Smithsonian boobs job. They (the girls) were now all dented and deflating, and my plan (while married) was to wait to have another baby before I fixed them. It just seemed to make the most sense, because I knew another baby was just going to literally suck the life out of them too. I had seen it happen to many of my friends. Oh, and that *other* baby idea? *C'est la vie.* With this divorce came many consequences, and one of them was the foreclosure of my birth canal. Kaia and I would be a team. Just the two of us. Like Punky Brewster and her dad, but different and without a penis.

For my midextreme makeover, I went conservative (at least for me). I didn't want to look like stripper-mom, I was going for PTA mom *lite*. Plus, big fake racks—much like skinny jeans—seemed to be on their way out. Both were very early nineties. Armed with a black Sharpie marker, my plastic surgeon told me the best way to communicate what I was looking for was to come armed with visual aids. I pored through *Playboy* magazines, tried my best to ignore

the fact that the centerfolds were born in the late eighties, and circled examples of "good" breasts and "no way
please don't you dare!" boobs. It was like a to-do list, only
sluttier. I went for slightly smaller, as natural as fake can
look, teardrop-shaped boobs, and flew up to San Francisco
to meet them. In L.A. there was over a six-month wait for
Dr. Garth Fisher, and even though he is known as the best
boob guy, he was also twice as expensive, so technically I
could only afford one of his. He was the Bentley of tit doctors. With no idea where my future finances sat, I decided
I just needed a nice sedan with leather seats instead.

Next in line for my soul redecorating was selling
my ancient (with over a hundred thousand miles on it)
exterior-dented and interior-torn Lincoln Navigator. The
married-girl plan was to get a sensible mom-mobile.
Something hybrid made sense, with enough room for an
expanding family that didn't cost too much. Maybe a Ford
Escape, or Toyota Highlander? Instead, the newly single side
of my brain decided to splurge on a "Fuck it! MILF [Mom I'd
Like to Fuck] mobile." My divorce Porsche. Or as my friend
Lisa Ann Walter called it "my Divorsche-a." To go with my
new . . . "Di-voobs." Laughter was the best medicine. Unless
I could get my hands on some good pot. Truth be told, even
if I wanted to do my impression of Cheech and Chong and
escape life's troubles with a big smoky bong hit, I couldn't.
If there were a custody battle, I would be drug tested. I also
couldn't get some much-needed Lexapro. I had to just pretend to be balanced. Acting in real life sucks that way because you can't just yell "Cut!" when you want a do-over.

———

I T WAS AROUND this time that I also started fervently
seeing my therapist. She encouraged me to write in my
journal. I was looking for enlightenment in all the wrong
places. Her intentions were good. The goal was to have
another Oprah "aha! moment," cathartically writing and
getting closer to the ultimate goal of mental stability—that
promising oasis—just out of my reach. So, I wrote until
my hand felt like it had carpal crumpled-up syndrome.
This was especially true when I was feeling vulnerable
or near my period (a.k.a. dropping eggs, that time of the
month when women hormonally reassess everything that
is wrong with their lives, and their thighs). One of the first
things I did the night I found out about Tim's new girlfriend in particular, after replacing his ringtone on my cell
from Sheryl Crow's "My Favorite Mistake" to "The Devil
Went down to Georgia," was to grab my journal and a pen.
I enjoyed what had become the irony of writing in what
I now called my "divorce diary." My divorce diary was a
fierce red leather book with a sacred heart carved onto the
cover. I had found it at one of those overpriced stationery
stores over four years ago while I was in wedding-planning
mode. It was purchased to write my wedding vows in,
and was prominently displayed in all the photos of a-hole
and I getting married. Now it was a tiny piece of salvation as I scribbled my most private thoughts. I was told:
"Just write down whatever you are feeling. Don't judge
it. Don't reread it. Don't think. Just write." And so I did.

Nothing was off-limits, from my secret worrying "if my vagina was stretched out" post–baby birth, or the sheer terror of pondering what Tim's new girlfriend, my replacement, might look like. "Oh God, what if she's like a young Jessica Alba?" Or worse, what if it *is* Jessica Alba?

The weirdest part about all the aftermath and wacky high jinks that ensued was that Tim started to treat me as if *I* were the one who had been doing what he had been doing. He seemed to be so angry with me that if he could have bottled that rage, he could have a hell of a career as a pro wrestler, or at the very least as a bull in Pamplona, Spain.

Around this time, Tim realized I had no intention of giving him half of the house I owned before I got married. Tim was not a big fan of my decision and I came to this conclusion based on the fact that he started expressing himself with a very specific, very special noun choice. His word du jour became the famous C word that Eve Ensler devoted an entire chapter to in her work of art *The Vagina Monologues*. Nothing like some cunt napalm to really start up a shit storm. I don't think I would have minded the cunt bombs so much, except that it happened in front of Kaia. Sadly. When I tried to reason with him that this was "considered universally inappropriate," particularly in front of our eighteen-month-old, boy genius retorted, "Well if you don't *act* like a cunt, I won't call you a cunt!" While math isn't my strong suit, I did note that that resulted in two more "cunts." All cunts aside, I wasn't gifting him half my damn house. Step back Tim. You wordsmith, you!

The house in question was what I called the beach house. I had purchased it by myself a few months into our dating. It was a beautiful, Mediterranean, brand-new construction home, with a startling view of the ocean. I loved it. It was the third house I had bought since I turned twenty-five. I kept upgrading the homes, making money, selling that house, and using the profits I made for the down payment on whatever the next house was. TV doctor by day, and house flipper by night. It was a time when everyone was making money on houses, before anyone had uttered the word "recession," and therefore the beach house doubled in value and was considered my best investment since the first set of implants (of which I have one, proudly displayed and framed on my bedroom wall).

It took me a week after Tim stormed out of the house and left, to conclude that he was not a good packer. He had forgotten a stainless steel suitcase that I had given him from a celebrity gifting suite. Celebrity gifting suites are about the greatest perk to being in show business. You literally go from display table to display table where the vendors are eager, almost desperate for you to take some of their free merchandise in exchange for free publicity. It's like looting, but luxurious, legal, and they take pictures of you doing it while packing you a nice to-go bag. The latest celebrity gifting suite left me with a pricey, stainless steel suitcase, which Tim immediately claimed as his. It looked very James Bond and I would watch as Tim organized his ticket orders (with the Super Bowl tickets that every player was given the opportunity to buy at cost). He probably felt cool carrying it around, and maybe even like he had a job like a normal guy—an issue I tried gently to get him to think about now that his career had taken the bench.

One curious night I looked at the combination lock near the handle and thought, *I wonder what he keeps in here exactly, and what's the code?* Tim used 2424 (his college football number) for everything—ATM, Internet, house alarm, etc.—so I was sure it couldn't be that simple.

I tried his last four digits of his social security number. Nothing.

I tried his birthday. His birth year. Kaia's birthday. Nothing.

I tried 6969 because he was immature. Nothing again.

So I tried 2424, and when I heard the entry *click*, the sound confirmed that Tim, or rather "Dim," was in fact a moron. Jackpot!

Literally a Kodak moment. I started clicking away like Annie Leibovitz doing a cover shoot for *Vanity Fair*. Inside the silver suitcase were about fifteen bottles of his human growth hormone (*click*), two hundred syringes (*click*), a receipt for the syringes with *my* name on it (news to me, like everything else! *click*), a giant bottle of about a hundred steroids with the words "For Equestrian Use Only" emblazoned on it (did we have a horse I didn't know about?—*click, click, click*), along with some Cialis (like Viagra but longer lasting—*click*), some Percocet (surprise, surprise—*click*), Valium (*click*), and a lot of receipts from Federal Express, which I pocketed. There, among what looked like the contents of Elvis Presley's bathroom cabinet, was a

distinct FedEx-receipt paper trail. The names of I'm guessing dealers and their addresses written in the familiar
handwriting I saw once a year on anniversary cards. Unlike the Hallmark cards, I was keeping these. Plus, there
were the scribblings of what looked like sports games he
had bet on, and the total amounts. Unders, overs, negative
marks, and positive signs—like the world's most expensive
math equation. I cursed myself for my financial prudence
during our marriage. Why the hell was I shopping at Target when there was a perfectly good Gucci going to waste
just a few miles away?

It took me an hour to sift through all the new bounty.
I figured my new photo album might come in handy one
day. This fucking guy was busy to say the least.

Aside from Tim's suitcase, other discoveries and information seemed to just fall into my lap. See, the thing is,
when people know you are absolutely getting a divorce and
there is no shot of your getting back together they like to
share stories. It's very show-and-tell. Heavy on the tell.
When people know there is a kid involved and a potential
custody battle? Then normal people, people who have feelings of remorse and a conscience, tend to get attached, and
they feel morally obligated to let you in on some info you
may not otherwise be privy to—as it was in this case.

Around this time I could have really used a service like
www.fyimessages.com, which was not yet in existence.
This website is an Internet messenger system to let you
know things, anonymously, "for your information." Things
like "FYI: you have rancid breath." Or "FYI: you need to

grow the hell up." Or, in my case, it would have been nice to find in my e-mail inbox, "FYI: your husband has thrown his hotdog down many, many hallways." No, I received no fyimessages, but much like James Taylor, I was informed that "You've got a friend."

Enter: "Friend."

(Now, I'm going to be referring to "Friend" as Friend—in an effort to prevent having an actual dead friend.)

Tim's from Jersey, remember.

O NE NIGHT I was driving to acting class when I got a phone call. Friend said that we needed to talk. There was some stuff about Tim that he knew, and that was keeping him awake at night, knowing that I didn't have an ounce of a clue. I was pretty damn sure I had found out everything there was to know (besides maybe gory details), so I kind of sarcastically laughed and snorted, "Don't think I don't know—'cause I know! Tim's a special kind of douche bag of epic proportions!"

"Yeah . . . but . . . I don't think you really know . . . "

"No. Unfortunately I do know!" I said as confidently as David Caruso on *CSI: Miami*, just not as challenged in the pigment department, or playing with my sunglasses. "I know he's a cheater. I know about the gambling. I know about the drugs."

"Yeah . . . um . . . there's a bit more . . ." Friend seemed jumpy and nervous, like he didn't know if I had Tim on a three-way call or not.

"Well Jesus, just tell me!" I was losing patience. I didn't have time for the buildup, and this wasn't *Deal or No Deal*.

"I can't tell you over the phone. It might be dangerous for you to drive," said Friend cautiously.

"Dangerous how?" It was official. His little guessing game was annoying me.

"Dangerous in that I should wait to tell you in person." Friend definitely got my attention there.

"Well, I'm not waiting," I said definitively, and pulled the Divorsche-a over. I even put the phone up to the car ignition so Friend could hear it had been turned off.

"There. Now what the hell is it?" I was starting to get annoyed.

"Tim slept with someone *on* your wedding night. She's one of your best friends."

What?

Since when was Friend into drunk dialing? I thought.

"Who?" I spat, as evidenced by some saliva spray on my windshield.

"Who was the girl who was married to the hockey player?"

Friend was asking, genuinely not knowing. He was referring to Amy. Amy was one of my *best* friends, who married Moose's roommate, and whose wedding I was a bridesmaid in!

"Amy? No, no. There. Is. No. Way. No!"

I was furiously shaking my head back and forth, a bit more frantically than intended and with no one to see it except people driving by. As the silence from Friend dragged on, I started shaking it more vehemently, uncontrollably giggling, and repeating, "There's no way! There's no way!" a few octaves higher than my normal range. It sounded more car alarm than vocal chords.

Finally I said smugly, "I don't believe you."

"It happened, Rosa."

"How? How did it happen? I was there!"

"It happened when you went to bed for the night."

"I'm sorry?" I countered sarcastically. "You mean after Tim and I consummated our eight-hour-old marriage?"

Friend said nothing. This time he didn't have to.

I don't know which was more deafening: the sound of the silence that confirmed it or the sound of my own heartbeat, which I could hear banging away in my eardrums like it was on speakerphone.

The nausea was rather abrupt. Like a surprise party for the honorary guest . . . named bile.

"There's more . . ." Friend sighed heavily. (I'm sure delivering this information couldn't be up on anyone's list of good times.)

"What else could there be?" I said as I searched my car for a Kleenex. I opened every nook and cranny and there was nothing. I looked down at my T-shirt and decided that using it as an impromptu snot catcher was the least of my problems.

Friend was right. There was indeed more. Not only from Friend. The universe clearly wanted me to know everything, as the discoveries kept falling into my lap as the days and weeks moved on. I wasn't even looking for clues.

They just got delivered to me via different people, different messengers. You know the saying that when God wants you to know something, he knocks on the door, and then again a little louder, and then even louder? Well, in this case I think God had me in a headlock, was giving me a noogie, and he wanted to really drive the point home. The night I found out about Amy and the wedding night was a Thursday night. Ironically, on Tuesday, just five days later, I was set to see Amy and have drinks with her *for the first time in almost four years.*

Cheers, bitch!

MY STRANGE RECURRING DAYDREAM . . .

9 have often wished for a twelve-step program to assist
me in my quest for athlete sobriety. Amid the comfort
of my peers perhaps these ladies and I would sit in a
circle in some dingy church basement, clutching crappy
black coffee, listening to Carrie Underwood's "Before
He Cheats" play softly in the background. We'd spend
the time recounting our past and/or current temptations
underneath a large banner that read: "Welcome to
AAAA: Actresses And Athletes Anonymous."

Our mantra would be: "Recovery is not a sprint
but a marathon—just take it one game at a time" as
they passed out sobriety chips with the picture of our
inspiration, our founder, Marilyn Monroe, on them. It
was no accident she went from DiMaggio to the anti-
DiMaggio, Arthur Miller, in record time. The closest
thing Miller ever swung was a pen.

The members of AAAA would include:

Halle Berry, Jenna Jameson, Pam Anderson, Ashley
Judd, Khloe Kardashian, Bridget Sampras, Alyssa
Milano, Kate Hudson, Madonna, and Eva Longoria,
just to name a few. Some in recovery, some currently
facing their demons . . . er . . . athletes. As we'd chant in
solidarity,

Athletes are overrated.
Athletes are overrated.

Our holiday card that year included the strikingly
beautiful, taller-than-you-can-imagine, lucid-ish (late)
Anna Nicole Smith.

TWELVE

Instant Replay

The year after my wedding, Amy seemed to be drifting further and further away from me. I knew she was going through her own shit and her own divorce and all the mourning that goes with the loss of any relationship, so I gave her space. But when my calls started going unreturned—and ignored as time passed—I couldn't justify what was obvious. I called several times over several weeks and heard nothing back. I gave up on the reaching-out-and-touching-someone by Christmastime and decided to try and get a response from Amy via one of my Christmas cards. I prided myself on sending out cards that were funny, as opposed to the usual dogs and/or kids in front of the fireplace in their holiday turtleneck sweaters. I also never send out a year-end newsletter, which I don't think you should ever receive unless you specifically sign up for it. I'm always baffled by the oversanitized Norman Rockwell information that's trotted out in these things. To be honest, I'd be dying to read them if people were real and cut out the bullshit.

For example, "Dear friends, This past year has been a real bitch! Of one. Santa Claus ain't coming here! Our marriage is dangling by a thread (Dan is a total dick!) and then we found ourselves pregnant with our third baby (whoops!) and he's less cute than the first two—sort of a cross between an old man and Verne Troyer. We've been at each other's throats ever since. Tick tock, huh? According to my watch, we're on borrowed time. This newsletter could be our last . . ."

That one would make the fridge for sure.

The first year Tim and I were married, I was asked to be a guest on the last episode of Sharon Osbourne's talk show. Wouldn't you know that when I got there I found out that Anna Nicole Smith was going to be a guest that day as well!

"Tim," I said to my precious one. "We're getting our picture taken with her, and it will be our Christmas card." I was a woman on a mission.

This was during the year Anna was a hot mess on her late-night E! reality show, and years before her tragic untimely death. This was Anna fresh off the diet drug and featuring her slim new body. And slim she was! She was way thinner than me, and at least a solid foot taller. I couldn't believe how statuesque she was. Everything really is bigger in Texas! And beautiful. She truly was pretty, especially when her eyes were all the way open and she wasn't slurring her words like a half-tanked contestant on Bret Michaels' *Rock of Love*. It was obvious she had a good heart, and was genuinely interested in the orphanage in Tijuana, Friends of El Faro, where I was talking about volunteering. She seemed to have a soft spot for kids.

Anna agreed to take a picture with us. She was twirling a cream-colored rose in her acrylic nails and decided to place it in her cleavage at the last minute for the photo op. Appropriately, she stood towering in between Tim and me.

This card was going to be even better than the year we posed with Hugh Hefner at a dog fashion show for charity back in the days when Hef had a baker's dozen of look-alike platinum-blond girlfriends, and not just a mere trio. My ultimate goal was a Christmas portrait with Gary Coleman from *Diff'rent Strokes* if we ever ran into him. This was prior to his tragic and untimely death, and I mean no disrespect, but back then I would have paid a lot of money to ask him to pose as our baby Jesus. I doubt he would have agreed to the whole cloth diaper part of it but I had an artistic vision at the time. For those of you with the similar artistic visions, Babies R Us does not carry mangers. (I checked.) The objective was, of course, to be humorous. I wouldn't have wanted someone on the A-list—just someone that would ignite smiles—to be a part of our Christmas card merriment. We signed them: "Happy Holidays! Love, Rosa, Tim and

Anna Nicole"—as if she was part of the family and on a first-name basis. This confused the hell out of my eighty-year-old aunts. They thought we adopted her.

As I was addressing the cards at Christmas, I thought, *Amy and I have always bonded through our senses of humor.* I totally loved that about her: We were able to crack each other up with ease. Once while she was still married, her husband kept noticing "Jimmy Choo" on the credit card statements. Month after month, it was the same thing, similar charges. Finally, somewhat frustrated he asked, "Who is Jimmy Choo?" Amy, without missing a beat, quipped, "That's *Doctor* Choo. My dermatologist. You said you loved my skin! Well, it doesn't get that way by itself, Sam." Sam was a victim of several ice concussions. And she took advantage of it. She also took advantage of the fact that his bank account could afford it. She felt a sense of entitlement, after all, for having to move to from L.A. to Boston, where she knew no one, gave up her "career" as an actress, and had to buy more conservative, Bostonian Talbots pumps.

I put our photo Christmas card in and sealed the envelope. Then I scrawled on the back of the envelope, to make sure to entice a chuckle—or at the very least a response out of my recently distant friend—"And the award for worst caller-backer friend of the year (drumroll please) . . . goes to Amy!"

I did the quantum physics math of the post office, figuring if I mailed it on this date and she got it on that date, she'd probably call me on this date. But again, nope, no response.

Instead, when I ran into people who knew how close we were, and they asked, "So, have you talked to Amy lately?" I would have to eat a slice of humble pie and say "Um . . . no. Not so much. Amy broke up with me."

"What? You guys were so close! Weren't you her brides-maid?" They thought I was kidding.

"Yeah. I know. I haven't had a friend break up with me since Holly Dunham in the sixth grade. But when someone no longer returns your calls, that's pretty much considered the universal sign of a breakup. So . . . she dumped me."

Of course, I was hurt and confused. We had never even had a fight, or a falling out. As time went on, I'd say to Tim, "I just want to write her a letter. I want to address the situa-tion! People who are thirty don't do this! I want her to take responsibility for the breakup." I sounded like a wounded character on *The L Word*. Tim would try to console me in the compartmentalizing and overly easy way that men do. "Fuck her! She's a whore!" I actually envy men's ability to see things as so black and white and not have to live with a hamster wheel of thoughts that go round and round and round. It must be nice to be a simpleton.

When a guy dumps you, it hurts. When a friend dumps you, it stays with you. This is especially true when you don't have a reason to back it up. About a month before I found out the truth about the wedding night, I was at

the gym working on my revenge body. I went to the restroom to wash off any trace of what I call gym finger—the
disgusting germs that can only be found in gyms and
that I try not to think about. Focused on scrubbing away
at the sweaty, fecally, staphy, not-everybody-washes-
their-hands-after-using-the-bathroom-and-touching-the-
equipment gym finger, I looked up in the mirror and
made eye contact with the platinum blond washing her
hands next to me.

It was Amy.

I hadn't seen her since almost four years before. She
laughed as if we were on the best of terms and reached
out to give me a big hug, grab my shoulders, and look right
into my eyes, her teeth dazzling white. "How *are* you?" she
said, as if she had been looking for me, and I was lost. It
was as if I was on a carton of milk somewhere, or as if my
number had changed, or as if I hadn't tried contacting her
(read: stalking her) a half a dozen ways.

"I'm good!" I answered the way you are supposed to answer that question (and not divulge that your life looks like
the remains of a disaster movie). And up until that moment
I was relatively "good." Right up until that moment. You
know when you are caught off guard and someone asks
you something innocent and it evokes a stream of tears? I
was suddenly that girl. I was so embarrassed by the sudden waterworks and so nervous to see her and so mad at
her for ditching me inexplicably, but at the same time I
was so grateful and so pissed at myself that I couldn't stop
the crying. I was furious at how my tear ducts betrayed

me. I could barely see; the tears were flying out of my face. *Rosa, can't you have some control of this shit? What's happening? Get it together!* I thought, as I scolded my own body parts. I couldn't even cry easily on cue for my job, and here I was a friggin' faucet. In public no less. I felt like such a loser.

Living in the same small town by now, I assumed everyone had heard about Tim and my impending divorce, so I talked with her as if it weren't news. "Well, you know Tim turned out to be a real a-hole, and we are getting a divorce." She seemed genuinely concerned and surprised. She hadn't heard.

"Can we get together for drinks? I would love a catchup," she said with her arms still on my shoulders.

"Yeah, Amy, I would love nothing more."

I felt kind of relieved. For sure, she was going to tell me why in the world she had broken up with me, and most likely apologize and ask for my hand in friendship back. Surely, she would want to bond again over the fact that we were now having the similar experience of divorcing athletes. "Friends don't let friends marry athletes" was my new motto.

Being at the gym that day was meant to be. We set a couple of dates for plans, and then Amy always canceled on me a few days before. It was weird. Finally, we had attempted to set plans again, with an "and I promise not to cancel this time!" attached from her. So by the time I was fed the information about Amy and my wedding night we were set to see each other face-to-face in five days. I was hoping she wouldn't cancel again. My therapist said, "No way. She wants to tell you! That's why she made plans in the first place." The day we were supposed to meet she texted me. "We still on?"

"Yes," I texted back. Holy crap, this was going to happen. Tonight.

I was as nervous as if I had a big date. I was hoping the random crying jag wouldn't happen again like the last time at the gym, and I was looking forward to getting some much-needed answers.

I got to the restaurant Mediterraneo on the Hermosa Pier, and waited shakily for her to arrive. Normally I would have asked for a white wine spritzer but it was a little embarrassing how much of a lightweight non-drinker I was and I decided to man up with a mojito instead. I like ordering them and mispronouncing them on purpose just to see the waitress's face. "A mo-jee-to please?" Waiting for Amy, I was a little sweaty and I kept taking long, deep breaths, hoping to convince myself that I was calm. My heart sank at the sight of anyone with any shade of light blond hair who passed by. Was it her? But that had been happening for years in our small beach town, thinking I was always going to run into her. Finally I saw her outside the restaurant window, talking animatedly to someone I didn't know. *Hmm . . . I wonder if she slept with her husband, too,* I mused. Amy had always been in great physical shape. She had the fake rack, supertoned Angela Bassett arms, big blue doe eyes with fake-looking—but real—long lashes, and the hair extensions, but the good ones. Not the doll-hair kind. She was pretty, in a semi-stripperesque way. But that was her intention. She used to idolize Pam Anderson and Carmen Electra, even during that phase when Carmen wore that too-dark-brown lip liner. I'm not judging. I did the same thing. It took me years to figure out where my actual lip line was, and not my wishful-thinking lip line.

As Amy entered the restaurant in what I felt was slow motion, I couldn't help but let all the insecurities I've ever had creep in and announce themselves with a gusto. I heard the self-doubting voices (that all women are equipped with) loud and clear inside my head. That, and the superhuman ability to recall every single detail from memory when we are in a fight with the opposite sex. Seriously, why ever fight with a woman? Not only is she going to remind you of the details, but she will tell you what kind of hair day she was having, what you were wearing, and who was on *Regis and Kelly* that day.

I could see she was scanning the place to see if I had arrived yet as I thought, *Hmm. I always thought Tim's type was exotic-looking brunettes, not some bitch from the slutty Malibu Barbie collection. Damn it, Rosa, shut up! Why do you even care?*

Finally, I waved her over to the table.

"Hiiiiiiii!" she beamed as she hugged me. "It is so *good* to see you!" she squealed as I was embraced with gusto in an instant, tight hug. I tried replicating her enthusiastic "hiiiii," but half my face was buried in a sea of her platinum hair.

Okay, this is weird. This is not at all how you start a conversation about letting someone else's husband enter your vagina, I thought.

"Tell me everything. How *are* you?" She was playing concerned friend again, just like at the gym with the emphasis on the wrong vowels.

The waitress came by and Amy ordered an apple martini. That was her drink of choice back in the day; some things hadn't changed—except the part about my husband falling into her. I couldn't stop the inner dialogue if I tried. I wanted to give myself a gag order.

"Well . . . um. Wow . . ." I stuttered like Stuttering John from the Howard Stern show. "Gee, there's a lot to cover. But I'll give you the CliffsNotes. Turns out—I believe Tim is a sociopath. I also believe he is addicted to prescription pills. He admitted to gambling almost a hundred thousand dollars from our savings, and . . . get this, he's been cheating on me, well, from the wedding night"—I paused to gesture in her direction—"until the present."

I waited for her to react to my not-so-subtle gesture toward her.

She was stone-faced. There was nothing there. I knew she possessed a SAG card and was a wannabe actress, but come on! Her face revealed nothing. It was the same look we were about to give the waitress when she came over and rambled on about the specials of the evening: the fish they couldn't sell that was about to rot and the crap food that doesn't necessarily go together normally that the chef got creative with.

I wasn't expecting the stone face. I momentarily second-guessed the information that Friend had conveyed to me. What if I had the wrong girl? But who else do I know that was married to a hockey player? The way I had it planned, that first speech about the CliffsNotes was where she was going to jump in and confess. So I changed my course, to try and provoke a reaction from her.

Take two. I decided to take out my nerves on the paper straw cover, shredded it into a small pile on the table, and twisted the remains around my fingertip until it went purple from lack of circulation. I released the paper noose.

"Look, Aim"—I used her nickname, like that would close the four-year gap—"we can sit here and bullshit for twenty more minutes, or we can be honest like we used to be, and you can tell me from your perspective what happened the night of my wedding with you and Tim."

Now Amy took a deep, dramatic, Stella Adler Studio of Acting breath. And then she took another, this one from Meisner studies.

I didn't have the patience to watch her gulp down all the oxygen in the room, so I encouraged her to start talking, and stop with the yoga breaths.

"Aim. There is *nothing* you can tell me about Tim that I don't already know. There is nothing that will surprise me, unless you tell me you have a four-year-old son with him." I meant business, but I wasn't threatening, because the sick part of me wanted the dirty little details that only people who have been cheated on long for. Less was not more. I wanted to know, to paint a vivid picture, to make sure that my torture was sketched out for me on a full-blown color canvas. So I said it with a smile: much like a school counselor for troubled teens.

"Rosa, I was in a really dark place at the time . . ." she finally said, grabbing my hands in hers. I didn't remember her being this hands-on before, but that might explain how she got into this whole debacle in the first place. "What I did was inexcusable, but I was a different person back then. I was trying to deal with the worst depression I had ever had in my life. I'm an insecure person anyway, but I was at an all-time low. I acted out. I did things I am not proud of, things I wish I could take back. . . ." She looked very vulnerable, but the way she looked at me was also familiar, like when an actor or politician fucks up and has to apologize in front of a slew of microphones at a press conference.

"There were a lot of drugs at your wedding, you know . . ." She continued matter-of-factly, as if it was also printed in the wedding program.

"No. I did not know," I said, wondering how much more I could possibly have been unaware of. Was I female? Was my name even Rosa? Was I invited to the same wedding? How could I be so Helen Keller about what was going on around me? Did Amy get her lips done? If I could stop my inner dia-tribe and stop analyzing the whole situation from across the table like Simon Cowell, I would have been better off, and more focused on what she was actually telling me.

"Well, Rosa, there were. I was doing coke, and I think Tim was doing coke? Anyway, after the wedding, I went back to my hotel room and there was a knock on my door. It was Tim. I thought it was weird he had come to my hotel room, but we were fucked up so nothing was that weird. We decided to go into the hot tub, and when we came out, he sort of threw me down on the bed and we started screwing around."

Surely, there was throw-up in my near future. Although I had only ingested the few tiny sips, some acidic mojito mintiness started creeping north and making its presence quite known.

"Didja . . ." I thought if I said it really, really fast, it wouldn't sound so bad out loud," . . . havesexwithhim?"

I was wrong. It still sounded bad.

She wrinkled her forehead as much as her Botox would permit. "I don't think so, but it's hard to tell. You know when you've been doing coke and you're screwing around and it's unclear?"

Again, no. I do not know. It isn't a common denominator, I thought.

But I said nothing, because I wanted her to spill as much information as possible and I thought the more I nodded the more she'd reveal. Tip: If you ever find yourself in this situation, confronting one of your best friends about potentially sleeping with your husband and you can remember to nod—well, nodding works. They go into more detail if you don't react like Edvard Munch's *The Scream* painting.

Amy went on to tell me that a week after the wedding night, while I was in Japan filming *The Grudge*, Tim left our "Tokyo honeymoon"—as we were calling it—and met up with Amy. Amy called him to talk about what had happened in Maui on the wedding night. She blamed herself and said she had a lot of guilt and she desperately wanted to apologize to him, addressing what had happened. They met for Mexican, had too many sangrias, and instead of addressing what happened they ended up undressing. They fucked that night at Amy's house, unbeknownst to me (and apparently unbeknownst to my informant Friend because he didn't even know this part of the story until I later told him) while I was having shabu-shabu somewhere in Japan with Sarah Michelle Gellar.

Of course, Amy apologized profusely and begged for my forgiveness. "If I could even get back one-tenth of our friendship I would take it, gratefully!" Part out of shock and part out of knowing that if a custody battle were to take place I would need her to possibly testify about Tim's character (or lack thereof), I put my hand on top of her hand and said, "You know, Amy, I forgive you. You were one of hundreds of girls. You weren't the reason. But I have to ask . . . were you going to tell me this tonight if I hadn't brought it up?"

If possible, Amy looked even guiltier as she shook her head no. "I was going to take it to my grave, Rosa."

I was running out of surprised reactions. I went to my go-to nod.

"But *why* wouldn't you have told me?" Before she could answer, I interrupted myself. "Wait. No. You know what? Doesn't matter. I'm glad you didn't. Because maybe I would have dumped his ass, then never had Kaia. It was supposed to be like this."

She kept talking, and I kept trying to listen, but I was interrupted by my own private monologues. Maybe it was her depression and insecurity that drove her to the brink of insanity? Maybe it was jealousy? Maybe it was so I could have the bragging rights to owning the worst judgment of all time? Ultimately, the why didn't really matter. Bottom line is that there is no excuse for what she did, Tim didn't accidentally fall inside her vagina, and nobody drugged her apple martinis that night. There was no magic sentence or explanation she could have come up with to justify what happened. Twice. When she bent down to get her credit card out of her Marc Jacobs bag to pay the bill (of course I didn't stop her or offer to pay half), I noticed a massive, new, horizontal, scrolly tattoo that danced above her ass crack like an ink target. You can throw in all the butterflies and curlicues you want, but at the end of the day you still just have a nice tramp-stamp.

How fitting, I thought. *The icing on the tart!*

BETWEEN FRIEND'S NEW info, my confrontation confirmation summit with Amy, more people coming out of the woodwork like hungry news-delivering termites, and a ten-thousand-dollar retainer I shelled out for a private investigator (and former shady LAPD guy), I uncovered a shitload more information—all while adding six new gray hairs to my growing collection. I was aging a little too fast for comfort that year. It was all very Chia Pet gone wrong. I highly recommend private investigators. They are like superheroes you can hire to let loose—committed to serving justice and bringing down the cheaters of this world. Ladies, when in doubt? Have his ass checked out.

It didn't take Sherlock Holmes to figure out that if Tim had been having sex *on* our wedding night (lest we forget, Valentine's Day 2004), chances are he was playing musical vaginas throughout our entire relationship.

Also on the menu throughout our entire marriage? Turns out that Tim *allegedly* enjoyed hookers. Yeah. Lil' bit. Specifically Craigslist hookers. Yep. I became aware that everything is for sale on Craigslist, and not just used lawn furniture. Was I living under a rock? Who knew? You should go on the site under "casual encounters." Some of the girls are okay-looking, most only show body parts (because really, who needs a face?), and some of them look like Eddie Murphy in drag and a fat suit.

Now, I don't want to give you the wrong impression of Tim. That would be unfair. I don't believe he was specifically biased to, say, Craigslist prostitutes. Oh no. He seemed to be an equal-opportunity employ-*whore*. One sworn court declaration I obtained detailed him having international dalliances as well. Ironically, this would have been the same weekend when we were trying to get pregnant at a friend's wedding trip in Cabo San Lucas, Mexico, and where, ironically, I was busy warning him that "the hot tub could harm his sperm count." I would never have found out about this specific gem, but he left Mexico without paying the concierge who made the arrangements, and the concierge was out close to a thousand U.S. dollars. So he (the concierge) talked, being under pressure for the reimbursement. Tim told me that morning in Cabo that he was "going golfing." So technically it was my bad, because I didn't ask him how many holes he was playing, or what kind specifically.

And because hiring hookers isn't risky enough to, well, my health and his, Tim—whose rapper name could have been Sir Sleuth-A-Lot—upped the ante, by *purportedly* bringing these lovely working ladies into our home while I slept (apparently quite soundly), and while the baby slept.

All the times I've watched *Family Feud* I have never once seen the category: "Name the one room in your house your husband would most likely take a prostitute. Survey says!" The answer (if my sources are accurate) would have been "the baby's playroom." God, I hope Lysol really is 99.9 percent effective on germs as advertised.

The discoveries came faster than I could process them— like I was working overtime on a conveyor belt. According to Amy and Friends, Tim was occasionally using cocaine. He just dabbled in it from what I gathered (and from what the sworn declaration from his former teammate gathered). He was not like Scarface bad. But apparently pills are helpful for coming down off of cocaine. People on coke also commonly like to talk, which in the end might have been Tim's downfall. His Achilles heel was that he seemed to get off on bragging about what he was doing behind wifey's back. In the end, that boastfulness must have rubbed Friend the wrong way because he could ultimately only keep Tim's secrets inside for so long.

So many things started to come into focus at this time—bits and pieces—that finally make sense. I felt like a reluctant jigsaw-puzzle champion. During my marriage, I naively thought it was just standard NFL practice to come home from time to time and have a pee-tester guy waiting in your driveway, surprise-requesting a urine sample. I just thought they (the NFL) were really diligent about the "just say no to drugs" campaign. What I learned was that once you fail a random drug test in the NFL, they test you a lot more stringently, and do things like "randomly show up at your house for pee tests." What the NFL does not do is tell the spouse, so I never got confirmation of this, just my educated guess that Tim wasn't tested this way "just because." Personally, I think it is a really dumb policy on the NFL's part, keeping the wives in the dark. It's not at all conducive to keeping healthy, sober athletes, but neither is handing out prescription pain pills like they come from a PEZ dispenser. They should really just cut to the chase and put prescription pain pills in vending machines inside the locker rooms, alongside the herpes medication Valtrex.

Thanks to those "friends and family phone plans," spouses everywhere are able to assist in their covert-operation shenanigans by obtaining different private phone numbers. Some, and I'm not naming names, kept the secret phone (set on "silent") hidden in our home behind the electronic equipment. It's the perfect spot because you couldn't pay me to go back there. Like most women I am equally repelled and bewildered by simple electronics, let alone remote controls that look like NASA equipment. Friend told me the "secret phone" had been nicknamed the "bat phone." Except Batman was less of a degenerate—and quite possibly anally probing Robin.

I tried to wrap my head around all the information that had come at me. I felt like I was playing a real-life game of Ms. Pac Man, going through the maze and gobbling up all this new information with ease. And frankly I was somewhat tired of people's stories starting with the three words: "Did you know . . . ?" My head swirled with fun facts: the wedding night, the prescription pills, the coke, the gambling, the hookers, the suitcase, the fact that Carlie was his serious girlfriend months before we separated and not "just an oops-this-one-time-at-bandcamp temptation."

If what doesn't kill you only makes you stronger, then I was one strengthened bitch. Oddly, you would think all this information would shatter someone. But it had the opposite effect. It actually took any guilt or burden of a failed marriage off my shoulders. And this wasn't just something my therapist told me I should feel. It was the truth. I felt better than I had since the day we separated. I knew that if he was fucking Amy on our wedding night and the rest of the new bullshit I found out was going on, then we had no chance, ever, at marriage. Because really? We had no marriage. Saving that marriage would have been like trying to hold the *Titanic* up post-iceberg, or, for instance, getting Paris Hilton to live in a mirror-free home. I had won the epic douche-bag-for-a-husband lottery and there was no shot of anyone stripping me of my title. The fact is that I think I was married to a socio-path and that wasn't just a sound bite. I actually Googled it to confirm my diagnosis.

HOW TO TELL IF YOUR MAN IS
CHEATING (OR FREQUENTING HOOKERS)

1. *Prostitutes don't take MasterCard. (Check his ATM statements.)*

2. *He is no longer interested in kissing (even during sex— or even interested in sex for that matter).*

3. *He suggests trying some crazy shit in bed that has never fascinated him before and starts an "I wonder if open relationships work" line of dialogue.*

4. *He comes home with sparkles on his face like he just went down on Tinkerbell—after a day of golf/work, meeting/workout.*

5. *If you suspect it, it's probably not by accident. Obtain a special (spy) GPS system without his knowledge and attach it underneath his car to see exactly where he is going. (About three hundred dollars online. You're welcome.)*

6. *His phone history is completely deleted.*

7. *He goes to Vegas more than church.*

8. *He thinks Tiger Woods was misunderstood.*

9. *Go to his computer, look up www.craigslist.com, and see if "casual encounters" has already been clicked once. If it has, it will be a different color than the other options on some computers.*

10. *He is a professional athlete.*

Just ninety days athlete-sober, and channeling
my inner cougar.

THIRTEEN

Getting Tackled

My therapist, Kristin—along with every other concerned friend who heard my *Jerry Springer* saga—encouraged me to go and get tested for every disease you can think of and maybe even throw in the Ebola virus test, just because. I nervously went to schedule an HIV test and a physical with my gynecologist. While I was waiting in the sheepskin covered stirrups (how considerate is that?) Dr. Shirley Cohen waltzed in.

I've never understood why some women choose male gynos. It's like a woman deciding to be, say, an erection analyst. Despite any medical training, or background, I'm just not sold on the idea that a woman could be as competent about what it feels like to get or have an erection. Therefore, personally, I would choose someone who sports a dick for any penile situation, and I believe that having a vagina is a prerequisite for someone observing any downstairs situations of mine. Plus, unless your male gynecologist also subscribes to *Hustler* magazine, chances are most men aren't used to seeing things quite as brightly lit and spread eagle as they are in those damn stirrups. Dr. Cohen, with pen and clipboard in hand, started the Starbucks chatter, while peppering the conversation with necessary directives.

"Hi Rosa! Long time no see! How's the baby? Scoot down for me. You had a baby girl right? I bet that's no fun shopping for a little girl huh?" She laughs likes it's her go-to joke. "Nothing cuter than little girl clothes. Scoot down for me more please. And she's what now? One? One and a half? Open your legs up a bit more for me. There you go. Okay. Looks good. Healthy pink. You can scoot down just a bit more. So what are we doing today? Annual pap smear?" At this point I felt so embarrassingly "scooted down" that I wondered if there was a window open or if I was really feeling intermittent puffs of breath from her rapid-fire monologue. And how long might it be before she accidentally dropped the confident doctorspeak and utter, "Uh-oh."

I am certain of three things: death, taxes, and that it was a man who thought up the words "Pap smear." It's the worst phrase: Pap smear, it's not just for bagels. Nevertheless, I had bigger fish to fry with this visit.

"Um, no. I mean yes," I said sounding giggly despite feeling rather paranoid. "Yes, I need a Pap smear, but I also need some, um . . . sexually-transmitted-disease test-ing done. I need, you know . . ." I lowered my voice an octave and said the following words so fast I'm pretty sure it sounded like one syllable. "IneedanHIVtest."

I waited for her to judge me.

"Oh." She tried not to sound surprised, but I'm sure she anticipated a typical postbaby "I wanna go on the pill again" visit like most normal people besides Angelina Jolie, who has a new kid every season.

"So Rosa, do you have any reason to believe you are at risk?" she asked as she got various long-ass Q-tip swabs out of her drawers.

"Yeah. Yep. I do . . ." At this point, I wasn't even aware I was shredding the bottom of my paper gown. I was oblivi-ous to the fact that I was creating a fringe hem and it was all very Pocahontas, but disposable and paper. "My hus-band, well, soon-to-be ex-husband, we are divorcing . . . He cheated. A lot. A lot lot. With people. A lot of people and, well . . . um, probably prostitutes too." Why did the English language suddenly fail me and feel like my second language? I was talking in staccato sentences like a three-year-old. Except three-year-olds don't use the word "pros-titutes," and if they did it would sounds like "pasta-toots."

"Well, I can do that!" said Dr. Cohen as calmly as if every patient that came through her Beverly Hills stirrups were in my exact situation. "And lucky for you, the sex-worker industry is really great about utilizing protection with their clientele." She said this with a smile, like it was a late-night infomercial for hookers. As if she expected me to shred some more of my paper gown into pompons and give a "gooooo Trojans!"

Outside in the little nurses' den I could see there was some whispering going on. Or were they talking about what takeout they'd get for lunch? It's hard to read lips, particularly since Chinese, sushi, and HIV look so similar when mouthed in hushed tones. Maybe it was just extreme paranoia, but I felt some judgmental, darting looks as they took me into the blood-draw room to tie that druggie rubber band thing around my biceps. It's like a push-up bra for your veins, which I didn't need. I have naturally massive veins. I know what you're thinking. Every girl's dream, right? Who doesn't want giant drug-addict-looking veins? It was so weird, I thought as they were drawing blood. I had been in that exact room, that exact seat so many times before, but praying for a positive pregnancy test result. This time I was praying not to end up on the cover of *People* magazine. With headlines that would read: "No Strong Medicine Could Help Dr. Lu's Deadly HOOKER Virus! ROSA BLASI on Women Who Love Men Who Love Whores—the Exclusive Interview!"

Thank you God. The tests all turned out negative.

The next step in relationship recovery and new singledom? Off to the Internet. Specifically, I needed to obtain the ownership to the domain names www.epicdouchebag.com and www.douchebagolympics.com. Plain old www.douchebag.com was already taken, much to my pal Lisa Ann Walter's and my dismay. Lisa Ann had dated a "special guy" who fathered her twin boys, so she was a fantastic recovery partner and had lots of helpful hints about how to deal with, well, douche bags. We didn't know exactly what we were going to do with the web addresses yet, but it seemed like we were the right people to own them.

After I changed my e-mail password to "FuckTim" and signed up for Facebook, I trolled on to Match.com. I had to sign up in order to take a gander at L.A.'s finest. I chose the name Beach Beatch, and had an overwhelming urge to post: "Cavernous vagina seeks soul mate" on my Match .com summary just to be funny. I didn't have the balls to actually post a picture. I just wanted to see what was out there. What did normal single people actually look like? It was crazy how many people were on there, and even crazier that people were cheesy enough to use modeling shots, some clearly from the eighties. There were thousands of people to scroll through. At the time, although I was looking for someone of some substance, I would still bypass anyone vertically challenged by my standards—or under six feet. Old habits die hard.

I met one guy who was as smart and funny as he was adorable. Based on lobbing some witty e-mails back and forth, I guessed that he was a writer. He said he was, which threw me. This guy looked more smoldering Calvin Klein ad and less Woody Allen hunched over a typewriter. Did I have beginner's luck or what? I could have sworn that the background of one of his photos was reminiscent of the whole paparazzi red carpet experience. Hmm. You can only research/stalk so much without a last name. I told him a little about myself, and said he could Google me if he wanted to see a picture. Obviously I didn't think this out too clearly, and as soon as I suggested it I realized I sounded as classless as some of the dudes looked on the dating site.

Match guy number one didn't "believe it was me" and sent me an e-mail that basically said he felt sorry for me, to be impersonating this actress in an attempt to get men interested. Ouch. He also mentioned that "whoever I was, I should know that Rosa Blasi is married to an NFL player." Yeah, not so much anymore. I wrote him back: "Dude. If I was impersonating an actress, I would choose one with a really successful career, who's about seven years younger, with no ex-husband baggage. We are currently in the process of a divorce." I urged him to listen to my voice on some fan websites that posted late-night talk show interviews. Unless you're Rich Little, it's really hard to impersonate a speaking voice. Then, when we spoke on the phone, he would know it was me. He called, confirmed it was me, and I on the other hand couldn't believe my Match jackpot! This guy was outstanding. We talked for over an hour that first phone call. He went to Princeton (where yes, he played football, but I forgave him because it was Ivy League and not a really good "competitive" school—football speaking). He came from a great, close family. He was also from Chicago and he used to be an actor on a soap opera (that explained the matinee-idol good looks and the red-carpet mystery, and kudos to him for giving up the crappy career choice!), and now he worked for—wait for it—ESPN.

Dear God? Seriously? What's up with all the obstacles here?

Seriously, he works for ESPN? I have often joked that I am sure I star in God's favorite sitcom, and this little tidbit almost came with its own laugh track. It was like Sarah Palin trying to date the head of Planned Parenthood—a major hurdle to say the least. But I didn't want to be so prejudiced. After all, he seemed so great on paper, and it had been a long time, six-plus years, since I had been on a date. Plus, I had been urging all of my single friends to try Internet dating whenever they became frustrated. Now that I had no single friends left, and only knew moms of toddlers, I wondered if I was ever going to meet anyone. I didn't go out out anymore. I rarely left the five-mile radius beyond the local Target in my town, and I couldn't stay awake past 10:00 p.m. Even if I did run into someone, I was all caught up in "mom mode," which included not having the time or patience to look like you've showered, even if you did. "Makeup" to me was an attempt to cover a few picked zits, usually while driving (which is safer than texting while driving, but still up there with drunk driving). My mom-look consisted of beat-up baggy jeans that looked like they were carrying a back*pack* not my back end, Uggs or flip-flops, and hair tied up in a bun. It wasn't the chic "Evita on the balcony bun," but the I-couldn't-have-bothered-to-pull-the-ponytail-all-the-way-through-the-rubber-band bun. As if I needed any help in my now-depleted self-esteem department, I noticed something else kept happening around this time: I started to feel a little invisible.

I really noticed it now when I saw a cute (younger) guy, and the guy literally looked right through me. It was like

I was the Ghost of Christmas Past, but older—and minus the clanking chains. I had to face it. This was not the same dating game as in my twenties. I had gotten significantly older and more frazzled. Perhaps it was less than a decade in chronological years, but in dating years—well, that was like dog years. And I don't think it can be chalked up to being a "vain actress." I think when you are celebrated in any way, shape, or form for your looks—whether by the public or just people in your hometown—once your looks start to fade and the aging sets in, it is a brutal awakening. The only solace I found in all of this was that it must be far worse for people who are less smoke-and-mirrors (like I was) and more truly natural knockouts. Poor Cindy Crawford. Yeah right. I saw her recently at a U2 concert and wanted to commit suicide on the spot. She's six feet of perfection and glow—Baby Jesus with legs! Compounding this problem is that a woman looks in the mirror (especially those lit-up, magnified, should-be-illegal mirrors!) and judges herself against incredibly cruel and unreasonably high standards (thank you Barbie Dolls and fashion magazines). Whereas a man can grip his spare tire, ignore the "I want to get as far the fuck away from my eyebrows as possible" hairline, bypass the pasty *Twilight* complexion, and think happily, *Not bad!*

I couldn't fathom meeting someone unless I was all decked out in my full war-paint, on a film set working (and even that felt like it was nearing a looming expiration date). Plus, I had no desire to date an actor. You can only have one narcissistic person in the relationship, I think.

M R. MATCH AND I decided to meet a couple of days later. I worked really hard to achieve sexy without trying too hard—and young. The young part was hard. You can only do so much with an ass that's surrendered to gravity. It had no real buoyancy, just a memory of what once was and a crack in the middle to let you know it wasn't a back leg. The last six years had been unkind. Plus, when a person falls out of you (or in my case, just one little seven-pound girl) I was pretty sure it sped up the aging process. Crap. This used to be so effortless! How was I going to achieve that dewy Gucci runway look? I would figure that out for date number two, but in the meantime, I had no choice but to overmoisturize, pick a restaurant with low, flattering lighting, and spray-tan the years away.

I finally got to meet Mr. Match, and he was ga-ga-ga-gorgeous. He was funny, charismatic: The conversation was nonstop. He was better looking than his pictures, and I just wanted to reach out and caress that little divot between the biceps and the elbow that really-in-shape people have. You know, that Angela Bassett part that swoops down and then up? Snacky. I had a random thought shoot into my mind on the day of the date. One of Tim's outings for "work" was meeting up with a guy who went to Princeton and worked at ESPN. I now wondered if it was Mr. Match, and thought it would be foolish to pretend like I didn't know this information. So I asked.

"Um . . . okay . . . so this is random. But I know you

work for ESPN and well . . . do you know my ex-husband by any chance?"

Mr. Match exhaled loudly, as he if were blowing out an actual match. "Yes! I didn't know if I should say? I didn't know. But yes, Tim met with me about his business plan." The conversation got a little awkward from there, but after that roadblock, it picked up and got all flowy like before. This guy was great. And who cared if he casually knew Tim? I thought I did a good job of trying to convey that I was over Tim, that the divorce was for the better, and my now-constant sound-bite line: "And you know, I'd do it all over again if it meant having our daughter." I did mean it, but I felt like people also wanted to hear it. I wanted them to know that I was, in fact, okay. And not recently diagnosed with something terminal—besides bad judgment in men.

Mr. Match gave me a hug good-bye after our marathon three-hour date. *That was odd*, I thought, as my head by-passed his lips and went into the shoulder/hug territory that he initiated. Maybe he was just Joe Gentlemanly? He really seemed like the perfect guy and I felt I deserved him after the fiasco that turned out to be Tim and all his—Timness. I waited for him to call, like he said he would, and—well, nothing. A day and then a couple days went by, and I realized that this had never happened to me before in my past dating experiences. And I felt even older and more vulnerable than the week before. Was this what I had to look forward to? Was this dating as single moms know it? Wouldn't a guy call to at least see if he could get in your pants? And didn't we have a connection or was

I totally out of touch? I decided my friends would have the answers. Turns out they were the least helpful people to ask. I might as well have seen a priest for as useful as my friends were. Their memories of dating predated my own. Their advice was a combination of sisterhood positive thinking straight out of *Oprah* magazine and a Nike slogan: "Call him! Women should take charge! They can call the guys now! Just do it!" I knew I had to immediately become more current in my dating education, and called on my team of gays to ask the tough questions. I collected two on a conference call.

"You guys, I need your help. Is this normal? Is this a sign? Is he 'just not that into me'?" I awaited the verdict on the other end of the phone, which I knew would be brutally honest. I was in the dark ages about current dating trends and badly needed a brush-up course. Initially they were very positive. "Well . . ." Too many syllables and too long a pause followed. "Every guy is different. Maybe he's intimidated by your strength . . ." blah, blah, blah. They were talking to me like I was fragile, and proceeded very cautiously. I told them the timeline from our first date until now. Their tone totally changed and they were suddenly the mean English judge on *Dancing with the Stars*. "Oh. It's been four days? No, no. Not a good sign, girl."

Two weeks later, I got an e-mail from Mr. Match. He acknowledged that we had insane chemistry and if the situation were different, we would be going out—most likely again and again. But (and I hate that word, it's used far too often on finale episodes of *The Bachelor* right before he shit-cans some sweet young thing), he thought it "was too close for comfort with me being the ex of Tim Fish." Ugh! Tim fucking Fish was ruining every aspect of my life.

I kept trolling on Match, but there weren't any guys that even remotely piqued my interest. There was one guy I met for drinks who was an attorney, but he was too attorney-y. He just seemed like kind of an egomaniac, who was already involved in a love affair with his sports car. I love it when I get a surprised look once I start conversing, followed by a nice backhanded compliment like "Wow. I didn't expect you to be . . . so smart!" Just melts me every time. The lawyer dude was not my type, and not cute enough to put up with for date number two. Finally I Googled the question: "Where do good-looking people meet online?" It directed me to an article written about the CEO of a newer online dating site, who started the company out of frustration with the caliber of "talent" on the online sites that were already out there. The website was named HotEnough.com, and the concept was that you had to get "voted on the island" so to speak. You had to submit two photos. Only one of the two could be professional (a.k.a. retouched). The other members literally voted you in or not, to see if you were hot enough. They assigned a number, and if you got less than an eight, you were a no-go. It reminded me of my pageant days but seemed that much more cruel. The sadistic, competitive side of me of course was intrigued. I got my "approval" rating into the site, after shaving five years off my age. Once in, I was frustrated to see that there was only one guy I would even consider going out with. The rest were so trying too hard—like Larry-from-*Three's-Company* looking, all shiny hair-gelled—that I almost dry heaved while surfing the site. What did I expect? Who knows. Whoever was looking for girls on that site in the first place was bound to be about as deep as a puddle, but part of me didn't care. I knew the only way to survive the recent events was to jump back into the dating world with both high heels.

I was one month separated, and totally okay with the concept of meeting a cute, take-your-mind-off-things "transitional guy." This transitional guy would aid and assist me in becoming ready to date a "real guy," whenever that was. I figured I was a long time away from a real guy—seeing as how I couldn't really trust any guy as far as I could throw him. Tim had left my trust issues as exposed as a raw nerve. I was skeptical of anyone with a penis. Once, during this time, a pregnant friend told me she found out she was having a baby boy. "Yeah. Good luck with that . . ." I found my inner self scowling. It was not my finest hour.

There was a guy on HotEnough.com named Paul who caught my eye: a cute, six-foot, thirty-year-old, Greek, Adonis-looking, Sagittarius Midwesterner! *Yay for mama!* He seemed like a tasty treat. We had a great time talking on the phone beforehand, in what's commonly known to the online dating world as the prerequisite "trying to sniff out potential psychos" conversation. Paul passed with flying colors. He didn't seem weird at all. But I still took separate cars to meet him. (I wasn't a daredevil, and I didn't want to end up in the trunk of some overly zealous *Dexter* fan copycat!) I decided on a local restaurant that

283

had more of a nightclub vibe (read: low lighting). We had a nice enough first date. It would have been better had I not developed such a high school crush on Mr. Match. The date with Paul was fresh on the heels of the Mr. Match blow-off. But I was intrigued by Paul's confidence and we decided to go out again.

A BOUT A WEEK later, one of the football wives (who was in the minority: one of the ones I tolerated), sent me a huge arrangement of flowers. They were basically "sorry I heard your life is in the shit hole" flowers. Word, especially bad word, travels fast. It was incredibly sweet and thoughtful of her, and I was able to put them to great use. I knew Tim would be nosy as he waited in my foyer to get Kaia for his next visit, so I tossed the card from Tamera, and wrote, "Rosa, I had an amazing time. I can't wait to do it again. Love, Paul" on a new card. I placed the arrangement on the foyer table, and knowing Tim would snoop, waited for him to make a comment about it. So it took him no time at all before he yelled, "Who's Paul?" to me from downstairs.

"He's . . . he's a guy that I am dating, Tim," I said intentionally casually, yet intentionally evasively. My high school tactics worked, because a couple of days later Tim said snottily, "So, what's Paul do?"

I was anticipating this follow-up. I had heard long ago that when women are cheated on, the first thing they want to know is: Is she prettier than me?

The first thing men want to know is: What does he do? Sadly, this theory sort of drives home the point that women are more defined by their looks and most men are defined by their jobs, or their power. I knew Tim was among the latter, so I had an answer ready and waiting.

"Paul? Um . . . yeah. You don't want to know, Tim." I suppressed a giggle. "It's unimportant."

He bit.

"What does he do, Rosa? Just tell me."

"Fine. Well, Paul—this is awkward—happens to be a divorce attorney." I smiled sweetly. It infuriated Tim. Here he was thinking that I was getting all this free advice, and all these war tips from a pro. The reality? Paul had less money than the bartender from Chicago I dated ages ago. Although Paul was kind, and we had a great time for the three months we were together, he was also dead broke. Never a restaurant were we to see the inside of the entire time we were together, with the exception of the time I took him and paid. He cooked like a five-star chef and he was the perfect postmarital boyfriend, but it was always meant to be just that. He was a gift on borrowed time from the rebound gods. Plus, he reminded me what kissing was like. The first time we really made out I reported to my friends: "Kissing is *so* fun! I forgot how fun and how exciting a good old-fashioned make-out session is with a new guy." Crap, if I had known this I might have considered cheating on Tim years ago during our kissing droughts. Because all of my friends were married, they lived vicariously through me: seeing the world through my new dating-colored lenses, yet fearing the world of divorce through my new depleted-bank-account and impending-legal-fee lenses.

Sure, I tried going out on other dates here and there, including one blind (never again) date, and another with a guy who suffered from what I call don't-floss breath. This is the kind of breath that comes from a person who seldom, if ever, flosses his teeth. A piece of chicken left over from a dinner in 1997 begged to be released from betwixt his tight back molars, with no relief from a toothbrush in sight, which caused waves of heinous dead-meat smell every so often. I hate don't-floss breath. It makes me dry heave. And then I fixate on it with every exhaled breath, which only exacerbates the problem. With every word he spoke, I got a tiny smack of don't-floss breath in the face, until I was forced to hold my breath and beat a fast retreat. I also discovered, during this short but abundant dating spree, that there was a reason to date guys your own age.

While I was waiting at an audition, I met a cute guy so young he'd have gotten carded anywhere, any time. There was something familiar about him that I couldn't place, and a cockiness that I was attracted to in a sort of cougar-licious way. I was too young to be a real cougar, but this guy was also too young to be my boyfriend at twenty-three. The familiarity mystery was solved when I Internet stalked him, and discovered his father was one of the biggest movie star legends on the planet. That explained the legendary chip on his shoulder, but nothing could have prepared me for how useless kissing boys under twenty-five was. The thrill of the chase was fun and the attention flattering, but the actual execution was a waste of my time. I was having flashbacks to college, and not the good kind. They were the kind that involved guys trying to finger-bang you, leaving you simply confused—and a bit sore. Young men: Just because you saw it in a porno once does not make this okay. For the first time ever, I thought of the Elton John song (with reference to the guy's famous father) sung in an entirely different way: "Don't let the *son* go down on me. . . ." The date ended promptly—followed by a new "no dating men under twenty-five rule" that I have religiously followed ever since.

It was becoming tedious to go out with someone only once and become annoyed with them before dessert was served. Perhaps I was less annoyed than fixated on something I perceived as a flaw (like not being able to imagine myself kissing them). I was becoming the one-date wonder.

THE BIGGEST OBSTACLE I found was that it was really hard to be myself. Myself has verbal diarrhea, and no boundaries. It's almost impossible for me to think before I speak, and so when anyone asked, "So, why did you and your husband separate?" I was torn about how to reply. I had two choices. I could either say, "It just didn't work out" (read: lie) and risk looking like a cliché Hollywood actress with a ten-minute marriage and a cavalier attitude toward divorce (when the truth is that I couldn't hear about someone else divorcing after less than five years and not judge them myself). I always thought if the age requirement to get married was thirty and people just worked a little harder in therapy, there would be a lot fewer divorces. On the other hand, if I started to tell the tale of what actually happened it was so crazy that I seemed crazy, too. Not many people I confided in actually believed me. Some (even close friends) asked if I had proof. Luckily, I have a sweet manila file marked "Declarations—Oy Vey!" It used to just say "Declarations," but as the folder started to fatten up, I added the "Oy Vey!"

Thankfully, one of the sworn declarations I obtained was from Amy, in case I ever needed it in court. She detailed what happened the night of the wedding and even ended her sworn statement with: "Having been married and divorced to a pro athlete, I have witnessed the feelings of hopelessness and anger that follow the end of a professional athletic career. No longer having the stadium or field in which to release their aggression, this often leads to depression, rage, and substance abuse." She saved the best for last, and ended her letter with "I have also witnessed a grandiose sense of entitlement in most athletes, as a result of being coddled in their profession." I was grateful for the letter, but I also felt like it was the least she could do—after doing my husband.

Through all the new crazy of the divorce and impending child custody case, I was forced to go to what is called a PACT class (Parents and Children Together), which was basically a "how not to be a crappy parent" class required by all parents engaged in custody battles. The crowd was less than savory. Lots of faded black concert T-shirts, gang tattoos, the smell of cheap stale draft beer seeping from their pores, and suspicious-looking men you'd think you'd find in a "domestic violence is a no-no" course. There was one lady there with a fake Chanel bag, so I tried to make eye contact with her. She noticed, and pulled her purse a little tighter toward her. I was trying to establish a class friend, someone to take our food breaks at the vending machines with in the Superior Court of Los Angeles cafeteria. But then I remembered I was wearing a gray college hoodie, ripped jeans, and no makeup on my tired-ass face, and I realized she thought I was one of *them*. I was going to have to step it up and try to get it together, or at least try to fake looking together.

One day I arrived about ten minutes late to my home, where Kaia and Tim were waiting for me after a custodial visit. I hadn't changed the locks yet (dumb rookie mistake) and when I got there, Tim had been rifling through my dresser drawers. While I was very pleased that he found the Magnum Trojans I bought before I'd ever laid eyes on Paul's penis (wishful purchasing on my part—but I believed in the power of *The Secret*), I was mortified when I realized Tim had stolen my divorce diary! It was gone. He had been looking for his metal suitcase filled with the human growth hormone, syringes, and steroids, but found my diary instead (and the condoms, which he laid out in the middle of my bed as if to say "I found these too!").

Although I was blindsided by Tim faxing and sharing pages of my divorce diary, nothing prepared me for the day

I went inside our first courtroom on opposite sides. In all of my life I have never wanted to climb into a deep hole and press PAUSE on life the way I did that day. I had been advised to try and get Tim randomly drug tested from what's called an "ex parte" source. Ex parte is a fancy legal term for hideously expensive and an immediate court appearance if you have reason to believe that you or your child is at risk. Considering that I believed he was eating Vicodin like they were bar nuts, and considering that every bottle of pain pills I have ever seen clearly advises against operating heavy machinery, I thought I should try and get his pill-popping under control. Because if you can't operate heavy machinery, chances are your parenting might suffer as well. I even imagined him joining the cast of *Celebrity Rehab with Dr. Drew* (one of my favorite shows). I was sitting in a courtroom after being handed a copy of Tim's attorney's side of the argument of why they "should not" drug test Tim, which was mainly the genius argument that if he had a prescription what could possibly be the problem? Most of it is legal bullshit, which should just be written in plain English so more people can defend themselves, but some of the argument came in the form of exhibits. Such as the exhibit A, which was a Xeroxed page out of my divorce diary. I immediately recognized my own handwriting. My most intimate thoughts poured out on the page. And there it was in front of me. I couldn't take it back, or even have the chance to explain myself. I just had to read it.

In my very own handwriting it said, "I wonder if my vagina is stretched out . . ."

The words leapt off the page and I imagined that every person sitting in the courtroom now was wondering the same question. Oh. My. God.

This isn't happening.

This isn't happening.

This isn't happening.

I immediately felt a blazing hot flush, followed by an outpouring from every sweat gland my armpits possessed, and some from places I didn't know I had.

On the next page in the same handwritten scrawl was another entry: "I want revenge," written on the night I found out he had a girlfriend during our marriage. They included that page as Tim's entire defense, that I was a scorned, bitter, vengeful, overly dramatic actress, and in my very own words and handwriting "wanted revenge." Talk about taken out of context. This was worse than any *Star* magazine bikini-clad celebrity cellulite issue! I was "so sad he had left me," they claimed—and all this other garbage page after page written from his lawyer that I could barely read. Words blurred and I wondered if the burning from my cheeks could possibly set my whole body on fire right there. Had anyone ever actually died of embarrassment? Would I be the first? Would this be my legacy? Could my literal dying of embarrassment land me on the cover of *People* magazine or *Us Weekly*, finally? His defense had cleverly included the entry "I wonder if my vagina is stretched out" simply for humiliation's sake. And mission accomplished—because that worked. I don't blame them for taking "I want revenge" and using it against me (even though it was from the first night I found out he had cheated). Score one for team a-hole! Touché douche.

Also in the exhibits was something that was fair game. During the time I discovered all the bonus information from Friend and "other sources"—we'll call it the trifecta of info, like the Wizard of Odd: Coke and hookers and Amy? Oh my!—there was a six-week period when I had to keep all that information strictly to myself. I knew we would be using some of the information in court at the ex parte hearing, and not saying *anything* about it was one of the most difficult things I have ever had to do. Including childbirth. I had to see Tim every single day for a custodial visit with Kaia. Every single day. This was combined with Tim's admission that Kaia was sharing a bed with him *and* Carlie during overnight visits (only six weeks postsepa-ration), and compounded further by Kaia's return from these visits reeking of another woman's perfume, her hair in perfect pigtails, and her tiny nineteen-month-old nails painted an obnoxious sparkly blue. Gag worthy. Knowing what I knew, and not being able to talk about it or con-front him was the ultimate exercise in self-control. The only time I got close to a full-on blurt was one time Tim actually called me a "whore" during a custody exchange. I smiled my former pageant-survivor smile, and said, "Well, Tim, a whore is someone who is *paid for sex*. Just so you know. *You* know?" He looked momentarily confused but blew it off and got into his car. I was like a lit firecracker waiting to explode on the inside.

After holding all this new Tim-formation inside for a

whopping ten days, I had taken Kaia on a long road trip to visit friends. It took an hour and a half to get from the beach town we were at back to Tim's house for his visitation time. I didn't want to be late, so despite the fact that I had to pee so badly I was literally in physical pain, I didn't stop the car. I made it just in time, dropped off Kaia, and got back in my car. *Oh God. I wasn't going to be able to make it even the twenty blocks away that I lived.* I hobbled to Tim's front door and rang the bell. From inside the house, without opening the door he yelled, "What do you want?"

"Tim, I have to pee *so bad*. Can I use your bathroom please?" Pride aside, I was officially begging through a shut door. "I'm dying. I've had to pee for over an hour!"

"Fuck you!" he chortled.

Oh no he didn't.

"Fine!"

I was beyond fuming. I clenched my teeth so hard I am shocked I didn't chip a tooth. I lifted up my sundress, pulled aside my bikini bottoms, and peed like a racehorse all over his front doorstep. Just as I finished and pulled down my dress, Tim opened the door with a video camera and filmed me leaving the "crime scene."

"Thank you." I said walking away from the urine puddle.

As momentarily satisfying as that was as I waltzed back to my car, I later regretted it. And by later I meant as soon as I saw pictures of my personal piss lake also known as exhibit D in court documents. Obviously, this was not my finest hour. There have been far worse acts committed in the history of relationships using the defense of "temporary insanity." And I think my life during this time certainly qualifies as insane. Plus, as a bonus, nobody was murdered.

DATING NIGHTMARES, STOLEN diaries, and uncontrollable bladder incidents aside, there was one guy I met at a charity benefit who offered me hope that there were men out there I could be interested in, who had never been part of any stupid team or even seen the inside of a gym for that matter. He was about my age, surprisingly more handsome in person, and I recognized him instantly from a show I have been a fan of since I remembered. He was a cast member of *Saturday Night Live*. He was as funny as I expected him to be, and he seemed to be really self-deprecating and just a sweetheart. Not Hollyweird at all. I didn't even mind that he was on the shorter side and I was so excited for our first date that I went shopping for the occasion. My outfit was very carefully planned. I was going for "show that I have a cute body, but don't scare him with the sexy." I wore jeans and a white silk shirt, some killer shoes, and an old-looking, beat-up leather belt that incidentally cost a lot of money to look that "old" and that "beat up." What guy doesn't like jeans and a white shirt? I thought. Plus, he was a supertalented intellect, so I wanted to play up my brain instead of my rack (like I did back in yesteryear).

We had an amazing date. It lasted from 8:00 p.m. till 1:00 a.m. He couldn't have been more of a gentleman, even jokingly getting out of the car to come around to my side and buckle *my* seat belt, and I could have talked to him all night long. I had a mad crush in the making, and I was excited to find out if we had any sexual chemistry as well.

At the time, Tim and I had put the house we co-owned on the market and it had sold in just five days. There was the world's fastest escrow, and I found myself homeless just twenty-one days later. I had to figure out where to live for six weeks, as my beach house was being rented until then. I felt the healthiest decision for Kaia and me was to move in with my parents in their spacious, one-bathroom, 800-square-foot log cabin. Kaia would require a room to herself (or she would never sleep) and I was fine sleeping on the couch. My parents were in the guest bedroom (which was really an office, because it had no closet). All five of us were on top of each other in this cozy beach hut. It was embarrassing to say "I'm living with my parents and sleeping on their couch" out loud, even if it was temporary. Plus, directly across the street was my former residence, the P. Diddy McMansion, and *the* biggest house on the block monstrosity that I used to call home. It was definitely one of those "truth is stranger than fiction" stories at that point.

Whether he believed me or not, my fabulous date walked me to my (parents') front door to say goodnight and to tell me what a great time he had. As we approached the door, I heard my parents' six-pound maltese, Leila, start her familiar, territorial, Napoleon-complex barking. She barked, or rather shrieked, like a rabid dog defending her life.

Suddenly, the awful barking stopped, and more abruptly the front door swung open. There stood my seventy-six-year-old father, holding Leila, in what looked like a pair of seventy-six-year-old Fruit of the Loom underwear. The crotch of his once-white briefs now hung loosely midthigh. They were more like vintage culottes than tighty whities. I made a mental note to make sure Dad ponied up and invested in underwear that was worthy of an audience the next time he decided to answer the front door in them.

"Oh Rosa! It's just you." His eyes were half closed, and he shut the door again and shuffled back to his bed. I was officially mortified. And what if it wasn't "just me, Dad"? Jesus. Who else would it be? A burglar who couldn't resist the lure of a tiny log cabin fixer-upper? And who opens the door in his underwear carrying a handbag dog? Besides maybe Paris Hilton? I was lost in humiliation when my dream date interrupted my inner diatribe.

"Was that . . . ?" he started.

"My dad, yeah," I affirmed quietly, wondering if it was possible to feel any more humiliated, and wondering if despite the dark and my olive skin, my date could still see that I was feverishly blushing.

"Was he in . . . ?"

"His underwear? Yeah." We were already finishing each other's sentences but not exactly the way I pictured it happening. It was beyond awkward. He smiled, planted a sweet kiss on my cheek, said that he'd call, and gave me another friendly cheek kiss. I couldn't decide if it was a pity kiss, if he was just the world's most polite dude, or if he was European.

I was so excited to see him again but even more per-plexed than I was with Match guy when I got the extreme high-def blow-off. We had a couple of phone conversa-tions, and I know that the "easy out" explanation of why he couldn't have been less interested was that in less than a week he was going back to New York to start work on the new season of SNL. I never heard from him again. As much as I'd like to label him "must have been gay" to mas-sage my ego, the harsh truth is that he probably just didn't dig me. Or he had a girlfriend. Or he was freaked out that a kid had fallen out of me only two years before. Or that I was still technically married on paper. Or that I lived with my parents who answer the door in their ancient tighty whities . . .

Last I heard he was dating a beautiful . . . rocket scien-tist. Yes, really. What does she have that I didn't? Besides the not-counting-on-her-fingers thing when she needs to do simple math?

PROFESSIONAL ATHLETES' RETIREMENT GUIDE . . . FUN FACTS!

1. *The bad news is:* Fewer than half of pro athletes get to choose when they retire.*

   The good news is: When they do, this gives them more time to play golf and retreat to their mansions to endure lifelong worship.

2. *The bad news is:* The divorce rate for retired athletes in the major professional leagues is over 60 percent.*

   The good news is: Lawyers everywhere rejoice in this statistic and have ample access to season tickets.

3. *The bad news is:* There is a 60–80 percent divorce rate in the NFL. According to the NFL Players' Association, "50 percent will divorce after the first year they are done playing."

   The good news is: It's not technically cheating when you are no longer legally married. Then it's just called good old-fashioned whoring around.

4. *The bad news is:* Offensive and defensive linemen have a 52 percent greater risk of dying of heart disease than the general population.*

   The good news is: This takes some of the pressure off of funnel cake consumers and most amusement park patrons.

5. **The bad news is:** *Two-thirds of football players retire with a permanent injury.**

   The good news is: *They have had so many head collisions they won't remember how it happened.*

6. **The bad news is:** *The average American life span is seventy-six years. For NFL players it is fifty-five years, and only fifty-two for offensive and defensive linemen.*

   The good news is: *People will remember you for how you looked in your glory. More Walter Payton, less John Madden crepey-skin-looking.*

7. **The bad news is:** *By the time they have been retired for two years, 78 percent of former NFL players have gone bankrupt or are under financial stress (because of joblessness or divorce).*

   The good news is: *Because some of them can't read, they just see the first part of that word and think they got "bank."*

8. **The bad news is:** *At five years postretirement, 60 percent of former NBA players are "broke."*

   The good news is: *"Broke" to some of the players just means downsizing your diamond-studded necklace chain, or forsaking the rims you really wanted.*

9. **The bad news is:** *The suicide rate among retired NFL players is six times the average rate.**

The good news is: *The suicide rate among retired NFL players is six times the average rate.*

10. ***The bad news is:*** *According to Judd Biasiotto, from his article "15 Surprising Facts About World Class Athletes," "Less then one percent of all athletes who participate in competitive sports ever reaches an elite level. As an example, consider the odds of making it in professional basketball. Each year approximately 250,000 high school seniors participate in interscholastic basketball. Of these seniors, approximately 12,000 will receive college scholarships. Out of that 12,000, around 200 players will be drafted by the NBA, but only about fifty will actually be offered a contract. Of these fifty, only five will eventually earn a starting position. Of these five, only two will stay in the NBA. for more then five years."*

The good news is: *Odds are you won't have to worry about this being your retirement guide.*

Article source: Iron Curtain Labs.

Racing Against the Sunset: An Athlete's Quest for Life After Sport, by Scott Tinley (Lyons Press, 2006)

**New York Times, August 9, 2009, with information obtained from the Athlete Outreach Program conference speaker.

If only my life as a single mom came with directions like the Barbie Cadillac.

FOURTEEN

Game Over

A year and a month after our separation, I opened the mailbox, as I did every day, praying for a residual check from anywhere from *Married with Children* to the new *Melrose Place* (and every show I had done in between), when I saw that I received something official-looking from the State of California. I tore open the envelope to find that I had been issued an official divorce decree on May 7, 2009. Our battles were far from over. I had been told "custody is a revolving door." This is just lawyerspeak for "you are going to be hemorrhaging money via legal fees until your child's eighteenth birthday." Tim had decided he suddenly wanted 50 percent custody, and he wanted me to pay him child support.

The sign as you enter the state should read: *Welcome to California! The No-Fault State!* Christie Brinkley was my new idol; she did it the right way. Get divorced in a state where you can air your ex's dirty laundry and get compensated while doing so. Not true in California. They don't care about any of the circumstances—just numbers and which partner makes the most money. In our case, that happened to be me because Tim was collecting unemployment by the time we got divorced. Ah yes, herein lies the drawback for being a responsible working woman.

Holding that divorce decree in my hand, I thought of how much my life had changed in just a year. I didn't have much time to rejoice. I was rushing off to the set of the new hit television series *Make It or Break It* on ABC Family. I had been cast as a two-timing trophy wife and mother of two teenagers aged sixteen and nineteen (played respectively by twenty-three- and thirty-year-old actors). The days of my being an ingénue were long gone, and the days of HDTV (which shows every flaw and then some you didn't know about) were here, much to my chagrin. But I'm not complaining. I am grateful for the work during this crazy recession. The irony, however, did not escape me that my husband on this television show was supposed to have been a former professional baseball player! Welcome to God's favorite long-running sitcom: *Rosa's World*!

I slipped into the driver's seat of the now year-old Divorsche-a, smiled at the cute horse on the emblem, and called Mitch, my boyfriend of nine months. I wanted to share with him the "goodness." That was the word he engraved on the back of the gold Tiffany locket he gave me for my birthday, with a photo of him and me on one side, and Kaia and me on another. "Goodness" was how he described us, and so many things we had to celebrate. Simple pleasures, like watching his three children (ages four, six, and eight) playing with my daughter at the local park, or just finding a really good hot spinach and artichoke dip.

Mitch was my neighbor across the street from the last house I lived in with Tim. We shared an alleyway and our houses were so close I would often use his driveway to complete my three-point turns. I always thought he was cute, but short, and he seemed like a single dad because I had never seen his wife. I knew they were separated and divorcing, but they had not moved out of the same house. She even had her new boyfriend's name tattooed like a gangbanger across the back of her neck in the ghetto-fabulous script usually reserved for graffiti artists and concrete walls. Classy broad. Mitch reached out to me via Facebook to "see how I was doing." In turn, I wrote back to him asking, "If you ever want to get an adult beverage not served in a colorful plastic cup, call me?" (I think we were both used to being at kid-friendly restaurants and I knew he'd appreciate the minor attempt at "parental humor.") He accepted immediately, and the first date (or was it even a date?) was a go. Mitch and I bonded over tales of "whose ex got weirder toward the end of their marriage?" I won even though his wife seemed to be wearing mostly midlife-crisis cologne these days—"for the

woman who has everything . . . yet wants to piss it all away."
He had never seen me with makeup on until our first date,
and often saw me as he was piling his kids into his minivan.
I was usually in my oversized robe, not yet free of my morning eye boogers, and scooping up a jumbo English mastiff
poop the size of an economy sack of rice. Yet Mitch thought
I was "beautiful."

This was a first in my life: meeting a man without "the
mask" of all my heavy tranny-fabulous makeup, without
those security layers, or my forced "sexy look" that I had
grown accustomed to and couldn't feel "beautiful" without. When I looked in the mirror I saw what was wrong,
what used to be, and what had changed. I was embarrassed about how I really looked after a freshly scrubbed
face, yet found comfort in the fact that I "cleaned up well"
when I needed to. Armed with a blow drier and some necessary face spackle, I could whip up a makeover montage
(just like the ones in the movies set to snappy songs) in the
blink of a smoky eye!

I didn't believe Mitch for several months when he told
me that I was beautiful to him even without makeup on. I
even challenged him. "If women are so beautiful without
makeup on, in all their basic rawness, then how come the
men's magazines haven't caught on to it, smart guy? How
come they don't feature that au naturel look? Why can't
they come up with a lip gloss that isn't like fly paper for
your hair to stick to when the wind blows?" That last one
made Mitch suppress a smile before answering.

"Rosa, that makeup look, that 'hot girl look'?"—he actu-

ally did air quotes as he said it, mimicking me—"I'm not
saying that doesn't make men think about having sex with
them. But how you really look without all that? That's how
real men prefer the woman they love." I was speechless,
which has never happened before or since. The realization
that I didn't have a smartass comment or a quick comeback rendered me useless, and I had to sit with the lingering smell of the truth-spray he had just blasted me with.

MITCH WAS THE opposite of everything that was familiar to me about dating and men. He was a five-
foot-seven Jewish Jersey boy who graduated from Penn. He
was also the most hands-on, caring father I had ever met
besides my own. When he and his wife of a dozen years
had separated, he had 90 percent custody of his children
and had taken a year off of his work to help them with the
transition. He coached all their activities, was extremely
involved in their school boards, and even more involved in
the neighborhood. He was "that guy," the man who had no
enemies and only admiration. He was the quintessential
good guy.

Lucky for the shallow side of me, the good guy also
happened to possess a beautiful face, and better abs than
you see featured on a men's underwear package. He was
a successful entrepreneur, basically a technology nerd,
who knew nothing about Hollywood, nor cared, and he
was always smiling like he was some kind of a tooth
ambassador, or a cheerleader of his own life. I had to

admit it was contagious. I came home from our first date and told my mother, "He's great. But, I think he might be *too nice.*" My mother put down the magazine she was reading and just shot me a look of pure exhaustion. She had heard this report before and it usually meant the guy was a distant memory by the time the restaurant valet returned my car to me. "But I'm willing to have a second date with him!" I added quickly, retrieving myself from the hole I had just dug. It couldn't hurt, I thought, and we did have a lot in common, being single parents and newly divorced and all. He was the first dad I had ever gone out with. I didn't tell my mother that as much as I wanted to date a guy like Mitch I was secretly worried we would have zero chemistry. But the chemistry gods were smiling on that second date because when Mitch kissed me—boy, could he deliver. I learned something valuable that night. Forty-year-old men know what they're doing. Younger men are useless. We started dating.

Mitch was an outstanding planner. He arranged surprise couple's massages, wrote me poetry, took me to musical theater (because he knew I loved it), concerts, minivacations, and hiking trips. We even tried Bikram yoga (yes the stupidly hot kind for overachievers) and a sushi-making class together. He wanted to do things, and go places. He truly didn't give a crap about sports. He was creative, and best of all treated me better than anything even I had seen scripted in a movie. I sincerely hope that someday Kaia will grow up to marry a man just like Mitch. It was easy for me to love him. Mitch, on the other hand, had to be patient with me and my permanent Heisman pose keeping him at arm's length. With each new discovery of what I had been missing, I had a feeling of mourning. As much as I realized how great life was postdivorce, it was also a reminder of what was missing from all of my past relationships, and what I had settled for. My low self-esteem had compromised my entire life up until now. I had to remind myself to just love him, because finally, after all this time, I believed I deserved it. I deserved him. The greatest part was knowing that without traveling down Tim's shit-highway, I would have never gotten off on Exit Mitch.

Pre-Tim, I would never even have gone on a date with a Mitch. But I am grateful that Tim ultimately led me to Mitch, and I realized that although I had no idea what the future held for us, I knew I could never go backward. I couldn't pretend I was unaware, now that I was in the know. I had to go down that crazy path to ensure that I would never, ever even entertain the thought of dating anyone that even remotely resembled Tim, *or any athlete*, for the rest of my life. I had finally found the cure to jock itch . . . just a few steps from my own front yard.

As for my daughter, now age three, she came home from preschool acting extra giggly and silly on the day of their class Halloween party, when everyone got to dress up in their costumes. I thought it was just the high fructose corn syrup buzz she was experiencing, or the fact that I let her wear her little plastic high-heeled princess shoes to school, until I realized the reason for this excitement.

"Mom! Brody . . . was dressed as a *football player* today!"

Brody was a little boy in her classroom, and she punctuated her report with a squeal, as high-pitched as stepping on a doggie chew toy. She had the biggest smile on her face that I'd seen since I took her to the American Girl Doll emporium and I wasn't prepared for what followed, but it has kept me up most nights ever since.

"And I *love him!*"

Oh my God.

The sequel.

CHEATERS HALL OF FAME AND THE LESSONS LEARNED

1. Tiger Woods (PGA)

And they all came out of the Woods-work to talk about it. *Lesson learned: Don't date dumb sluts. They like giving interviews.*

2. Michael Jordan (NBA)

Not only did he break NBA records, but also a few divorce $$$ records as well. *Lesson learned: Sometimes you end up paying for strange vagina—even when you aren't with a hooker.*

3. Magic Johnson (NBA)

"Magically" turned his scandal into becoming the most beloved athlete of all time, the philanthropist of the decade, and obtained many multiplex cinemas and restaurants bearing his name. *Lesson learned: Smile and the whole world smiles with you. Also, admit your shit. People will love you for it.*

4. Alex Rodriguez (MLB)

Publicly and with Madonna. *Lesson learned: If you want to cheat on your wife with someone superfamous, you run the risk of being the Brad Pitt of athlete cheaters, Mr. . . . Rod.*

5. Kobe Bryant (NBA)

Bought a bazillion-dollar-cheater-apology bauble ring for the wife and offered an apology. *Lesson learned:*

Your apology is only as good as the giant rare diamond that accompanies it.

6. Chipper Jones (MLB)

Had a baby with a Hooters girl he had an affair with. Lesson learned: There are items for sale not necessarily listed on the menu. Ask your wait staff for details!

7. Steve McNair (NFL)

Most famous dead cheater. Lesson learned: Don't piss off your crazy-ass mistress. You may not live long enough to file a restraining order.

8. Tie Domi (NHL)

After getting caught the "second time" according to his wife, she finally divorces him, but not before doling out all the details for the press. Lesson learned: First, don't let your alleged mistress (and famous actress) wear your jersey to the NHL awards as it could upset the wife. Second, don't follow that move by next allegedly cheating on her with someone who has dated Bill Clinton. Neither act is subtle.

9. Jason Kidd (NBA)

Allegedly. Jason has denied it and claimed he was a victim of spousal abuse by his wife, who (surprise!) accused him of cheating, which kind of makes sense if he was cheating. Lesson learned: You could potentially look like a pussy once you get beaten up by a girl.

10. O. J. (NFL)

"Allegedly." Lesson learned: Don't make him mad.

ACKNOWLEDGMENTS

WITH DEEP GRATITUDE from the depths of my loins, I love and thank the following people:

Mom (for your gift of honesty and sarcasm) and Dad (for your gift of writing and goal-oriented, go-for-it attitude), you have not only stood by me my whole life but bragged about it—mostly at Dominick's grocery store in Mt. Prospect, Illinois. You have also not been incinerated from the hot shame of being my parents . . . yet. Your unconditional love held me up when life was crashing and burning all around me, and you still call after every time I'm on TV to tell me that I am the second coming of Meryl Streep. Most of all, you inspire me to be the kind of parent to Kaia that you were to me. That says everything!

Tasha, who read this and gave notes . . . as if this book were an assignment for English class, complete with red pen markings. Rocky, because you are one of the most sarcastic, quietly funny people I know, and you and Alicia's opinions matter to me. Marina: you would be mentioned, but you're terrible at returning e-mails.

Sue Carswell, my "ghost editor" who whittled down my first 210 pages to 92 and told me "I rant too much," and "go off on tangents" and wrote many, many more helpful and inspirational words across my pages like "NOT FUNNY," "TRY AGAIN," and "I DON'T GET IT." Without your input, this book would be a hot mess of an Attention Deficit Disorder roller-coaster ride, and I am grateful for your keen eye to perfection and flow. You are my ghost wife.

Claudia Cross, my literary agent, of Sterling Lord Literistic, Inc., who did exactly what she said she was going to do, with supreme class, and in record time. As well as assuring me through my second guessing-ness that all was well and "the book would happen."

Mauro DiPreto and the Harper Collins/It Books peeps: Jeremy Cesarec (marketing), Milan Bozic (cover), and Alberto Rojas (publicity) for getting it, getting me, and then getting it done. If I had a dollar for every time I said "HarperCollins bought my book!" I'd never have to work again. I am so proud to be a part of your legacy. Thank you for making this a positive and truly collaborative experience. Thanks for making such a great cover come together: Jan Cobb (photographer), Shawn Finch (hair master), Deb Altazio (makeup). You guys were perfect!

Cheryl McClean of Creative Public Relations, my publicist and friend. You work magic!

John Kelly and Sandy Bresler, my only talent agents for the past fifteen years . . . for a reason. You are trustworthy Hollywood rarity, and I am grateful for you both.

Nick Halloran for having a conscience. Colette Daniels and Jori and Jed Weaver. Emily Hegenberger, my best Southbay friend, and my Mommy and Me ladies, Marni Licursi, Albin Gielitcz, Kathleen Nies, Cathy Herd,

Cindy Ambuehl, Sheila Kerrigan, Leigh Kilton-Smith, and Joanne Presgraves, you were all there for the ride. You all watched in horror as my life events unfolded, loved me, and never judged me—at least not to my face. My "Big Bear" drunken chorale, including Migey, Mark, Dohve, Cookie, and Quilty, who said "Rosa! This is the funniest fucking shit I have ever read." (I'm paraphrasing, yet I'm okay with that.)

Sarah McCormick, for your constant therapizing friendship and many words of wisdom. Kelly White, MFT, my actual therapist. Alexa Sidaris and Liza Barry, thanks for introducing me to the "baloney 'n' carrots" reference on page 1. Nick M: you did nothing to help with the book, but you are a hot . . . mess. Not necessarily in that order.

Kristin Datillo, thank you for reading this early on, supporting the crap out of me, and being my (non-blood) soul sister. Lisa Ann Walter, for allowing me to ride your standup comedy coattails, hold my hand, and wipe me the whole way. Smartest chick I know.

Jennifer Mazzone. My BFF. The Gayle to my Oprah, and more. Not that I'm Oprah (I don't even like to use the Lord's name in vain.).

Mitch Gordon. The kindest, most loving man I have ever known besides my Dad.

Kaia: Never forget that everything happens for a reason. Everything. And that God gives us gifts beyond our wildest dreams. You are one of them, and you are also holding another in your hands as you read this. I never knew I would write a book until I knew I was supposed to. You are the light of my life and the inspiration for everything. I love you beyond words, and I am proud and grateful that you chose me to be your mom. Learn from my mistakes, continue to shine brightly, and for the love of God . . . please don't bring home an athlete.

ROSA BLASI is a native of Chicago and has appeared on many TV series, including: *Married with Children, Drew Carey, Frasier, CSI: Miami, 90210, Melrose Place, The Whole Truth, Mr. Sunshine,* and (voices on) *American Dad!* She made her silver screen debut in the successful film *The Grudge.* She is best known for her starring role as Dr. Lu on Lifetime's *Strong Medicine.* Rosa has performed stand-up at the Laugh Factory, Comedy Store, and L.A. Improv and has written articles for the *Huffington Post.* She has been featured in many publications, including *Time, People, US Weekly, Entertainment Weekly, In Style, Stuff, Maxim, In Touch, Self, TV Guide, Rosie,* and *Razor.* Currently, Rosa is on the ABC Family series *Make It or Break It.*